PAUL ON TRIAL

THE BOOK OF ACTS AS A
DEFENSE OF CHRISTIANITY

John W. Mauck

Foreword by Donald A. Hagner

THOMAS NELSON PUBLISHERS

Nashville

Published in Nashville, Tennessee, by Thomas Nelson, Inc.

Unless otherwise indicated, Scripture quotations are from the *New King James Version of the Bible*, © 1979, 1980, 1982, 1990, Thomas Nelson, Inc., Publishers.

Front cover illustration, "The Apostle Paul" by Rembrandt van Rijn, is from the Widener Collection of the National Gallery of Art, Washington, D.C. Used by permission.

Book design and composition by Bob Bubnis, Booksetters, White House, Tennessee

Mauck, John W.
    Paul on trial: the book of Acts as a defense of Christianity
    ISBN 0-7852-4598-7

2 3 4 5 6 7—06 05 04 03 02 01

CONTENTS

FOREWORD

Just as ministry is the work of the people and not the clergy (who are to equip the saints for ministry according to Eph. 4:11-12), so too the Bible is the book of all the people of God, not the domain of biblical scholars only. Indeed the writings that make up the Bible are meant to be studied by every Christian. The Word of God was written, after all, not to scholars but to the people of God in communities of faith. Although scholars may well contribute to a more adequate understanding of Scripture, there is often much to be learned about the Bible from those who are not professional scholars.

William Tyndale in the sixteenth century, with his English translation of the New Testament in mind, once said to a learned scholar, "If God spare my life, before many years I will cause a boy that drives the plough to know more of the Scriptures than you do!" When a Luther or a Tyndale brought the Bible to the people in their own languages, they made possible not only knowledge of the scriptures, but also the universal study of the Bible.

If the study of the Bible is not only for specialists or technically trained scholars, then they are certainly not the only ones who can shed light on its meaning. It is a great pity that many people in the churches who are otherwise intellectually engaged in all sorts of matters often seem content with a minimal knowledge of theology and biblical studies. It is not simply a matter of our too busy lives, but of a mistaken idea that these things are somehow so esoteric that they are beyond the average person. For this reason church members turn over the responsibility for the study of scripture to the clergy and the academy. The sense that one must depend on the experts results in a passivity that often keeps Christians from the joy of discovery. This failure is all the more disappointing given the ready availability in our day of superb tools that can assist every serious student of the Bible to an extent impossible just a generation ago.

Personally, I take great pleasure in seeing laypersons engaged in the serious study of the Scriptures. I am eager to encourage them in this, and I have in a few instances supported them in getting their work published. This is one reason I was pleased to encounter the present work by John Mauck. It demonstrates the very point I have argued above, namely, that the non-specialist can produce work that is not only well-informed, but also fresh, stimulating, and enlightening—work, in short, that benefits the Christian public and builds up the church.

Furthermore it is a fact that nowadays the discipline of New Testament studies is being enriched by many ancillary disciplines—literary criticism, sociology, anthropology, linguistics, to name only a few. It is really quite wonderful in the present instance, and in keeping with this current diversity of approach, to have an accomplished lawyer bring all of his skill to bear on the study of a narrative that is filled with legal matters. Indeed Mauck's hypothesis is that the Book of Acts contains such a large amount of trials and legal material precisely because it (together with Luke) was written as "an evangelistic legal brief" for Paul's defense at his final trial in Rome. Regardless of whether one finally agrees with this bold conclusion, no one can doubt that the Acts of the Apostles is filled with material that is fruitful for the study of legal process in the ancient world. As seen through the eyes of a lawyer, the narrative of Acts is illuminated again and again in Mauck's book.

Events of the recent past have brought to the public a new awareness of, and a quite amazing interest in, the law. Not only are we an increasingly litigious society, as everyone knows, but lawyers, the courts, and the law have all made their way into our living rooms via television—now not by means of Perry Mason, but the real thing, which can be far more interesting. We are beginning to be familiar with the language of plaintiff, defendant, counsel, brief, witness, cross-examination, deposition, and so forth. Law and litigation have become fascinating subjects. What charges are being brought and why? What defense is being offered and how? What do the laws in fact say? What is the evidence? On what grounds will the final adjudication be made?

Now, for the first time that I know of, we can view the legal aspects of the Book of Acts from the perspective of a practicing lawyer. I like to think of John Mauck as similar to the expert lawyers that now appear regularly as commentators on TV. The Book of Acts presents an exciting story, with Paul frequently in trouble and facing litigation, particularly at the end of the narrative. Now Attorney Mauck is available for commentary to help us to see and appreciate the various legal aspects of the story and to understand the case that would be presented in Rome. His direct knowledge of how the legal process works and his study of law in the first century make the narrative of Acts come alive in fresh ways. And never far from the surface is the reality, as Mauck reminds us, that the story of Paul and the early church on trial is also in the last analysis a matter of the Christian faith on trial.

This is a book to be welcomed in its own right, but also as a model of the insight that a layperson can bring through study and the application of his or her own specialized knowledge to the understanding of Scripture. I am convinced that readers will find this fresh approach to Acts both fascinating and enriching.

Donald A. Hagner
George Eldon Ladd Professor of New Testament
Fuller Theological Seminary

ACKNOWLEDGEMENTS

The information revolution is reaching back two thousand years. In the Gospel of Luke, chapter 1, verse 3, the reader, Theophilus, is introduced with the title "most excellent." Those two words raise a flurry of questions. Even a decade ago it would have taken weeks of study at a university with the right research facilities or consultation with one of the few scholars possessing a lifetime of accumulated specialized knowledge to answer one of the simplest of those questions: what people were addressed as "most excellent" in Roman times? Traditional Bible teaching explained "most excellent" as a title for a Roman official. Was that teaching correct or could those words or that title have been used with any person?

Intrigued, I located a Tufts University classics website to search an extensive database of Greek and Roman writers, using English, Latin, or Greek words, to quickly locate the usage of "most excellent" among ancient authors. The Bible teachers had been generally right on this point. "Most excellent," as a form of address, was used primarily as a title for rulers or governmental officials (except by the obsequious Cicero, who would call a cow "madam" if he thought she would give him more milk).

The technical revolution has empowered researchers in every field to retrieve and synthesize information with remarkable speed and increasing quality. Even biblical and classical studies, often esoteric domains, have been shaken, refreshed, and energized by the rapid influx of new scholarship and even swifter correlation of previous scholarship from related fields. For example, one *magnum opus* on *Acts* during the 1990s is a five-volume series by Eerdmans Publishing Company[3] containing titles on Acts in its literary, Graeco-Roman, Palestinian, and Diaspora settings. It utilizes dozens of experts with disciplines ranging from numismatics to Greek linguistics, as well as presenting a thorough analysis of Roman legal procedures by Brian Rapske in a separate volume on Paul in Roman custody. These and many other scholarly resources that will be cited in this book were essential to its writing.

Accordingly, as an author, despite occasional jabs at theologians, I must first acknowledge the astonishing breadth and cogency of academic achievement on which I have been able to rely in bringing the conclusions of this book to a broader range of intelligent, educated, but less academically immersed readers. I hope those conclusions will be seen as the fruit of a long progression of collective efforts. My original contributions to an understanding of *Acts* come primarily from my professional insights as a lawyer who litigates on behalf of religious freedom. Even at that, law school professors, judges, fellow lawyers, and clients have sharpened insights which undergird this book. As well as these people remote, I have been aided by and thank people near: typist/encouragers Carol Riley and Lisa Freeman, mentors/friends Jhan Moskowitz and Dan Gruber, readers Ben Llamzon and Dan Sharon, copy editor Art Toalston, editing assistants John, Elizabeth, Andrew, Allyson Mauck, and Amanda Freeman, constructive academic critics Don Hagner, David Gill and Bruce Winter, literary agent Tom Ciesielka, Thomas Nelson director, special sales, Kathleen Dietz, editors Jim Weaver and Lee Hollaway, and marketing director Julia Hoover. Others who have helped with business contacts, letters of support, or other helpful advice include Jeff Whetstone, Sam Casey, David Brickner, Erwin Lutzer, Roy Schwarcz, Nancy Hice, my patient law partner, Rich Baker, Murray Tilles, Randy Weiss, Dave Oseland, Derek Lehman, Seli Groves, and William Anderson. Also, the members and staff of First Presbyterian Church of Evanston, the downtown Chicago Bible study group, and the discipleship group have been supportive in many ways. To Rosemary, my wife, adviser, and partner, thank you for always supporting me. Also, to Garrett Evangelical Seminary, thank you for use of your library. Most of all to God, thank You for the Light.

Introduction

Far beyond other historical sources, the Book of Acts documents the early years of the small Jewish sect which arose in a remote province of the Roman Empire and has shaped—and continues to shape—the thoughts and hearts of many civilizations and billions of people. The thirty-two-year time period covered by *Acts*, roughly A.D. 30 to 62, begins when Jesus' followers are told they will be "witnesses" beyond the land of Israel. Soon their worldview is shattered by the realization that being witnesses includes telling Gentiles they can be included in the plan of salvation of the God of Israel! *Acts* then continues through a period of persecution by Jewish leaders and ends at what we now know was the beginning of more than two centuries of Roman persecution of believers in Jesus.

To acknowledge *Acts* as a "historical" source extraordinaire is not to imply that it was written as history *per se*. The dynamics of *what* Luke wrote—resurrections, miracles, persecutions, and the explosive spread of faith in Jesus—have obscured the dynamics of *why* he wrote. The question which generations of scholars have posed and to which no self-evident answer has been found is "*Why* was *Acts* written?" Culminating with Paul, the mentor of the author Luke, in prison awaiting trial before Nero, one must ask, "Does the *ending* of Acts have anything to do with why it was written?" Luke was neither a historian nor a theologian in any modern sense. Although he wrote an account of events which occurred (history), it was not intended primarily for future students or for scholars of his generation. Nor was he seeking to teach or encourage his fellow Christians.

I contend that Luke investigated, gathered facts, borrowed from other sources, and edited[1] them for a different and definite purpose: He wrote a legal "brief" to defend Paul against charges of fomenting civil insurrection and, by extension, to defend all of Christianity against the charge that it was an illegal religion. His original reader, Theophilus, was, the evidence will show, the Roman official responsible for the judicial investigation of trials to be conducted before the Emperor Nero. Luke, true to his reputation as an evangelist, crafted his brief to present the gospel so that even the very investigator would come to believe in Jesus.

The events which Luke records are, to some worldviews, outrageous or ridiculous. The gospel message continually proclaimed by his protagonists in *Acts* claims eternal relevance to every person. Is it truth, lies, a clever mixture of both, or ignorant rantings? To judge the truth or falsity of Luke's account, one needs to understand to whom he was writing and why.

To the modern Christian who believes Scripture to be inspired by God, this book will be helpful, disquieting, and possibly radical. Helpful, as it enables the reader to understand the who, when, where, and why of this longest book of the New Testament and to better apply the message to his or her life and faith. Disquieting, as it echoes the question asked of lovers of sausage and law—"Are you sure you want to watch it being made?" And radical in that the twenty-first-century reader's "Christian identity," or understanding of what a "Christian" is, may require reconsideration.

To the reader inquisitive about the identity of Jesus, the history of Judaism or Christianity, and the truths which those faiths claim to express, *Acts* is an important primary source. To explore it, I recommend a four-wheel-drive, all-terrain vehicle. The roads, where they exist, will be unfamiliar. Sometimes we will need to traverse risky country. The rewards for the adventurous traveler will soon become apparent as we safari back two millenia to remote lands, encountering characters whose actions and ideas appear both weird and contemporary and discovering treasures overlooked by previous expeditions. Much of the analysis of the many events recounted in *Acts* will examine their veracity from a lawyer's perspective.

Because the period covered by *Acts* immediately follows the gospel accounts of Jesus' life and because resurrections, healings, miracles, and appearances of Jesus abound, the modern reader may wonder whether early Christianity was swathed in sociopathy or truth. No safe middle ground will be found between these polarities. The reader who presupposes that *Acts* was written a generation or two after the last events recorded in the book will adjust his thinking or be troubled.

The Book of Acts is one of history's hinges. First, it is a hinge to the New Testament. In the Christian canon, to its left, are the four Gospels: Matthew, Mark, Luke, and John. They recount the life of Jesus from various vantages with different, but overlapping, agendas. However, the Gospel of Luke, as will be discussed in its own chapter, has a special relationship to *Acts*. To the right of *Acts* are twenty-two letters to particular churches, individuals, and groups within the church. Beyond its central placement within the physical text of the New Testament, *Acts* is pivotal in the New Testament because of:

1. **Chronology:** The Gospels tell of the life and passion of Jesus. *Acts* picks up where they leave off. The Letters do not begin until about twenty years after the Resurrection. So *Acts* spans the period from the Resurrection, about A.D. 30, to about A.D. 62. In many respects, it is the only record of the believers in Jesus during the formative years of the church.

2. **Theology:** While the letters instruct believers *how* to live and *why*, *Acts* balances those teachings by describing how the believers, and particularly certain leaders, *actually* lived without directing the reader how he or she must live. Rightly under-

standing *Acts* is thus an indispensable link to understanding both the Gospels and Letters and how they relate to each other.

3. **Judaism:** Beyond the New Testament, *Acts* is a hinge between the Jewish and Christian faiths. The multifaceted and temple-centered Judaism of the first century was, after the destruction of Jerusalem in A.D. 70, to become the rabbinic Judaism of the next two thousand years. Its sister belief system, Jewish faith in Jesus as the Messiah, was to become known as Christianity and, through the influx of Gentiles, the world's largest religion. *Acts* is a seminal source to understanding the emergence of each faith. The question is often asked: "How did Christianity and Judaism become separate religions?" Beyond doubt, *Acts* is our most important original source for the answer to that query.

THE LAWYER'S APPROACH

As a lawyer approaching an analysis of one of the foundational documents of the Christian faith and one of the primary original source records of Judaism, Christianity, and the Roman Empire, one is moved to be both humble and assertive. Humility flows from reading many of the hundreds of books and scholarly articles on *Acts* and realizing my deficient expertise in such areas as theology, ancient literature, and sociology and confronting my ignorance of Greek, Hebrew, and German.[2] Assertiveness flows from a habit cultivated in my profession: law. An advocate, especially a litigator, which I sometimes am, must present his client's case vigorously. Equivocation at critical junctures can be fatal. Of course, a litigator who shelves his objectivity can just as surely crash himself and his client into hard realities.

THEOLOGIANS

Historically, the study of *Acts* has been dominated by theologians and biblical scholars. In my research, I have studied, slogged, and delighted through the jungles, tundras, and Edens of their writings. I have begun to understand their language, have incorporated many of their insights and, I think, fathomed some of their game rules. Empathizing with you, the reader, I will let you in on their secrets to help you understand the scholarly debates which form a background to this book and enjoy the many ironies which arise from those controversies.

Debates between biblical scholars often resemble a multi-player/multidimensional table tennis game. One theologian pings a few dozen spheroids replete with footnotes into the ether. Light years away, with paddle ready and specially tinted theological goggles tightly fitted over his bifocals, another professor gazes into the firmament hoping one of the stars is actually a hypothesis that will float into the range of his swat (his "area of expertise"). When that long-awaited opportunity arrives, perhaps years after the serve, he pongs the incoming air-filled sphere back into the cosmos, having attached his own footnote. Or, if he is particularly adept and his theological filters signal danger, he will destroy the incoming footnotes with anti-matter footnotes of his own, preferably in Greek or German. (Footnotes in irrefutable Old Syriac are reserved for special academic heresies.)

After repelling or redirecting the uncautious hypothesis, the gallant theologian then lofts his own shots into the unknown. Of course, many of those insights are never confirmed, never refuted, and never returned. They drift forever in the eternal void. And so the struggle continues. Perhaps a dozen times a century some scholar will score a point and the other players declare "progress." For example, finally in the late twentieth century a "consensus" has developed that the Gospel of Luke and the Book of Acts have the same author! Whether this author is the Luke mentioned in several New Testament letters, however, or a "putative" (i.e., reputed) Luke as some scholars describe him, or Luke Skywalker, is still not a matter of academic agreement.

I won't pretend to play in this league. My Old Syriac is rusty. If anything in this book is of value, it may be because my theological goggles don't fit so comfortably over my bifocals. Not that I lack theology—I subscribe to several theological paradigms—but I don't *see* everything theologically. Theologians see the Bible theologically, of course, whether "liberal" or "conservative," and they approach *Acts* with certain common presuppositions. After all, *Acts* is part of the Bible selected by Christians to comprise their sacred writings and is the second half of *Luke-Acts*, the first half of which, the Gospel of Luke, is child to the Gospel of Mark, sibling to the Gospel of Matthew, and cousin to the Gospel of John. For the Christian, the Gospels are in the main the accounts of Jesus, the Son of God and son of Man. How, then, the theologian reasons, can *Acts* not be theological?

Let me conclude this introduction by suggesting that not all theology derives from primarily theological works. Certainly, God put the sun in the sky to warm and brighten our lives, but a sunrise can also tell us of God. As a lawyer, I have this habit of taking off my theological goggles and slipping on my legal lenses when reading *Acts,* helping me see some things that might have been missed by those more theologically learned or analytical than I by virtue of my legal vantage point.

Glossary

Most key words and terms used in the Book of Acts are a part of our modern vocabulary, but the meaning of many of those words today differs significantly from how they would have been understood by a first-century reader. To understand on a primary level what Luke intended to express when he wrote *Acts*, we must suspend our modern definitions and, as far as possible, adopt the thinking of the times. Because *Acts* was written to a Gentile Roman reader, the definitions used will attempt to conform to what a Greek-literate first-century Roman would understand:

APOSTLE – literally "a sent-out one."
1. An itinerant evangelist such as Paul or Barnabas (see Acts 14:14), a messenger, a missionary.
2. A leader of the church exercising authority with elders in matters of doctrine and governance (see Acts 15:22-3).

BAPTISM –
1. The Jewish *mikva* or ritual cleansing bath.
2. A Jewish ritual accompanying conversion to Judaism.[4]
3. An immersion of repentance associated with the Jewish prophet John, the cousin of Jesus.

CHRIST – The Greek word for the Hebrew "Messiah" or anointed one. When we hear the word we think of Christians, but a first-century Roman would have associated the word with Jews.

CHRISTIAN – See "Jew" and Chapter 1.

CHURCH – An assembly,[5] or congregation; a Roman would have understood this term in its normal usage. The religious connotation was new and had not come to describe the believers in Jesus, clearly distinguishing it from Judaism. When Paul uses the word in Acts 20:28, "Be shepherds of the church of God, which He bought with His blood," it appears that the "of God" is added to distinguish the "assembly" from a secular "assembly"; otherwise Paul would have been redundant. Although the "church" had leaders and structure, the word in *Acts* is not used to refer to leadership or structure but only to the believers as a group. Of course "church" would not have been understood with the theological meaning it connotes today nor with the meaning it acquired in the second and third centuries.

DISCIPLE –

1. A student. Many rabbis (teachers) surrounded themselves with young men whom they would instruct in the Jewish law. Paul was a disciple of Gamaliel (Acts 22:3).

2. A believer in Jesus (see Acts 14:21, 28).

EASTER – See Passover.

EVANGEL – Evangelist, evangelism, literally the "good news." The apostles tell the evangel. Although the message of Jesus was new, the concept of seeking affirmatively to spread the message about the God of Israel was, in the first century, much more a part of normative Judaism than it is now (see Book of Jonah, Acts 19:2, Matt. 23:15).

GOD-FEARERS – Gentiles who worshiped and believed in the God of Israel, but had not become Jews and did not observe all aspects of the Jewish Law. They are mentioned seven times in *Acts* (Acts 13:16, 26, 50; 16:14; 17:4, 17; 18:6-7). The context indicates they attended synagogues and were manifoldly connected to their Jewish mentors.

JEW – Who can define? The Romans definitely tried. In the first century, the religious and ethnic identity of a person as a Jew was more tightly linked than today. The Jewish belief system at this time was biblical, priestly, and temple-centered, as opposed to rabbinic. The rabbinic system of ancient, medieval, and modern/orthodox Judaism had some antecedent elements in place at the time *Acts* was written (A.D. 61-62), but it essentially traces its origin to the era between the destruction of the temple in A.D. 70 and the destruction of political Israel during the Bar-Kochba revolt in A.D. 125[6] The Jews of A.D. 62 consisted of:

Sadducees – the politically ascendant party which controlled the priesthood. They accepted only the Hebrew Bible as authority and did not accept the oral law tradition. They did not believe in life after death.

Pharisees – Very strict observers of the Law (Torah) who widely applied regulations concerning ritual purity. They believed in the resurrection of the body, angels, demons, and the possibility that God spoke audibly to people.

Christians – In Acts they were also called Nazarenes (Acts 24:5) and followers of the Way (Acts 9:2).

Essenes – An eschatologically focused separatist group believed to have written the Dead Sea Scrolls.

Zealots – Vehement opponents of Roman rule who saw their opposition as biblically mandated.

Some sources indicate that many other sects also existed during this era, but no detailed records of those groups have survived.

MIKVA – See Baptism.

PASSOVER – Also referred to as the Feast of Unleavened Bread (Acts 20:6), memorializing to all Jews the Exodus and to the Jewish followers of Jesus also pointing to the Crucifixion and Resurrection of Yeshua.

PENTECOST – (Shabuot) The Jewish Feast of Weeks occurring fifty days after Passover (Acts 2:1; 20:16).

SANHEDRIN – The Jewish governing council of elders presided over by the high priest. It was given broad leeway by the Romans to govern but could not administer the death penalty. Communities within Israel appeared to have had a measure of self-governance apart from the Sanhedrin (see Acts 6:1-4, commentary on Acts 18:17 and Acts 1:15).

SCRIPTURES – The Hebrew Bible, or the Hebrew Bible as translated into Greek, now commonly known as the Old Testament or Old Covenant. These scriptures are also referred to as *Tanakh*. The Greek translation, known as the Septuagint, was widely used by Jews of the first century. None of the New Testament writings would be accepted as inspired for several centuries. Luke gives no indication in the Book of Acts that he understands himself to be writing Holy Scripture.

TALMIDEI YESHUA – "Students of Jesus" - disciples.

TANAKH – See Scriptures.

TORAH – Literally "teaching" or "instruction." Also used to mean the Books of Moses (Genesis, Exodus, Leviticus, Numbers, Deuteronomy) or the Law (see Acts 13:15).

WITNESS – Literally "martyr." This important word is used throughout *Acts* in its judicial courtroom sense of one who is called to testify. The secondary sense of providing a testimonial to the reality of Jesus arises from the first usage and it's also apparent in *Acts* (see Acts 1:8).[7] The third sense, that of Christian martyrdom, is beginning to be seen in *Acts* (see Acts 22:20) but does not develop fully until the next several centuries.

YOM KIPPUR – The Day of Atonement, also referred to as the Fast (Acts 27:9)

TIME CHART OF ACTS

Date	Event
A.D. 14-37	Reign of Emperor Tiberius
c. A.D. 28	Beginning of Jesus' ministry
c. A.D. 30	Passover, Crucifixion, and Resurrection
c. A.D. 30	Pentecost (Acts Chapters 1 and 2)
c. A.D. 37	Saul converted on Damascus Road
A.D. 37-41	Reign of Emperor Gaius a/k/a Caligula
A.D. 41	Emperor Gaius assassinated
A.D. 41-54	Reign of Emperor Claudius
A.D. 41	Claudius issues edict reaffirming privileges of Jews
April 7, A.D. 44	Peter delivered from prison (Acts 12:6-11)[8]
A.D. 46-48	First missionary journey (Acts 13, 14)
c. A.D. 48.	Word "Christian" first used in Antioch (Acts 11:26b)
Early A.D. 49	Jerusalem Council (Acts 15)
A.D. 49	Expulsion of Jews from Rome under Emperor Claudius (Acts 18:2)
A.D. 50-52	Second missionary journey (Acts 15:36—18:22)
A.D. 51	Famine during reign of Emperor Claudius (Acts 11:28)
A.D. 51-52	Gallio is proconsul in Corinth (Acts 18)
A.D. 53 or 54	Third missionary journey begins (Acts 18:23—21:17)
April 7, A.D. 57	Paul celebrates Passover in Philippi (Acts 20:6) [9]
A.D. 54-68	Reign of Emperor Nero
A.D. 52-59	Governorship of Felix in Judea (Acts 24)
A.D. 57-59	Paul imprisoned in Caesarea (Acts 24–26)
A.D. 60	Revolts in Britain against Roman rule
June, A.D. 59-62	Governorship of Festus in Judea (Acts 25)
A.D. 60-62	Paul imprisoned in Rome (Acts 28:30), *Luke-Acts* written
A.D. 62	Nero sheds all restraints as adviser Sextus Afrianus Burrus dies and adviser Seneca retires
A.D. 62	Jacob (James), brother of Jesus, is killed in Jerusalem by order of the high priest
July 19, A.D. 64	Great fire of Rome, subsequently blamed on Christians by Nero
A.D. 66	Israel revolts against Rome
A.D. 69-70	Jerusalem besieged – Vespasian crushes revolt and destroys temple

1 Luke 1:1-4.

2 Next to English, more scholarly articles on Acts are written in German than any other language. I have, however, utilized my passable reading knowledge of French and Latin sources in researching the book.

3 Various editors, Grand Rapids: Eerdmans, 1993-96, and Brian Rapske, *The Book of Acts and Paul in Roman Custody* (Grand Rapids: Eerdmans; Carlisle, U.K.: Paternoster Press, 1994).

4 "Our rabbis taught: A proselyte who comes to convert at this time, we say to him: Why did you decide to convert? . . . we are not too lengthy with him nor are we too detailed. If he accepts this we circumcise him immediately . . . once he has recovered, we immerse him immediately . . . If he is immersed validly, he is an Israelite in all matters. (In the case of a woman, position her in the water up to her neck and make known to her some of the lighter and some of the weightier commandments.) (b. Yeb. 47 a-b)," quoted by Alan F. Segal, *Paul the Convert* (New Haven: Yale University Press, 1990), 101-2.

5 Acts 19:39, and Paul Treblico, "Asia" in *The Book of Acts in Its Graeco-Roman Setting* (Grand Rapids: Eerdmans, 1994), 356-7.

6 See generally Dan Gruber, *Rabbi Akiba's Messiah* (Hanover, N.H.: Elijah Publishers, 1998).

7 Marie-Eloise Rosenblatt devotes much of her excellent book, *Paul the Accused, His Portrait in the Acts of the Apostles* (Collegeville, Minn.: a Michael Glazier Book, the Liturgical Press, 1995), to exploration of the theme of witness in the Book of Acts.

8 Jerome Johnson, *At the Right Time: Dating the Events of the New Testament* (Havre de Grace, Md.: Bath Kol Books, 1998), 291.

9 David Gill, "Macedonia" in *Acts in Graeco-Roman Setting*, 399; see also Johnson, *At the Right Time*, 324.

CHAPTER 1

THE "CHRISTIANS,"
"*THE* JEWS,"
THE AUTHOR,
AND THE ACCUSED

What do you think of when you hear the word "Christian"? As we have come to understand it at the beginning of the twenty-first century, "Christian" is fraught with theological, socioeconomic, and political connotations. However, in A.D. 62 those connotations, to the extent they existed, differed in many ways. If you think of a swarthy Jew with a robe and sandals, you may have a good visual image of a first century follower of Jesus. In fact, the word "Christian" had only recently been minted when the Book of Acts was written.

Until Greeks in the Roman City of Antioch began to believe in the Messiah of Israel, about A.D. 48, all believers in Jesus thought of themselves as Jews. No one had ever used the word Christian. When necessary, to distinguish themselves from other Jews who did not believe in Jesus, they called themselves or their fellow Jews called them "Nazarenes," or followers of the "Way." They also called themselves the "church," meaning the "assembly," or literally, the "called out ones."

All of these appellations sufficed until the believers in Antioch began to admit many Gentiles into their congregations without requiring them to be circumcised and become Jews. At that point, certain Greek speakers took the word "Christ," which is Greek for the Hebrew title "Messiah," and applied it to this congregation of Jews and Greeks who were following the God of Abraham and believed that Jesus was the Messiah of Israel and the source of universal salvation. Apparently, these Greek speakers were not believers and the term "Christian" was derogatory.[1]

In fact, the word "Christian" appears only three times in the New Testament[2] in contexts which suggest that Gentile nonbelievers were applying the word to the followers of Jesus. Greek-speaking Jews who did not follow Jesus would have been unlikely to use this term initially, for that would have implied an admission of the claim that Jesus was the Messiah.[3] Thus, to the modern reader, the first century people who have come to be known as "Christians" can more accurately be described as "Messianics." Yet even that term can be confusing if the reader does not bear in mind that in the first century almost all Jews were looking for the Messiah. Accordingly, in this book the words Christians, Messianics, messianists, Jews who believed in Jesus, Jewish Christians, *Talmidei Yeshua* (disciples of Jesus), and similar terms are used interchangeably to express the greater Jewishness that the church had at that time.

As will be seen from the commentary on the text, the Jewish believers in Jesus were, in A.D. 62, struggling to keep the Roman Empire and the non-Messianic Jewish leadership from pushing them out of Judaism. Theirs was a struggle against powerful political, social, and religious forces still present today, a struggle that echoes in the ever-continuing question "Who is a Jew?" Parallel questions may occur to the modern reader: Who can call a Jew a Jew? Can a Greek, such as Luke, who believes in the Messiah and God of Israel but is not circumcised, call a Jew a Jew and not be seen as anti-Jewish?

A couple of years ago, I was sitting in my car in a Chicago neighborhood. A man carrying a golf club came walking down the street, stopped at every storefront, and took a big swing at each plate glass window, leaving a large hole. The man happened to be black. Immediately, I drove off to alert the police and was fortunate to spot two officers in a patrol car within a couple of blocks. After I hailed them and described a man breaking windows with a golf club, one of the officers, who also happened to be black, looked at me (I am white) and asked, "Was he white or black?" His question evoked cognitive dissonance because my first thought was that the race of the vandal was irrelevant and the question offensive. I must have been wondering whether the officer was suspecting that I might be reporting a black man swinging a golf club because I didn't like the looks of him in the predominantly white neighborhood we were in. Those thoughts were fleeting, however, when I quickly realized that the man's color would be one of the easiest ways for the police to recognize the perpetrator when they drove over to the scene of the vandalism. So I answered the officer's question and the police proceeded to investigate.

It may at first seem to us in the twenty-first century that Luke's use of the phrase "the Jews" and his portrayal of much of the Jewish leadership as corrupt evinces an anti-Jewish bias. Throughout *Acts*, Luke refers to Paul's opponents as "the Jews," "the Jewish leaders," or sometimes with greater precision, such as "the Jews from Antioch and Iconium."[4] In various contexts, he also refers to the Messianics as "the Jews."[5] Thus, the context of *Acts* indicates that the term was used in a descriptive rather than pejorative sense (see also the commentary on Acts 28:19).

Nevertheless, in the years leading up to A.D. 62, the Jewish establishment was persecuting the Jewish believers in Jesus severely and the *Talmidei Yeshua* were under serious suspicion if not threat by the Roman establishment as well. Thus, the description of the Jewish leadership in *Acts* (and the Gospels) is harsh. This opinion was shared by other Jewish sources and so is unlikely to be purely sectarian.[6] Although the priesthood and temple appear to have been respected by many Jewish people at this time,[7] two circumstances existed which tended to separate the temple authorities and particularly the high priest from the populace. First, the high priesthood, according to Hebrew scriptures, was to be hereditary. The Romans, however, through their military dominance, had usurped the prerogative of naming the high priest. He was their man. Second, the tax burden, partly to benefit the temple authorities, was heavy. "The total taxation of the Jewish people in the time of Jesus, civil and religious combined, must have approached the intolerable proportion of between 30 and 40 per cent."[8] "They [the Jews] had to pay two sets of dues, each of which was calculated with complete disregard of the other; the Jewish authorities were as little disposed to relax the temple dues in the light of the imperial tribute as the Roman government was to relax the tribute in the light of the temple dues."[9]

Proselytes to Judaism were also common, as were God-fearers. The proselytes are mentioned in *Acts* frequently by Luke perhaps because to the Romans they constituted an unknown or ominous political threat. For example, during the Jewish revolt in A.D. 66–70, the Adiabeneans, whose ruling dynasty had converted to Judaism in the middle of the first century A.D., joined in the war against Rome.[10] Thus Roman authorities would have been acutely interested in Jewish movements, and any Roman official reading *Acts* would have seen a *political*, as well as a religious, implication from the use of the word "Jew." The modern reader of *Acts* must be continually aware that the author and the original reader of *Acts* understood references to Jews and Jewish leadership in the preceding politically charged context.

"BUT LAWYER?"—LUKE THE AUTHOR

Luke, the author of *Acts* and of his namesake book *Luke*, has been described in many ways other than as a lawyer. In his letter to the believers in Jesus at Colosse, the Apostle Paul calls him a "dear friend," a "beloved physician."[11] In his letter to Philemon, he refers to Luke as a "fellow worker,"[12] and as Paul, under Roman arrest, senses the end of his life, he writes that "only Luke is with me."[13] From the passage in Colossians we also learn that Luke was a Gentile.[14] His self-description in the introduction to the Gospel of Luke is as an historian/investigative reporter.[15] Historian Philip Satterthwaite adds to our understanding of Luke: "He [Luke] gives clear indication of having received the kind of [rhetorical] education one would expect in a Graeco-Roman writer of this period who embarked on a work of this sort."[16]

Luke's use of the third person plural in Acts 16:10 and subsequent passages gives presumptive evidence that he joined Paul's evangelistic team during the second missionary journey and was an eyewitness to much of what he wrote. His name, proficient use of Greek, and possible origin in Troas or Mysia in Asia Minor suggest he was ethnically Greek. Although he is not named in the text as author, church tradition, most scholars,[17] and the text itself all point to the Luke mentioned throughout Paul's letters as the author of *Acts* and the gospel which bears his name.

Beloved physician, Greek, historian, reporter, disciple and friend of Paul, evangelist, educated speaker, fellow worker, Gentile, but lawyer? While we have no evidence that Luke ever argued before a tribunal, collected a fee, or wrote a will, *Luke-Acts* appears to have been written to defend Paul from charges pending against him as he awaited trial before the Roman Emperor Nero. I will argue that *Luke-Acts* is a legal brief, an extraordinary brief. And more than just a legal defense of Paul, *Luke-Acts* is written to defend all of the believers in Jesus *and* to win the heart of the reader charged with gathering facts for Paul's trial and the hearts of those reading over his shoulder. Thus, because he has written a defense for Paul's trial, Luke not only qualifies as a "lawyer," but also as the first lawyer/evangelist.

PAUL—THE FOCUS OF ACTS

Paul is the chief protagonist of *Acts*. Even though not introduced until the end of chapter 7, his personality and the events of his life, starting with his conversion in chapter 9, come to dominate the narrative which culminates with his imprisonment in Rome. In cinematographic terms, we might say the wide-angle lens scans and envelops the earliest years of the followers of Jesus in Acts 1–12, then narrows to Paul's missionary journeys throughout the Roman Empire from chapter 13 to 20 and, from chapters 20 to 28, purposefully and exclusively focuses on Paul and the legal charges and proceedings pending against him.

Acts and the New Testament Epistles give many details concerning and insights into the man Paul. Volumes about him abound[18] but for our purposes a few observations about his identity and a few observations concerning his role as a "legal client" are pertinent.

PAUL'S IDENTITY

Paul's self-description is as an "Israelite, of the seed of Abraham, of the tribe of Benjamin."[19] He was born in the Roman colony of Tarsus in Asia Minor and educated as a Pharisee (the then theologically dominant sect of Judaism) under Rabbi Gamaliel.[20] *Acts* details his dramatic conversion while journeying to Damascus to persecute followers of the Way. Thirteen of the twenty-four New Testament letters were written by him. Of those, five were certainly written while he was imprisoned in Rome from A.D. in 61 to 63 (or possibly during his imprisonment in Caesarea from A.D. 59 to 60).

PAUL AS A LEGAL CLIENT

The best clients 1) understand their legal objectives; 2) communicate well with their attorney; 3) carefully distinguish between facts and conclusions; and 4) understand some of the subjectivity of the legal system.[21] By these measures Paul was an ideal client. His stated life purpose was to "preach Christ [Messiah] crucified, to the Jews a stumbling block and to the Greeks [Gentiles] foolishness, but to those who are called, both Jews and Greeks, Christ [Messiah is] the power of God and the wisdom of God."[22] Although his oratorical abilities received mixed reviews,[23] his communication skills as a writer were extraordinary.

Certainly those skills would have been well used in collaborating with Luke, the lawyer, or more precisely, Luke the brief writer. Paul's rabbinic education, the argumentative aspects of his ministry, and his frequent debates with opponents of his message honed a rhetorician's mindset which carefully distinguished between first- and secondhand knowledge, between facts and conclusions, and between what he clearly remembered and what was vague.[24] Luke records Paul's main argument in defense of the charges against him: "[I am] saying no other things than those which the prophets and Moses said would come—that the Christ [Messiah] would suffer, that He would be the first to rise from the dead, and would proclaim light to the Jewish people and to the Gentiles."[25] The familiarity of Paul with the intricacies and vagaries of Roman jurisprudence will be apparent as the reader's perusal or re-perusal of *Acts* proceeds. As will be shown from the text or collateral sources, Paul, although not the author of *Acts*, was the perfect "client" to help frame the legal strategy for his defense and to collaborate with, direct, and assist his disciple, friend, and brother in Messiah, Luke, in writing the greatest brief ever written.

THE CHARGES AGAINST PAUL AND THE CHRISTIANS

The first question a criminal defense lawyer asks his client is "What are you accused of?" Because all serious charges against Roman citizens required an *inscriptio*, a written list of charges, we know that Paul had a number of specific charges pending as he awaited trial in Rome. Those charges could well have subsumed previous accusations made against Paul and the disciples of Jesus at other locations and times.

Consequently, if *Acts* is written to defend Paul we would expect to find references and rebuttals to those charges, explicit and implicit. The *Chart of Fourteen Charges Against Paul* correlates loosely with the *Chart of Sixteen Trials in Acts* found after the commentary to Acts 7, in that every "trial" referenced except one has associated charges. However, many of the trials result from multiple charges and many of the charges referenced or rebutted in *Acts* have no explicit corresponding legal proceeding. I suggest that Luke, in writing *Acts*, incorporated events which refuted actual charges against Paul or anticipated collateral accusations which he thought could arise during the trial itself. Consequently, the charges have been prioritized according to my judgment of the likelihood of having been pressed against Paul in Rome. The first four charges are highly likely to be pending as *Acts* is written. Numbers five through eight are possible, while nine through fourteen were not formally pressed. However, evidence concerning the events underlying charges five through fourteen would have been relevant to the primary charges by supporting or refuting Paul's pattern of behavior. In contrast, the overlapping *Chart of Sixteen Trials in Acts* is chronologized.

CHART OF FOURTEEN CHARGES AGAINST PAUL

	Acts	Charges	Probable Accuser(s) or Main Witness(es)	Location of Alleged Crime	Comment
1.	22, 24:5	*Vis*, inciting riots	high priest Ananias, Jewish leaders	Jerusalem temple, "all over the world"	Chapter 22 is explanation of "what really happened."
2.	19, 19:26, 19:37	Inciting riot; *Inuria*, blaspheming Roman Gods, particularly Artemis	Alexander, Demetrius	Ephesus	Explicit exoneration by Luke indicates charges. Blasphemy allegedly caused the riot.
3.	25:7–8	*Religio illicita*, (advocating illegal new religion), "serious charges," desecrating temple	chief priests and Jewish leaders	Jerusalem	Rebuttal by Luke indicates charge and letter from Lysias (Acts 23:26 is Ex. A for defense).
4.	28:17	Illegal religion	probably in *inscriptio*	everywhere Paul went	Explicit rebuttal indicates probability of charge pending.
5.	24:17	*Collegia*, having illegal common funds	possibly in *inscriptio*	on way to Jerusalem	See section on *collegia, infra*, which relates to illegal religion.
6.	23:2–5	*Inuria*, defaming and possibly striking the high priest	uncertain	Sanhedrin in Jerusalem	See discussion of that passage.
7.	17:5–9	Inciting riot, *maiestas*, treason	Jews of Thessalonica	Thessalonica	Echoes charges against Jesus, Luke 23:22.
8.	21:21	Illegal religion	non-Christian Jews in Jerusalem	outside of Jerusalem	16:21 is a charge of being *unRoman* while 21:21 is of being *unJewish*.

CHART OF FOURTEEN CHARGES AGAINST PAUL

	Acts	Charges	Probable Accuser(s) or Main Witness(es)	Location of Alleged Crime	Comment
9.	18:13	Illegal religion	Jews of Corinth	Corinth	Probably being accused of violating Mosaic not Roman law due to Gallio's response, but see text discussion.
10.	16:20	Upsetting social order	Slave owners	Philippi	Too vague to be a criminal charge.
11.	16:21	Illegal religion	Slave owners	Philippi	This charge though not particularly from this location is rebutted throughout Acts.
12.	16:16–19	Stirring up rebelliousness in slaves	uncertain	Philippi	See discussion of that passage.
13.	13:50, 14:5, 14:19	Inciting riots	Jews in Pisidian Antioch and Iconium	Pisidian Antioch, Iconium, Lystra, and Derbe	Civil disturbances followed Paul's preaching. Luke's explanation suggests rebuttal. Because events occurred about 15 years before trial they are less likely to have been the basis of charges.
14.	17:18	Advocating foreign gods, illegal religion	Jews of Athens	Athens	Text suggests prosecution in Rome was unlikely because *Areopagus* already heard charges.

Acts also recounts or implies charges against other Christians who would not have been on trial with Paul. These charges might have been cumulated against Paul to show that the Christians (and Paul as a leader) were seditious (see Acts 24:5).

CHART OF FOUR CHARGES AGAINST OTHER CHRISTIANS

	Acts	Accused	Probable Accuser(s)	Charge	Comment
1.	4:18, 5:28	Peter, John Apostles	high priest and Sanhedrin	teaching about the resurrection and violating order not to	These charges are not the basis of criminal prosecution.
2.	5:18–19 12:5–11 16:23– 29	Peter Peter Paul and Silas	none specified	jail breaking	Charges are inferred due to apparent rebuttal. See discussion of particular verses.
3.	4:44 5:1–2	Peter, church	none specified	*collegia* or possibly theft or running a scam	See discussion of verses.
4.	6:13–14	Stephen	members of the synagogue of the Freedmen	blaspheming the temple, advocating illegal new religion	Discredits prosecution.

1 Peter 4:16.

2 Acts 11:26, 11:28 and 1 Peter 4:16.

3 F. F. Bruce, *New Testament History* (Garden City, N.Y.: Doubleday, 1971), 268.

4 E.g., Acts 13:43.

5 E.g., Acts 12:43, 13:1.

6 Dan Gruber in the pamphlet, "The High Priests Who Condemned Jesus" (www.elijahnet.org) writes:

The Talmud speaks of how these particular high priests robbed the common priests of what was due to them and brushed off all pleas for restraint. For example, the common priests were customarily given the skins of the sacrificed animals, but these high priests demanded the skins for themselves. Attempts were made to reason with them:

"Yet the chief priests still seized (them) by force . . . Abba Saul b. Bothnith said in the name of Abba Joseph b. Hanin: 'Woe is me because of the house of Boethus; woe is me because of their staves! [The Soncino edition footnote adds: 'with which they beat the people.'] Woe is me because of the house of Kathros; woe is me because of their pens! [The footnote adds: 'with which they wrote their evil decrees.'] Woe is me because of the house of Ishmael the son of Phabi; woe is me because of their fists! For they are high priests and their sons are temple treasurers and their sons-in-law are trustees and their servants beat the people with staves!'

"Our rabbis taught: Four cries did the temple court cry out. The first: Depart hence, ye children of Eli, for they defiled the temple of the Lord."

In calling these high priests and their families the "children of Eli," the rabbis meant that these high priests had the same character and behavior as the sons of Eli . . .

Josephus remarks:

"As for the high priest Ananias, he increased in glory every day, and this to a great degree . . . for he was a great hoarder of money . . . He also had servants who were very wicked, who joined themselves to the boldest sort of the people, and went to the threshing-floors, and took away the tithes that belonged to the priests by violence, and did not refrain from beating such as would not give these tithes to them. So the other high priests acted in the like manner, as did those his servants, without anyone being able to prohibit them; so that (some of the) priests, that of old were wont to be supported with those tithes, died for want of food . . .

"A sedition arose between the high priests, with regard to one another; for they got together bodies of the people, and frequently came from reproaches to throwing of stones at each other; but Ananias was too hard for the rest, by his riches, which enabled him to gain those that were the most ready to receive. Costabarus, also, and Saulus, did themselves get together a multitude of wicked wretches . . . but still they used violence with the people weaker than themselves. And from that time it principally came to pass, that our city was greatly disordered, and that all things grew worse and worse among us."

The particular Annas, or Ananias, to whom Josephus refers is not the same as the one depicted in the gospels. He is of the same family, only a generation later. The leaders of this family were ungodly, greedy, and violent men.

Alfred Edersheim wrote of the commerce that this family conducted in the temple:

"This (temple) market was what in Rabbinic writings is styled 'the bazaars of the sons of Ananas' (Chanuyoth beney Chanan), the sons of that high priest Annas, who is so infamous in New Testament history . . . From the unrighteousness of the traffic carried on in these bazaars, and the greed of the owners, the 'temple-market' was at the time most unpopular. This appears, not only from the conduct and words of the patriarch Simeon [the grandson of Hillel, cf. Ker.i.7] and of Baba ben Buta (as above quoted) [Jerus.Chag. 78a], but from the fact that popular indignation, 3 years before the destruction of Jerusalem, swept away the bazaars of the family of Annas, and this, as expressly stated on account of the sinful greed which characterized their dealings."

The rabbis and Josephus characterized these high priests as brutal, greedy, and power hungry.

Gruber attributes the Talmud citation to Pesachim 57a, pp. 284-5, *The Babylonian Talmud*, Rabbi Dr. I. Epstein, ed. (London: Soncino Press); the Josephus citation from "Antiquities of the Jews" XX, 9, 2-4, *The Works of Josephus*, William Whiston, trans. (Peabody, Mass.: Hendrickson Publishers, 1985), 424; the Edersheim citation from his *The Life and Times of Jesus, the Messiah* Vol. 1 (New York: Anson D. F. Randolph and Co., 1883), 371-2, in turn citing Siphre on Dt. sec. 105, end, ed. Friedmann, 95a; Jer. Peah i.6. See also Steve Mason, "Chief Priests, Sadducees, Pharisees and Sanhedrin in Acts" in *The Book of Acts in Its Palestinian Setting* (Grand Rapids: Eerdmans; Carlisle, U.K.: Paternoster Press, 1995).

7   See Acts 23:5.

8   Bruce, *New Testament History*, 40, quoting F. C. Grant, *The Economic Background of the Gospels* (Oxford: Oxford University Press, 1926), 105.

9   Ibid., 39.

10 Irina Levinskaya, "Diaspora Jews" in *The Book of Acts in Its Diaspora Setting* (Grand Rapids: Eerdmans; Carlisle, U.K.: Paternoster Press, 1996), 3.

11 Col. 4:14 (NIV and AV).

12 Philem. 24.

13 2 Tim. 4:14.

14 Col. 4:10-14.

15 Luke 1:3.

16 Philip Satterthwaite, "The Background of Classical Rhetoric" in *The Book of Acts in Its Literary Setting* (Grand Rapids: Eerdmans, 1993), 378.

17 See Joseph Fitzmyer, *The Acts of the Apostles*, The Anchor Bible series (Garden City, N.Y.: Doubleday, 1998), 50.

18 See e.g., W. M. Ramsay's classic *St. Paul the Traveller and the Roman Citizens* (London: 1920).

19 Rom. 11:1.

20 Acts 22:3.

21 Whether Paul had that highly desirable fifth qualification of a "best" client, cash, will be discussed later.

22 1 Cor. 1:23-25.

23 Compare 2 Cor. 10:10 with Acts 17:22-31.

24 See 1 Cor. 1:10-17.

25 Acts 26: 22b-23.

CHAPTER 2

EMPIRE, EMPERORS, AND LAW

The period covered by *Acts,* A.D. 30–62, corresponds with the earlier Roman Empire. Two of the four emperors who reigned during that period, **Gaius aka Caligula** (A.D. 37–41) and **Nero** (A.D. 54–68) were base tyrants. The first, **Tiberius** (A.D. 14–37) does not figure significantly in *Acts*. The third, and only emperor mentioned by name in *Acts,*[1] **Claudius**, reigned from A.D. 41 to 54.

Gaius considered himself the brother of the Roman god Jupiter and required that sacrifices be made to him. He even ordered that his statue be set up in the temple at Jerusalem, but his legate in Syria delayed obeying the order, knowing it could trigger a revolt among the Jews. Gaius' death by assassination in A.D. 41 by a tribune of the Praetorian Guard prevented the implementation of the order and possibly averted a Jewish revolt.

Claudius, as did other emperors, insisted upon order but did so more in the context of developing the legal system. While he respected the Roman Senate and encouraged its active role in governmental affairs, he retained ultimate authority. He also created a cabinet ("*consilium*") or secretaryships for various duties:

1. *A cognitionibus*—for the judicial investigations of trials to be conducted by the emperor;
2. *Ab epistulis*—for imperial correspondence;
3. *A libellis*—in charge of petitions directed to the emperor; and
4. *A studiis*—in charge of the imperial library.

Although these offices are not mentioned in *Acts*, the thoroughness of Roman record keeping is highly relevant. The mere existence of a special post dedicated to pretrial investigation bears especially on the credibility of the thesis that *Acts* was written as a legal defense.

In contrast to his predecessor Gaius and successor Nero, Claudius was a relatively decent emperor. One of his first official edicts was to reaffirm privileges granted Jews under Roman law: no military prescription and no requirements to worship the emperor.[2] He did have at least one serious confrontation with the Jews when he expelled them from Rome in A.D. 49 (Acts 18:2).[3] Although Jewish believers in Jesus may have arrived in Rome as early as A.D. 31 or 32,[4] no direct historical evidence exists that the Roman emperor was aware of the spreading faith until the serious accusations against Paul[5] were delivered to Emperor Nero about A.D. 61.

Nero, although not mentioned by name in *Acts*, is a central behind-the-scenes character of the drama. By the time *Acts* was written about A.D. 62, he had been emperor for eight years. All of *Acts* (and its companion volume, *Luke*) could have been written with the hope that it would be read by Nero.[6] To understand *Acts*, it helps enormously to consider the possibility of Nero as one of the intended eventual readers of the legal defense of Paul and Christianity.

The nephew and adopted son of Claudius, the previous emperor, Nero married his stepsister at age sixteen and became emperor at age seventeen. Many historians believe his mother, Agrippina, poisoned Claudius so Nero could become emperor. Like his predecessors, he believed himself to be a god and required formal offerings from all but the Jews. Initially Nero relied on two senior statesmen, a military officer, Sextus Afrianius Burrus, and the philosopher/playwrite, Lucius Annaeus Seneca (Seneca the younger), to help him govern. Seneca and Burrus worked in tandem to govern Rome efficiently and, by Roman standards, fairly. Nero tried unsuccessfully to remove Burrus in A.D. 55.[7] In A.D. 59, five years after he assumed power, Nero had his mother murdered.

The reasoned and moderating influence of Seneca on Nero and his administrators may explain the tenor in *Acts* which suggests that facts, law, and reason may prevail over lies, politics, and fear in the adjudication of the charges against Paul. However, in A.D. 62, Burrus died. The Roman historian Tacitus reports Burrus' death broke the *potentia* (power, efficacy) of Seneca.[8] Seneca retired that same year, leaving Nero, at age twenty-five, effectively unrestrained. Because *Acts* was written in A.D. 61 to 62 while both this military adviser and this adviser/philosopher were still in power, it is reasonable to consider that Burrus and Seneca were within the circle of intended readers of *Acts* and to test the assertions of this book by asking whether *Acts* contains information or legal arguments of concern to a military adviser or philosopher at the highest level of the Roman Empire.

It would not be an exaggeration to describe Nero's reign as a progression from the libertine to a "sexual phantasmagoria."[9] "Nero's subsequent homosexual marriage in the capacity of wife to the freedman Pythagoras with the observance of all the ancient traditional rites of Roman matrimony . . . was a deliberately offensive (if entertaining) parody."[10] Historian Vasily Rudich concludes that Nero, in leading and pressuring the upper classes into debauchery may have been the primary object of Paul's denunciation of sexual promiscuity in his epistle to the Romans:[11] "Therefore God also gave them up to uncleanness, in the lusts of their hearts, to dishonor their bodies among themselves, who exchanged the truth of God for the lie, and worshiped and served the creature rather than the Creator."[12]

Nero was also feared for his murders of leaders who opposed him, his cruelty, and his wild suspicions. Most famously, he is remembered for blaming the fire which destroyed most of Rome, on July 19, A.D. 64 on the Christians after the rumor had spread that Nero himself was the instigator of arson. The historical portraiture which emerges is Josef Stalin in drag.

ROMAN CRIMINAL LAW

Rome had a sophisticated, proven, and at the time *Acts* was written, evolving criminal justice system. Under Augustus who reigned about one hundred years earlier, the regular, standing courts began to experience problems in handling certain cases. Consequently special investigations/special prosecutions, *cognitiones extra ordinem*, were instituted outside the regular court system to handle unusual or particularly difficult or important cases. "The trials in these *iudicia publica extra ordinem* [special public trials] were always conducted by public officials. Jurisdiction was exercised . . . chiefly by the emperor and the prefects."[13]

With the possibility in mind that Paul's trial before Nero would not have been a routine proceeding, let us consider the categories of Roman criminal law[14] so that we can compare them with charges against Paul and the Jewish Christians as well as the countercharges which Luke directs against Paul's accusers. This comparison may enable us to discern whether the charges correspond significantly to the existing legal categories or if they bear little relationship to each other. A significant correspondence will be evidence that *Acts* was written as a legal defense for Paul's trial.

Vis: (battery, violence; literally "force") bringing a group together to beat someone up or inciting a public riot. A subcategory, *vis publica,* included abuse of office such as killing, flogging, or imprisoning a citizen without a trial or who was appealing to the emperor.[15] The penalty, depending on the severity of the *vis,* could include death.

Iniuria: (outrage, defamation; literally "injury" or "law breaking") an offense "against a person's honor, his reputation, his dignity, or his physical integrity"[16] This crime required proof of malicious intent, and to the extent it pertained to defamation, truth was a defense. The penalties for *iniuria* ranged from a fine to imprisonment (exile) on an island: "*interdictio aquae et ignis,*" literally "removal of fire and water," i.e., deprivation of home and hearth.

Calumnia: a criminal procedural crime, including the bringing of false charges.[17]

Res Repetundae: (corruption) taking of or extorting of bribes or other forms of official corruption. The penalty was almost certainly exile (*interdictio aquae et ignis*) but could include death if the crime brought about the death of an innocent man.[18]

Maiestas or Perduellio: (treason, sedition) This crime overlapped *res repetundae* and *vis,* included *collegia* (discussed next[19]) and covered words as well as deeds.[20]

Actions which included treason were assembling a mob against the interests of the state, occupying a temple, writing or dictating a falsehood onto the public record and, for a judge, to enter a false judgment. It was also *maiestas* "to lay false claim to Roman citizenship."[21] The penalty for *maiestas* was usually death.[22]

Collegia: (unlawful assemblies, illegal associations) included any group "with a common fund and a treasurer or manager" which met without specific permission from the Senate or the emperor. This prohibition was designed to prevent groups that could incite electoral violence or represent a threat to the public order. Most importantly for our inquiry, *Jewish* religious gatherings were specifically exempted from this law.[23]

Tergiversatio: (dropping charges) The complete abandonment of a completed accusation.[24] No one in *Acts* is accused of this crime; however, it has an important bearing on the denouement of *Acts*. Although *Acts* ends with Paul awaiting trial in Rome, we can be sure his accusers from Caesarea followed through with the prosecution not only because of their motivations (to be discussed) which led them to bring the charges but also because they would face charges of *tergiversatio*.

RELIGIO ILLICITA

Rome recognized two religions as legal: Judaism and its own emperor cult/polytheistic pantheon of gods which served as an umbrella for devotees or cults of many gods (similar to modern Hinduism). This reinforced the political system and helped unify the disparate elements of the far-flung empire. Emperor worship, particularly, legitimized and helped sustain imperial authority. All other religions were illegal (*religio illicita*). We know that Christianity after the writing of *Acts* in about A.D. 62 and before its legalization under Constantine in A.D. 313 underwent long periods of illegality accompanied by shorter periods of severe persecution. While the fire which destroyed much of Rome in A.D. 64 was blamed by Emperor Nero on the Christians, the anti-Christian Roman writer Tacitus concluded that Nero was just making them scapegoats.[25]

Against this background, it is a conclusion of this book that the Jewish sect called Christians was in A.D. 62 fighting for its legal life. On one hand, they were persecuted by the Romans as Jews when other Jews were being persecuted and as Jews they were politically suspect:[26] The Jewish revolt against Rome, which would culminate in the destruction of Jerusalem and the Temple in A.D. 70 by Vespasian, was simmering and would soon erupt in A.D. 66. On the other hand, *Acts* details the intense and often vehement persecution of the Messianics by the Jewish leadership in Jerusalem and the Diaspora. The litigation strategy of Paul's accusers was to charge that he was creating an illegal religion thereby disrupting society. Although Christianity had a persuasive claim to legality as a sect of Judaism, it was caught in the cross-currents between Jerusalem and Rome. In the midst of this legal/political/religious cauldron, *Acts* was written to help this nascent sect survive.

PROCEDURES AND SYSTEMS

In addition to the laws we have just considered, every legal system contains procedures for applying those laws. Such procedures, including trials, are, at their best, searches for truth not Truth. Although ideally the individual participants should have truth as an end, usually their focus is narrower: a defendant seeks acquittal, a prosecutor seeks conviction and a judge must render a verdict. Even the legal system itself has forces which pull it from truth: politics, social order, limited time and resources, privileges,[27] the need for finality, and the effect a certain decision will have on the behavior of others. Given the brigands who would kidnap truth for their own ends, legal systems have stationed sentries along the procedural routes. The Roman criminal system had some safeguards that were unique to the needs of their society, some that are fairly universal, while in some areas safeguards were lacking.

To understand the import of the many trials referenced in *Acts*, it behooves us to know what the original reader knew:

<u>Judges, the Emperor and the Senate:</u> A provincial governor such as Felix (Acts 24) or Festus (Acts 25) was "commonly referred to simply as *iudex*, (judge), because that had become the most important aspect of his duties."[28] The same can probably be said of a proconsul, such as Gallio (Acts 18) or Sergio Paulus (Acts 13), whose job was to govern a Roman (as opposed to a provincial) colony. Because of the power these men held, the pressures and incentives to abuse were enormous and the countervailing penalties for corruption severe. Provincial governors were frequently rotated to lessen corruption. Each governor had a *consilium* (council) to consult concerning important decisions to help assure he was following Roman law and imperial policy.[29] The emperor too had a personal *consilium* with jurists on it and he could also refer to the Roman Senate which constituted a formal *consilium*.[30] Although the emperor had final decision making authority, any ruler/judge will, of necessity, delegate the investigation and trial preparation to subordinates. A written submission to the court such as a pretrial "brief," giving background, exculpatory explanations, and legal arguments, logically would be prepared in a major case such as Paul's; however, no parallel examples of "pretrial briefs" have survived, if any did exist.

<u>Recording of Trials</u>: "As [a] speech was being presented in court it was taken down in shorthand . . . these proceedings were being thus recorded no later than about A.D. 50 . . . all official proceedings are summaries. For all that, they were nevertheless regarded as accurate representations of what was said in court. These official documents were placed in government archives, for Rome attached great importance to the storage and preservation of all official documents, not least all those relating to legal proceedings."[31]

<u>Copies of Documents</u>: "Certified copies of official documents relating to judicial proceedings were available to a defendant, as was the forensic petition which initiated the judicial action . . . So too was other evidence such as petitions, letters and memoranda related to the legal cases. Therefore, a certified copy of any legal document was regarded in its day as genuine and there was no discrimination against a certified copy in favour of the original."[32]

Commentariensis (<u>Clerk of Court and prison supervisor</u>): "A rank below the centurionate, found on the office staff of most magistrates, his function was the keeping of records."[33]

The importance of written records and communications is magnified given the distances which the Roman Empire spanned and the right of a Roman citizen, such as Paul, in a far-off province to appeal to Rome. Such records also would be significant in the particular context of the charges against Paul and Christianity which involved events in many locations. The centurion, Julius, who takes the prisoner Paul from Caesarea to Rome in Acts 27, may have just been promoted from _commentariensis_. Or , because of the importance of Paul, this official may have been assigned by Festus, the Roman Governor of Judea, to transport Paul on his appeal to Rome. In any case, he functions as _commentariensis_ because he is the logical person to have kept Paul's criminal files, the letters from Claudius Lysias,[34] the Roman commander of Jerusalem, and from Festus[35] from getting wet[36] or being lost.[37] It is also possible that Paul's records were lost in the shipwreck described in Acts 27:39–43 necessitating a long delay while records were reconstructed in Caesarea, affording Luke the time to write _Luke-Acts_ and Paul to write many of the letters later incorporated into the New Testament.

The fact that Rome had a highly formalized system for record keeping, as well as a sophisticated regular courier system between it, its colonies and provinces, bears greatly on the credibility of _Acts_. Luke makes numerous assertions which can be verified by records, witnesses, or statements given by witnesses (depositions) before local magistrates. Paul had been under house arrest in Rome for two years when _Acts_ was written.[38] Thus, ample opportunity existed to collect and verify the evidence concerning the charges against Paul and the defenses raised by Luke.

<u>Prosecution</u>: Unlike modern legal systems, Roman law did not provide for governmental prosecution of criminal acts. Prosecution, with permission of the relevant court, could be initiated by any adult male citizen. "[O]nly one accuser was permitted for each offense; if there were several claimants, agreement first had to be reached on who should bring the prosecution."[39] (Of course, different accusers could have accused Paul of _different_ crimes. For example, one man could accuse Paul of starting a riot in Ephesus and another of inciting a riot in Thessalonica.) The accuser was put under oath that his accusation was not maliciously false but brought in good faith. _All indictments had to be in writing and signed by the accuser._ If the charges proved to be false, the court was then

required to investigate the motives of the accuser. If the accuser was found to have acted out of malice rather than ignorance or reasonable mistake, he himself could be punished.[40] Punishment could range from a fine to exile (*interdictio aquae et ignis*).[41]

When charges implicated state security, a special governmental investigator, *a cognitionibus*, could gather facts for use at a trial.

<u>Defendant</u>: A defendant had a right to be present when charged.[42] He could cross-examine and present documents and witnesses in his defense. Character witnesses (*laudatores*) were particularly important.[43] Although the prosecutor could compel witnesses to appear, the defendant could only request their testimony. However, the defendant could compel governmental records to be furnished.[44]

<u>Trials</u>: Normally, the prosecutor (complaining citizen) was required without benefit of lawyer to present the case against the accused and would open with a long speech detailing the charges.[45] The defendant, who usually had one or more attorneys to speak for him,[46] then gave an opening statement. The prosecutor next presented his witnesses who were cross-examined by the defense and the defense presented its witnesses who were cross-examined by the prosecution. Then the verdict was rendered.

<u>Juries</u>: For trials of Roman citizens held in Rome, a jury of various sizes was chosen from among a list of potential jurors from the Senate and wealthy men who would decide a case by majority vote. A trial in a province was decided by a governor sitting alone as a judge, but with legal advisers.

<u>Appeals</u>: Although a post-trial appeal procedure existed (*appellatio*), a Roman citizen could appeal before trial (*provocatio*) to have his case heard in Rome. Paul's appeal in Acts 25:10 is a *provocatio*.

<u>Emperor</u>: After Rome changed from a republic to an empire in 31 B.C., the use of juries diminished while the jurisdiction of the emperor increased for crimes involving the public interest. Procedures in trials before the emperor were not subject to formal rules but probably followed the pattern of other Roman criminal trials. The emperor's private *consilium* or a *consilium* from the Senate would act as an advisory jury. An *appellatio* and *provocatio* in Roman law appear to have been more trials *de novo* (new trials starting afresh) than a review of solely the court records and legal issues, as the word "appeal" means in current American jurisprudence. Probably Paul's appeal would have been investigated as a prosecution *extra ordinem* (special prosecution), heard personally by Nero, an imperial *consilium,* or both, rather than by a jury of citizens, because of the rapid spread of the faith in Jesus and the political, military, and fiscal implications of allowing Gentiles to become believers in the God of the Jews. Related factors likely would include the prominence of Paul among the Christians and the prominence of his accusers, as well as the number of cities within the empire where Paul or Christians allegedly broke the law.

The internal textual evidence in *Acts* explicitly supports the conclusion that Nero was to hear Paul's case personally.[47]

1   Acts 11:28, 18:2.
2   Harry J. Leon, *The Jews of Ancient Rome* (Philadelphia: Jewish Publication Society of America, 1960), 22.
3   Ibid., 24. Leon and the New Testament historian F. F. Bruce, *New Testament History*, 297–8, believe the expulsion may have been only of Jewish believers in Jesus rather than all Jews. Because I conclude that *Acts* was written for a readership of Roman officials and concerned the legality of belief in Jesus, I think that if the expulsion under Claudius had related only to Jewish believers in Jesus, Luke would have had reason to say so.
4   Acts 2:10.
5   Acts 25:26–27.
6   Acts 25:10–11.
7   Ronald Syme, *Roman Papers*, vol. 1 (Oxford: Clarendon Press; New York: Oxford University Press, 1979), 297.
8   Tacitus, Annals XIV, 52, 1, as cited by Syme, *Roman Papers,* 749.
9   Vasily Rudich, *Political Dissidence Under Nero* (London and New York: Routlege Publishers, 1993), 84.
10 Ibid.
11 Ibid.
12 Rom. 1:24–25.
13 S. Hornblower and A. Spawforth, "Roman Law" in *The Oxford Companion to Classical Civilization* (Oxford and New York: Oxford University Press, 1998), 407.
14 See generally O. F. Robinson, *The Criminal Law of Ancient Rome* (Baltimore: Johns Hopkins University Press, 1995).
15 Ibid., 80.
16 Ibid., 50.
17 Ibid., 99.
18 Ibid., 81–82.
19 Ibid., 74–75.
20 Ibid., 75.
21 Levinskaya, "Diaspora Jews," 6.
22 Robinson, *Criminal Law,* 78.
23 Levinskaya, "Diaspora Jews," 170.
24 Ibid., 99.
25 Ibid., 96.
26 Acts 18:2.
27 E.g., the American legal system in some contexts accounts certain testimonial privileges such as that between husband and wife and between pastor and penitent as more important than truth because of the larger social implications.
28 Robinson, *Criminal Law,* 10.
29 See Acts 25:12.
30 Robinson, *Criminal Law,* 10.
31 Bruce Winter, "Official Proceedings and Forensic Speeches" in *The Book of Acts in Its Ancient Literary Setting,* 307.
32 Ibid., 8.
33 Robinson, *Criminal Law,* 158.
34 Acts 23:26–30.
35 Acts 25:26.
36 Acts 27:43–44.
37 See Rapske, "Acts, Travel and Shipwreck" in *The Book of Acts in Graeco-Roman Setting,* 34; see p. 151 for the distinct possibility of the records being saved despite the shipwreck.

38 Acts 28:30.
39 Robinson, *Criminal Law*, 5; see e.g., Acts 24:1–2.
40 Ibid., 99.
41 Ibid., 102.
42 Ibid., 5.
43 Ibid.
44 See Winter, "Official Proceedings," 309.
45 Robinson, *Criminal Law*, 5.
46 Ibid.
47 E.g., Acts 25:11; see Col. 4:3, Eph. 6:19–20.

CHAPTER 3

THE INVESTIGATOR

Certain aspects of first-century Roman criminal law are readily apparent to the modern reader: the presence of lawyers[1] and the assertion of legal privileges of a Roman citizen.[2] Most of the aspects integral to *Acts,* however, are not readily discernable by us because Luke was writing to a different audience, to a man, Theophilus, and to men thoroughly familiar with both the substance and procedures of the system. They were part of it, they helped form it. While those men understood the legal *system,* they had little knowledge of the particular controversy: the identity of Jesus, the origin, teachings and leadership of Christianity, the identity of Paul, the history and context of his journeys across the empire, the events giving rise to the particular charges against Paul and the procedural background of the many "trials" of Christianity and Paul which led to the judicial proceedings in Rome. Consequently, in *Acts,* Luke concentrates on issues about which Theophilus needed to be further informed.

The modern reader is in a substantially opposite position, usually a Christian with a knowledge of Paul, basic Christian beliefs, and some early church history searching the pages of *Acts* for inspiration, but who has little knowledge of law, much less Roman criminal proceedings. To better understand *Acts* and to experience the power of its message to Theophilus, the modern reader is encouraged to learn what a first century judicial investigator would have known and to "unlearn" or set aside twenty centuries of historical hindsight. For legal terms like "brief," "lawyer," "judge," or "trial," the reader is reminded that modern usages are more often parallels than close descriptions of their ancient counterparts. One goal of *Paul on Trial* is to reorient those perspectives and thus give a fuller view of the message Luke intended to convey.

I often listen to my wife, Rosemary, speaking on the phone to someone who has called our home. By what she says or the tone of her voice, I sometimes discern the other side of the conversation. At other times, curious, I must ask, "Who were you talking to?" When she answers, I then better understand some of her comments which puzzled me moments earlier. Likewise, have you ever read the brief of just one party to a lawsuit? Pretty convincing, wasn't it? Also confusing. Each side has a "theory" of the case, an explanation, an interpretation, or, in the eyes of opposing counsel, a "spin" to explain the facts and legally justify the actions of the party for whom the brief is written. The problem, often, of reading the brief of just one party is discerning the controversy. Good legal writing should state the case so well that the reader will wonder how anyone could dispute the conclusion.

In essence, all legal briefs have two components: *facts* and *argument*. First, a brief must state:

1. Background sufficient to contextualize the issues.

2. Facts relevant to the particular charges in controversy.

3. Details –

    A. Time (date or chronology).

    B. Place.

    C. Who was present at events.

    D. Who said what to whom.

    E. What happened.

    F. What relevant written records or physical evidence exists.

Especially if the facts are in dispute, the brief should state the basis for the assertion of their truth, such as a public record, a court decision, or the name(s) and further identity of a witness(es) to the occurrence. (In modern practice, the fact portion of a brief is strongest when it contains a specific reference such as "deposition of Andrew Smith, Plaintiff's CPA in Chicago, p. 17"). Ideally, also in modern practice, the statement of facts is non-argumentative.

The second component, an argument section, then seeks to persuade the reader, in the light of common sense, reason, statutory law, public policy, or legal precedent, that the particular facts lead to conclusions in favor of the writer's client. The practice of "brief" writing in the late parchment, early codex era, would not have required facts and argument to be separated. Nevertheless, the essential logic of the elements necessary to present in order to convince a judge to rule a certain way is not dictated by an era of history but is a function of logic, the nature of the facts, and the charges made.

Also, a brief will vary depending upon the phase of the legal proceeding to which it pertains. A pretrial brief will seek to acquaint the judge with relevant background, facts, and legal theories to be presented either to convince the judge to rule in one's favor without the necessity of trial[3] or to predispose the judge to see the issues within the paradigm of the brief writer. The brief of a plaintiff will differ from that of a defendant, the former being explicit in the allegations of wrongdoing by the defendant and the latter attempting to show that the facts alleged or legal conclusions reached by the complaining party are groundless.

If *Acts* is an ancient counterpart of what today we would call a pretrial legal brief, written to defend Paul in his forthcoming trial by giving the immediate reader, Theophilus, necessary background and facts to the particular charges and legal arguments, we would certainly expect the elements of a properly crafted pretrial legal defense to be found in it. We know that under Roman law a petition or complaint would have initiated the proceedings against Paul. Thus the response on Paul's behalf would certainly address the particular charges against him.

Further, all, or substantially all, of the text should support other legal objectives of the brief writer *unless* the brief writer has an additional nonlegal agenda. A contemporary example may illustrate. In 1998, President Clinton was investigated for obstruction of justice. Certainly, his lawyers addressed the legal issues but they also needed to consider whether a counterattack on the president's accusers would alienate women's groups or whether cooperative actions with the special prosecutor could weaken the independence of the presidency. Likewise, Luke's defense of Paul had to consider the impact of his brief on two groups of people: 1. The believers in Jesus; 2. Theophilus and those to whom he would show the brief. As to the church, would they be given a greater freedom to serve God and preach the message of Jesus? As to the readers, would they be given the message of salvation in a clear and persuasive way?

I propose that Luke wrote *Acts* primarily as a legal defense of Paul against charges brought against him by Jews who did not accept the message of Jesus. As he wrote, Luke also was actively aware that the decision concerning Paul would determine the freedom of believers throughout the empire to follow and spread the teachings of Jesus. One of the vehicles of that defense (the brief), meanwhile, was constructed to carry the message of salvation to the reader.[4] If this thesis is correct, not only should all those elements be present in *Acts*, but all of *Acts* should further that agenda.

THEOPHILUS

He is the mysterious reader whose identity holds many of the clues to *Acts* and *Luke*. He is mentioned only twice in the Bible, at the introductions of *Luke* (1:3) and *Acts* (1:1). However, these mentions are highly instructive:

> Luke 1:1 Since many have undertaken to set down an orderly account of the events that have been fulfilled among us, 2. just as they were handed on to us by those who from the beginning were eyewitnesses and servants of the word, 3. I too decided, after investigating everything carefully from the very first, to write an orderly account for you, most excellent Theophilus, 4. so that you may know the truth concerning the

things about which you have been instructed. (New Revised Standard Version)

Acts 1:1 In the first book, Theophilus, I wrote about all that Jesus did and taught from the beginning 2. until the day when he was taken up to heaven, after giving instructions through the Holy Spirit to the apostles whom he had chosen. (NRSV)

From textual gleanings, and from the evidence which has preceded and will follow, we can deduce some aspects of his relationship to Luke and Paul and why Luke wrote to him. Theophilus probably was a Roman official. In his first book, Luke addresses him as "most excellent," a salutation used for a Roman official.[5] Although Theophilus is a Greek name meaning "lover of God," the name was common among Greeks and is serendipitous to the context. While some have suggested the name represents a generic "John Doe" who is seeking to learn of God, the salutation "most excellent" and the reference to his previous instruction[6] belie that suggestion. Numerous passages in *Acts* will support the conclusion that Theophilus was neither a believer in Jesus nor an inquirer. Also, from the omitted details in *Acts*, which Luke omits because he assumes Theophilus knows them, and from the supplied details in *Acts* which Luke supplies because Luke assumes Theophilus needs to know or be reminded of them, we get a firm sense that he is a particular real individual not a fictitious *persona*.

"THE EVENTS . . . FULFILLED AMONG US"

In Luke 1:1–4[7] Luke tells Theophilus he is writing to him because he wants to create an "orderly account" of "all things from the very first ... that you may know the certainty of those things in which you were instructed." Having been told that Theophilus has been "instructed," we deduce he already knew something of the story of Jesus, his disciples, and Paul: the "things fulfilled," the events which have come to pass by A.D. 62 and which Luke will show were God-ordained, foretold in the Jewish scriptures, and spoken by the prophets.

From this introduction many scholars have concluded that Luke had a "theological" agenda in writing.[8] They are correct, but only in a limited sense. A legal apologist for a man accused of creating, under Roman law, a *religio illicita* (an illegal new religion), would *necessarily* engage in a theological excursion. Consider a modern example: a minister charged by his denomination with ordaining a homosexual is threatened with removal from his position. An attorney defending him will ask the denomination the sources of its authority: is it the Bible, conscience, creeds, or a written constitution? How are conflicts between these sources resolved? Does that authority really forbid such ordination? Does it matter whether the ordained homosexual is active, inactive, or repentant of his or her sexual activity? If the ordaining minister repents of his action, is forgiveness required? As one can see, the theological issues in this hypothetical legal defense are manifold. A defender of the minister, writing a background summary of facts and authority (law) for the denomination tribunal, would *necessarily* engage many theological issues but would be writing *primarily* to help the minister keep his job rather than to teach theology.

The modern reader may protest that criminal courts do not consider theological issues. While modern *American* courts do try to avoid religious controversies, in Paul's case the courts of the Roman Empire could not. By declaring a mandatory state religion, using it to reinforce the political authority of the emperor, and by making Judaism the sole exception to that religion, Rome *necessarily* made religious issues into legal issues. Both Paul's accusers and Luke, his defender, skillfully framed their arguments in relation to this legal reality. When Luke tells Theophilus, in so many words, "I want you to know the certainty [I want to verify and give you the opportunity to verify] what we have been telling you about how Jesus *fulfilled* the promises in the Hebrew Scriptures [and thus faith in him is authentically Jewish] and how the Hebrew prophets foretold that the Jewish faith would spread to the Gentiles," he is not necessarily announcing that he will teach theology but may instead be propounding a legal defense.

Theophilus developed a close relationship with Luke and possibly Paul. Just from the text, we discern six interactions:

1. Prior to being given the Book of Luke, Theophilus had been given much information about Jesus, and/or the Messianics, and/or Paul.[9] Because Luke is aware of this, he will be writing to extend and organize that information.

2. Luke wants Theophilus to have a greater certainty about the information he has already received. The "careful investigation" recounted in Luke 1:3 coupled with Luke's expressed desire that Theophilus be more certain of his facts allows for the possibility that Luke may be giving Theophilus his compilation so that Theophilus can verify the facts himself.

3. Luke and Theophilus must have interacted when Luke gave him *Luke*. It is self-evident that Luke expected Theophilus to read his first book and that such a work would evoke many questions (such as what happened after Jesus was taken up to heaven) and possibly occasions to converse.

4. Luke and Theophilus knew each other over a period of time. As Theophilus was reading the first book, Luke was writing *Acts* which took, perhaps, at least a year to assemble and write.

5. The formality of the relationship between Luke and Theophilus between the writing of *Luke* and *Acts* changes. By the time Luke gives him *Acts*, the formal salutation "most excellent" has been dropped. He is called simply Theophilus.

6. Theophilus probably knew what happened to Paul since shortly after Paul arrived at Rome. The narrative of Paul's two years at Rome covers only his first three days[10] and then a few more days,[11] leaving a span of almost two years between Acts 28:28 and Acts 28:30. Of course, prison time may be uneventful,[12] but because the two years in Rome were closer in time to the writing of *Acts* than any other times covered in it, the memory of those events would be better and, if Luke's purpose is not forensic, the significance probably greater. Yet Luke covers two important years in one verse.

Joseph Tyson helps us further focus on the identity of the reader of *Luke-Acts* from the broader context.[13] This reader had:

A. At least general, but not necessarily detailed, knowledge of the geography of Galilee, Samaria, Judea and Asia Minor.

B. A detailed knowledge of the area surrounding Rome.[14]

C. Little extra-textual knowledge of most of the characters in *Luke-Acts* (all are introduced except as in D).

D. A general knowledge of Roman officials when identified by title and a presumed knowledge of Roman emperors; an acquaintance with and an acute interest in Simon Peter and Paul; and a prior knowledge of Jacob (a/k/a James, the leader of the Jerusalem church) as a person of authority within the community of believers in Jesus.

E. Educated at least to the point of literacy and fluency in Greek but no necessary knowledge of other languages.

F. Familiarity with first century political/historical events of importance to Rome:

   (i)   "First registration . . . when Quirinius was governor.[15]

   (ii)   Insurrection by Theudas and Judas, the Galilean.[16]

   (iii) Famine during reign of Claudius.[17]

   (iv)   Exile of Jews from Rome by Claudius.[18]

   (v)   Insurrection by an Egyptian with four thousand assassins.[19]

G. Knowledge of the Greek and Roman money system.

H. A basic understanding of Jewish religious practices but requiring information about Jewish sects. A general familiarity with the worship of Artemis,[20] Zeus, and Hermes.[21] Sympathetic to Judaism but not Jewish.

I. A predisposition to regard the Hebrew Scriptures as authoritative.[22]

Based on his study, Tyson concludes the reader of *Luke-Acts* is a God-fearing Gentile of the type shown throughout *Acts* as attracted to Judaism but not converted.

Philip Satterthwaite, based upon his study of classical rhetoric as applied to *Acts*, makes the following additional observation concerning the intended reader of *Acts*: "Such a person might have been alert to the importance of speeches in the structure of the narrative, and to techniques of implicit commentary..."[23] While Tyson's conclusions range from reasonable to sound and Satterthwaite's observation is logical, I think the legal insights into *Acts* can take us further. Although Tyson analyzes many attributes of the reader, he does not assess his familiarity with Roman criminal law which must have been considerable. Luke frequently mentions procedural irregularities or violations which would be patent to a Roman legal official. Because he does not label these irregularities as such, or explain them, it appears that Luke expects Theophilus to see them. Examples include:

    A. Felix's promise of a speedy trial.[24]

    B. Felix requiring Paul to testify against himself.[25]

    C. Lack of defense counsel for Paul before Felix.[26]

    D. Allowing multiple accusers before Felix.[27]

    E. *Ex parte*[28] presentation of charges to Festus as judge.[29]

    F. Multiple accusers before Festus.[30]

    G. Lack of defense counsel before Festus.[31]

    H. Relative lightness of Paul's pretrial imprisonment in Rome.[32]

One of the leading scholars on *Acts* has views of Paul's speech before Felix consistent with this analysis:

> The author of Acts intended his readers to see Paul handling his defense with great dexterity, and refuting these charges. He had done this by prescribing the limits of evidence based on Roman law, proscribing the charges of absent accusers, using forensic terminology, and, not least of all, presenting a well argued defense, even if preserved in a summary form. Paul conducted his own defense in an able manner against a professional forensic orator.[33]

From Winter's apt observation and the other evidence, we must conclude that *the original reader of Acts, Theophilus, was part of or had a close familiarity with the Roman legal system.*

THEOPHILUS WAS NOT A CHRISTIAN

Finally, the textual evidence will show that *Acts* was not written to a believer, but to provide the background of Christianity, facts relevant to the charges against Paul, and legal arguments germane to his defense. The following section, the Judicial Reader, will illustrate the pervasiveness of legal argument from a different analytical approach, but first let us consider what Luke does and does not explain catechistically:

	Issues Explained or Described	Issues Not Explained or Mentioned
1.	Legality of faith and admission of Gentiles	Theology of Jewishness and Gentile admission cf. Galatians 3:8–9; Romans 4
2.	Handling of money in the church	Theology of giving cf. 2 Corinthians 8–9
3.	No threat to Roman military/government	Theology of law and government cf. Romans 13:1–6
4.	Demonic encounters	Theology of spiritual warfare cf. Ephesians 6:12
5.	Paul's extensive education and Pharisaic credentials	Paul's extensive correspondence with the churches

This selectivity suggests a non-Christian readership. Second, the New Testament Epistles, not just those of Paul but of all the New Testament writers, *overflow* with praises to God. Yet in the twenty-eight chapters of *Acts* there are no first-person praises (there are several third-person elaborate praises in *Luke*). Third, all the salutations to believers in the Epistles are warm and usually effusive (see 2 John 1–2; Jude 1—2; 2 Peter 1:1–2), while the salutations to Theophilus are formal and lacking any references to his spiritual state either positional to God or personal. Finally, throughout the commentary we will note numerous passages which would appear to have been written for a nonbeliever and which would have been written differently if Theophilus was a Christian.

Following Tyson's methodology we thus deduce the following possibilities:

1. **Probably**, Theophilus held the office of *a cognitionibus* (investigator), was a member of Nero's *consilium,* or was, in some formal capacity, charged with the gathering of information for the trial of Paul in much the way modern judges delegate parts of complex trial preparation to magistrates or special masters. The charges against Paul and the import of those charges would most certainly have justified a special investigation under Roman law (*cognitio extra ordinem*) and a man assigned to the investigation. Such an investigator would have wanted much background information about Jesus and his early followers in order to contextualize both the accusations and the defense. Then he would have wanted the information to narrow the focus to Paul and the specific charges against him.

Because of the paucity of historical records concerning the men who held office under Nero, I felt compelled to go beyond published scholarship and therefore consulted with Professor Vasily Rudich of Yale and author of *Political Dissendence Under Nero*, concerning the office of *a cognitionibus*. His email response of 1/3/2000 contains the following helpful insights into Roman pretrial investigations:

> With your question you struck upon a tangled matter which was and still is a subject of a scholarly debate. Our knowledge of this particular *officium* (or "bureau") is very fragmented and depends on a few passing references in the literary texts and a few randomly survived inscriptions . . . What follows is information of which we are reasonably confident. First, regarding the *cognitiones*. *Cognitio* was the process of juridical investigation (or prosecution) undertaken by a direct order of a magistrate possessing the *imperium* (that is, the right of jurisdiction). Under the Empire it began increasingly to mean the procedures personally directed by the Emperor or his appointee (*cognitio extra ordinem*) which gradually tended to replace the system of the *quaestiones*, that is, traditional republican senatorial (and, at times, equestrian) courts. It is in virtue of such *cognitio*, for instance, that the Christians were prosecuted during the catacomb period of their history. Now, it is commonly agreed that no formal chancelleries on any permanent basis existed under the first three Emperors. It was Claudius who created such appointments, among them, presumably, the office of a secretary *a cognitionibus*, which he filled with his own trusted freedmen . . . One assumes that they were engaged in the preparation of the material for the Imperial prosecutions. We certainly do not know who was the secretary *a cognitionibus* under Nero. Various names were proposed but none of his known freedmen seems to fit the slot.

Because the duties of the office of *a cognitionibus*, pretrial judicial investigation, precisely correspond with the purposes for which *Luke-Acts* was written, I think Theophilus held that office or was a "special investigator" appointed to gather information concerning the charges against Paul and the Christians. The change in manner of address for Theophilus from "most excellent Theophilus" in Luke 1 to simply "Theophilus" in *Acts* makes it unlikely that Theophilus was an *iudex* because judges usually discourage familiarity.

2. **Possibly**, Theophilus was a Roman lawyer, a *rhetor*. Certainly, Paul and his friends at Rome would have hired a lawyer. Although Paul obviously would testify on his own behalf, having a good lawyer to organize the trial presentation, to present defense witnesses, and cross-examine prosecution witnesses, who would be familiar with the inner workings of the Roman system and the personalities of Nero's administration would be invaluable. Of course, to properly present the case and cross-examine the prosecution's witnesses, the lawyer would need to be familiar with all the facts of the case. Most litigation lawyers require new clients, as a first task, to chronologize their case in writing to solidify memories and provide a reference document.

Theophilus could be that lawyer and *Luke-Acts* may have resulted from a conversation like this: "Luke, the charges against Paul range widely. Nero's officials are collecting information from all over the empire, so I want you to write down the whole story about this Jesus and his disciples from the beginning. Who was this man? When you get to events involving the charges against Paul, be more specific: give me the who, what, where, and when. In addition, as you write, remember that I may circulate this brief to members of Nero's *consilium* and the Senate. This case has heavy political ramifications. Also, a lot of us have an interest both in Judaism and in this 'Christianity.'"

Against the possibility that Theophilus was Luke's *rhetor* stands the total absence from *Acts* of any coaching of lawyer by client. Because of the closeness which would necessarily develop between men working together over an extended period of time with the consequences of capital punishment looming, and because Luke and Paul would want to confide to their *rhetor* the vulnerabilities inherent in the witnesses and records and prior "acquittals" of Paul, it seems considerably less likely Theophilus was actually employed on Paul's behalf than he was a Roman fact gatherer.

Finally, throughout the text, by his careful chronology, geography, and participant investigation, Luke seems to be inviting, even challenging, the reader to investigate. If Theophilus was Paul's lawyer he would probably lack the capacity to do so. However, Nero's special trial investigator would have had the duty, authority and resources to check the facts.

3.   **Conceivably**, Theophilus was a Roman official, not directly involved in the case, but sympathetic to Christianity, and willing to intercede with Nero or other Roman officials and plead Paul's case out of court if given sufficient background information. However, such a man would also be unlikely to possess, privately, the resources or authority to investigate, confirm, or disprove the numerous events in *Acts* set forth in exoneration of the apostle. Consequently, if Theophilus is *functioning* as a pretrial investigator, it is far more likely he is the official responsible for that job than a freelance intervenor.

THE JUDICIAL READER

One approach never previously undertaken in an analysis of *Acts* and which is essential to discerning whether a "judicial" readership (a fact investigator, defense attorney, judge, or judicial assistant) is intended is to put oneself in the place of a putative judicial reader examing *Acts* as written to "Theophilus."[34]

Is it written:

1. To Theophilus as holder of the office of *a cognitionibus* or *a libellis* (which would insure that he would pass *Acts* around to other officials)?

2. To Theophilus as Paul's lawyer with the thought that Theophilus might

furnish the manuscript to Nero or circulate it to members of the *consilium* or Senate?

3. To Theophilus as a sympathetic aristocrat, perhaps a member of Nero's personal *consilium*?

If Theophilus, as reader, fits any of these categories, then we can expect to find certain issues addressed. Luke would have needed to anticipate how the charges against Paul would have appeared to Theophilus and those to whom he reported. In all cases a judge or investigator would already know the charges and would want to know from the defendant's viewpoint the who, what, when, where, and why in response to the charges.

In important cases, a jurist will also ask how this legal proceeding will affect:

1. Other potential litigants not before the court.

2. The judicial system.

3. Society at large.

4. His career.[35]

If *Acts* is written to defend Paul and, by extension, Christianity against the charges listed in Chapter 1, then in addition to the preceding general questions, following are some of the specific questions we would expect to be in the mind of a literate, reasonably well-informed, Gentile Roman judicial reader(s) of the first century, either initially, or as his reading of *Acts* progressed, and which we would expect Luke to anticipate in writing to him:

1. Who is or was this Jesus? This Messiah? This Christ?

2. Where did he come from?

3. What happened to him?

4. Where is he now?

5. How did his life intersect with Roman government?

6. What did he teach?

7. Are the teachings of Jesus dangerous to the:
   A. Civil order of Rome?
   B. Financial interests of Rome?
   C. Military conscription?

8. Who are the followers of Jesus?

9. Where did they come from?

10. What are their motives?

11. Where do the loyalties of the Nazarenes lie?

12. Where did they get their authority? Who is this "Holy Spirit" they are talking about?

13. Are they Jews? Are they from some particular region, tribe, or people group within Judaism?

14. Are they practicing the legal religion of Judaism or a new, illegal religion?

15. Who has the authority to say who is a Jew and what is Jewish?

16. Is not temple worship the defining practice of Judaism?

17. How does the priesthood fit in?

18. Why is Jewish leadership opposing the followers of Jesus?

19. What are their motives?

20. Who are the leaders of this sect called Christians?

21. What is their attitude toward the established Jewish leaders?

22. How are they organized?

23. What are their objectives?

24. How are they getting their money?

25. Are they building this sect for financial purposes?

26. Who is Paul and where did he come from?

27. What cities has Paul been in; when and with whom?

28. What did he teach, to whom, at what locations, and for how long?

29. What was the reaction to his teaching?

30. Did trouble follow him? How did it start?

31. Have charges been brought against Paul or other Christians previously? If so, by whom and what were the charges?

32. What decisions did our local military magistrates, consuls, and governors reach when they investigated or held trials?

33. What witnesses or written records can we check to verify these reports?

34. Why is this group growing so fast?

35. Where do they meet?

36. How do Gentiles fit in? Are they becoming Jews?

37. What about circumcision, dietary laws, and other Jewish practices for the Gentiles?

38. How does this teaching relate to:

   A. Other sects of Judaism?

   B. The followers of John the Baptist?

C. Worship of Roman gods or the emperor?

D. Greek philosophy?

39. Is this whole teaching ridiculous, or does it have implications for my personal life?

40. What recommendations should I make to that lunatic Nero and will I be punished if I don't make the right ones?

The foregoing are the interrogatories[36] of a legal thinker. If *Luke-Acts* substantially answers these questions, we can conclude that it is possible that *Acts* has an intended legal readership. While most of these questions would also be asked by curious Christians, if *Acts* had an intended Christian readership, many of the answers would be already known, irrelevant, or of limited interest to believers. Therefore, if Luke answers questions to which a putative Christian reader would already know the answer, or if he answers questions of limited interest to such a presumed readership, we can count those answers as relevant evidence that no Christian readership was intended.

Likewise, if Luke is answering questions which no Roman magistrate would care about, then that can be counted as evidence against considering *Acts* as written primarily for forensic reasons. In fact, the primary arguments against the hypothesis that *Acts* is a legal defense was articulated almost forty years ago by the noted authority on *Acts*, C. K. Barrett: "No Roman official would ever have filtered out so much of what to him would be theological and ecclesiastical rubbish in order to reach so tiny a grain of relevant apology."[37]

Barrett, who is now Emeritus Professor of Divinity at Durham University, continued to hold this view in 1998, thirty-seven years later:

> ...no Roman court could be expected to wade through so much Jewish religious nonsense in order to find half-a-dozen fragments of legally significant material. The same argument proves even more conclusively that the book was not written as a brief for the defense at Paul's trial; what would be the use of chapters 1–12 for such a purpose?[38]

Although Barrett's strong assertions are fair viewpoints and have seemed convincing to many scholars, they have weaknesses. Is it possible that Barrett and those who accept his argument have mistaken factual background or legally relevant arguments for "theological or ecclesiastical rubbish?" After all, the legality of the faith in Jesus may be *the* issue of *Acts*. It is also probable that the Roman emperor would have a special adjutant whose explicit job would be to gather and sift through information in anticipation and hope of simplifying complex legal issues and settling controverted facts. Finally, Barrett may be missing a hybrid purpose: to evangelize the reader. If so, we must consider all the substantial passages of *Acts* to see if those passages can be seen to further a legal or complementary agenda.

A scholarly consensus exists, with which I concur, that *Acts* (actually *Luke-Acts* as a two-volume set) was written to a Gentile Roman. However, many scholars regard that Roman to be a believer or seeker. The answers to most of the afore-mentioned interrogatories would be of interest *both* to a putative Gentile Roman believer/seeker and also to a Roman official weighing the charges against Paul and the *Talmidei Yeshua*. However *certain* of the interrogatories would have little or no interest to the believers. Some of the answers to these questions, such as 11, 14, 16, and 35, would probably be known to a believer. Based on my legal sense of those questions, after weighing the type of information generally given in the rest of the New Testament canon where believers were indisputably the audience, I believe interrogatories 7, 11, 14–17, 27–33, 35 and 40 would be of *secondary or minimal interest* to a Gentile Roman *believer or seeker*.

The text commentary will show that most of these questions are frequently addressed in *Acts* and thus provide persuasive evidence that the original reader was not a Christian or seeker and that Luke, in writing to Theophilus, answered questions that would be of primary interest to a judicial investigator. This section on the "Judicial Reader" has presented a specifically legal, and admittedly sub-jective, method of analyzing a text for forensic content/purpose in answering background questions. We have previously examined the possible charges against Paul and the Christians. Let us now consider whether any passages in *Acts* can function as *specific defenses* to the charges which appear to have been made.

---

1   Acts 24:1.
2   Acts 22:25.
3   See Acts 18:14.
4   See Acts 26:28.
5   E.g., Acts 23:25.
6   Luke 1:4.
7   The phrase in Luke 1:1 translated "the events . . . fulfilled among us" in the NRSV is elsewhere translated variously. The Jerusalem Bible renders it "the events that have taken place among us." The King James reads, "those things which are most surely believed among us." The Revised Standard: "the things which have been accomplished among us." This range of trans-lations tells us two important things:
   1.   The precise meaning of the Greek is uncertain in this context.
   2.   *All* of the different renderings are consistent with a hypothesis that Acts was written as a background and legal argument for Paul's trial.
   The modern reader must also be aware that sometimes the scriptures are translated backwards: e.g., the translator may have prejudged that *Acts* was written for religious instruction (cate-chism), therefore Luke 1:1 may *best* (in the translator's interpretation) be rendered as "the things most surely believed among us."
8   The reader should note that the Greek word in the title of Luke's second book "Praxeis" ("Acts" or "deeds done") is probably *not a part of the original text* but dates to the late second century. See Fitzmyer, *Acts of Apostles*, 48–49.
9   Luke 1:4.
10   Acts 28:17.
11   Acts 28:23.

12 Acts 24:27.

13 Joseph Tyson, *Images of Judaism in Luke-Acts* (Columbia, S.C.: University of South Carolina Press, 1992), various references.

14 E.g., Acts 28:13, 15.

15 Luke 2:2.

16 Acts 5:36–7.

17 Acts 11:28.

18 Acts 18:2.

19 Acts 21:38.

20 Acts 19.

21 Acts 14:11–18.

22 I think Tyson is too emphatic on this point because much of the presumption about the authority of scripture in *Acts* is not to make the point that the scripture was authoritative, but rather the point that, as loyal Jews, Peter, Paul, and the Messianics adhered to that authority.

23 Philip Satterthwaite "Classical Rhetoric," 379.

24 Acts 24:22.

25 Acts 24:10.

26 Acts 24:1–22.

27 Acts 24:9.

28 *Ex parte* is a legal term meaning contact by a litigant with the judge without the knowledge or consent of the other litigants.

29 Acts 25:2.

30 Acts 25:7.

31 Acts 25:8–12.

32 Acts 28:16.

33 Winter, "Official Proceedings," 327.

34 Acts 1:1.

35 See Rapske, *Paul in Roman Custody*, 69.

36 Interrogatories are written questions propounded by litigants in preparation for trial. The word is used metaphorically above.

37 C. K. Barrett, *Luke the Historian in Recent Study* (London: 1961), 63, as quoted by Robert Maddox, *The Purpose of Luke-Acts* (Edinburgh, U.K.: T & T Clark, 1982), 20.

38 Barrett, *Acts, The International Critical Commentary*, vol. 2 (Edinburgh, U.K.: T & T Clark, 1998), p. 50 of introduction.

CHAPTER 4

FOR THE DEFENSE

In writing about Jesus, the early church, and the travels of Paul, Luke weaves his defense against the many charges made against Paul and the followers of Jesus. The accompanying chart shows the defenses put forth to Theophilus just in *Acts* (most of the defenses raised in *Luke* are discussed in the chapter on *Luke*). Some defenses are subtle: assertions of verifiable facts which belie the accusations. Others are explicit: citation of legal precedent directly contrary to the arguments of Paul's opponents. In light of the number and breadth of charges, I have placed them into two general categories for ease in analysis:

1. inciting riots, civil unrest.
2. preaching an illegal new religion.

Even though Roman law had distinct provisions for crimes such as *inuria*[1] or *vis*, it will be helpful to place such charges in the incitement to riot category to more easily comprehend that the defense strategy in *Acts* is essentially two-pronged:

1. Paul and the Christians are peaceable.
2. Paul and the *Talmidei Yeshua* are faithful Jews and their Gentile converts are faithful to the God of Abraham.

Also, many defense arguments are repeated in different contexts, such as the Jewishness of faith in Jesus. The chart lists each separate argument I have detected, but only representative instances in which it is made. After the chart I explain how even the two broad charges are addressed by one comprehensive defense argument.

CHART OF FIFTY-NINE ARGUMENTS IN DEFENSE OF PAUL

	Defense	Charge Being Defended		Passage Illustrative of Defense
		Illegal New Religion	Inciting Civil Unrest	
1.	Our faith is based on Tanakh.	X		Acts 26:22b-23 *[I am] saying no other things than those which the prophets and Moses said would come—"that the Christ [Messiah] would suffer, that He would be the first to rise from the dead, and would proclaim light to the Jewish people and to the Gentiles."*
2.	The inclusion of Gentiles was always God's plan for the Jewish faith.	X		Acts 15:16–17 quoting Amos 9:12 *So that the rest of mankind may seek the Lord*
3.	We are a self-governing sect within Judaism.	X		Acts 1:15–26; Acts 3:42–47; Acts 4:32–35; Acts 6:1–7
4.	The rejection of Jesus by Jewish leadership can be explained.	X		Acts 3:17 (ignorance); Acts 5:17 (jealousy); Acts 13:45 (jealousy); Acts 5:28 (fear of blame)
5.	Jewish history shows its prophets are rejected.	X		Acts 28; Acts 7:52 *Which of the prophets did you not persecute?*
6.	The apostles and Paul are subject to duly constituted authority.	X	X	Acts 13:1–3; Acts 15:23 *The apostles, the elders, and the brethren, To the brethren who are of the Gentiles ... 15:23*
7.	The followers of Jesus are faithful Jews.	X		Acts 2:41 *Then those who gladly received his word were baptized . . . about three thousand. . .*
8.	The apostles were not sent out to stir up trouble but to be witnesses of Jesus.		X	Acts 1:7–8 *. . . you shall be witnesses to Me . . .*
9.	The resurrection is a fact verifiable by many witnesses.	X		Acts 2:32; also Luke 27:37–49 *This Jesus God has raised up, of which we are all witnesses.*

		Charge Being Defended		
	Defense	Illegal New Religion	Inciting Civil Unrest	Passage Illustrative of Defense

CHART OF FIFTY-NINE ARGUMENTS IN DEFENSE OF PAUL

	Defense	Illegal New Religion	Inciting Civil Unrest	Passage Illustrative of Defense
10.	The boldness of the apostles is God-given for the purpose of becoming witnesses.	X		Acts 2:16 *But this is what was spoken by the prophet Joel.*
11.	The presence of female prophets and evangelists is foretold in Tanakh.	X		Acts 2:17–18 quoting Joel 2:28–29 (Joel 3:1 in Heb.)
12.	The Jewish leadership had an immediate and timely opportunity to refute the Resurrection.	X		Acts 4:1–22 . . . *let us severely threaten them, that from now on they speak to no man in this name.* v. 17
13.	The authority of the apostles came from God and did not need to come from the existing Jewish hierarchy.	X		Acts 4:1–22 *Whether it is right in the sight of God to listen to you more than to God, you judge.* v. 19
14.	Neither the Christians nor Paul are chasing money; they seek holiness.	X		Acts 4:32–37; Acts 5:1–10; Acts 24:17 . . . *but they had all things in common.* 4:32
15.	The church is growing because of God, not because of conspiracy against Rome.	X	X	Acts 2:41; Acts 2:46–7; Acts 4:4; Acts 8:1–4 . . . *many of those who heard the word believed.* 4:4
16.	A prominent non-Christian Jewish leader refused to assert that the Messianics were not led by God.	X		Acts 5:34–40 . . . *if this plan or this work is of men, it will come to nothing; but if it is from God you, you cannot overthrow it* . . . (Gamaliel speaking) vv. 38–39
17.	Paul's opponents are hypocritical in appealing to Roman law because they ignore it when convenient.	X	X	Acts 7:57–58 (stoning of Stephen); Acts 23:14–15; 25:3 (conspiracy to murder Paul)
18.	The arguments concerning the temple are theological, not made to blaspheme.	X	X	Acts 17:24; Acts 7:48 . . . *the Most High does not dwell in temples made with hands*
19.	The church leadership is broad-based and open, not a cabal against Rome.	X	X	Acts 6:1–7 (choosing of deacons), Acts 13:1 (leadership at Antioch)

CHART OF FIFTY-NINE ARGUMENTS IN DEFENSE OF PAUL

	Defense	Illegal New Religion	Inciting Civil Unrest	Passage Illustrative of Defense
		Charge Being Defended		
20.	The opposition falsifies evidence.	X	X	Acts 6:11 *Then they secretly induced men . . .*
21.	Heart circumcision is the mark of a Jew, thus failure to physically circumcise Gentiles does not create a new religion.	X		Acts 7:51 *You stiff-necked and uncircumcised in heart and ears!*
22.	Paul's testimony is credible because he once persecuted.	X		Acts 8:3; Acts 22:4 *I persecuted this Way to the death . . . v. 4*
23.	Judaism becomes universal through Jesus.	X		Acts 8:26–39 (Ethiopian eunuch)
24.	Even when Saul (Paul) persecuted the church he did so legally.		X	Acts 9:1–2 (letters of authorization from high priest)
25.	Paul did not initiate inclusion of Gentiles, other Jewish leaders did so.	X		Acts 10 (conversion of Cornelius) Acts 15 (Jerusalem council)
26.	Conversion of Gentiles is not a threat to the Roman military or Roman civil order.		X	Acts 10 (conversion of Cornelius)
27.	The *mikva* is a part of normative Judaism.	X		Acts 2:38; Acts 10:48; Luke 3:3, 12 *Repent and receive mikva in the name of Yeshua the Messiah* (paraphrase of 2:38)
28.	The Gentile church and the Jewish church did not disconnect.	X		Acts 11:19–29 (many Greeks in Antioch believed and joined the Jewish congregation)
29.	Peter is a credible witness.	X	X	Acts 1–12 various references showing Peter as eyewitness to most events
30.	Herod Agrippa was disloyal to Rome.		X	Acts 12:19 (execution of Roman soldiers who had been guarding Peter)

CHART OF FIFTY-NINE ARGUMENTS IN DEFENSE OF PAUL

	Defense	Charge Being Defended		Passage Illustrative of Defense
		Illegal New Religion	Inciting Civil Unrest	
31.	The facts presented are verifiable.		X	Acts 23:25 and implicit everywhere a Roman city, official, or record is mentioned
32.	Paul and his students are non-violent.		X	Acts 14:19–20 Paul is stoned, disciples do not fight back.
33.	Timothy is a credible witness.	X	X	Acts 16–20 showing Timothy as eyewitness to most events.
34.	Paul's travels for ten years are detailed so he cannot be charged for riots in other locations.		X	Acts 16–28
35.	Paul is not preaching slave revolt.		X	Acts 16:16–18 deliverance of Philippian slave girl
36.	Paul was "acquitted" in Philippi.		X	Acts 16:35 (the magistrates order the release of Paul and Silas)
37.	The Thessalonica riot was started by jealous opponents.		X	Acts 17:5 (opponents become envious and stir up rioters)
38.	Paul's message was accepted by many Jews who checked the scriptures.	X		Acts 17:10–15 ... *they... searched the Scriptures daily ...*
39.	Preaching to Greek philosophers was not a departure from Judaism, but an offer into the faith through Jesus.	X		Acts 17:16–34 ... *but now [He] commands all men everywhere to repent* ... v. 30
40.	Our assemblies are not illegal *collegia*, but Jewish worship.	X		Acts 18:7–8 Paul moves preaching from synagogue to next-door home of synagogue leader.
41.	Gallio acquitted Paul and the Messianics.	X		Acts 18:14–15 ... *a question of ... your own law.*
42.	Jesus is being accepted by well-educated, intelligent people not just common folk.	X		Acts 18:24–28; Acts 17:34 (credentials of Apollos)

CHART OF FIFTY-NINE ARGUMENTS IN DEFENSE OF PAUL

	Defense	Illegal New Religion	Inciting Civil Unrest	Passage Illustrative of Defense
		Charge Being Defended		
43.	The teachings of the Jewish prophet John confirm the Jewishness of faith in Jesus.	X		Acts 19:1–7 (encounter with disciples of John in Ephesus)
44.	Paul avoided confrontation at Ephesus.		X	Acts 19:9 *And he [Paul] went into the synagogue and spoke boldly for three months ....*
45.	Demetrius incited the riot at Ephesus.		X	Acts 19:24
46.	Paul did not even speak to the Ephesian rioters.		X	Acts 19:30
47.	Paul was not teaching the Jews of the Diaspora to stop following *Torah*.	X		Acts 21:21–24 (meeting between Paul and James the leader of the Jerusalem congregation)
48.	Paul's opponents are anti-Gentile.	X	X	Acts 22:21–22 (riot when Paul uses the word "Gentile" in his speech)
49.	The Sanhedrin itself has sharply differing views on Jewish theology.	X		Acts 23:9–10 (internal dispute over resurrection of the dead)
50.	Lysias, the Roman commander, found Paul innocent of starting the Jerusalem riot or preaching a new religion.	X	X	Acts 23:25–30 *I found out that he was accused concerning questions of their own law.* v. 29
51.	Paul was never convicted by Felix of inciting the Jerusalem riot.		X	Acts 24
52.	Even those accusing Paul of leaving Judaism admit the Way is a sect of Judaism.	X		Acts 24:5 ... *a ringleader of the sect of the Nazarenes.*
53.	Paul was never convicted by Festus of inciting the Jerusalem riot.		X	Acts 25:7 ... *many serious complaints against Paul, which they could not prove.*
54.	Agrippa "acquitted" Paul.	X		Acts 26:31–2 *This man might have been set free ...*

CHART OF FIFTY-NINE ARGUMENTS IN DEFENSE OF PAUL			
	Defense	Charge Being Defended	Passage Illustrative of Defense
		Illegal New Religion	Inciting Civil Unrest	
55.	Paul's innocence is shown in that he did not flee when he could have.	Either or both		Acts 27:3 (Paul given liberty to visit friends and receive supplies)
56.	Paul is not on trial because he is guilty, but because God has sent him.	X	X	Acts 27:23–4 . . . *you must be brought before Caesar . . .*
57	God has used nature to show Paul's innocence.	Either or both		Acts 27:13–41; especially Acts 28:3–6
58.	Paul's God has even caused the Roman gods to attest to Paul's innocence.	Either or both		Acts 28:11 (Roman gods of truth and perjury convey Paul to Rome)
59.	Paul's condition of arrest at Rome confirms that the case against him is weak.	Either or both		Acts 28:30 *Then Paul dwelt two whole years in his own rented house . . .*

Both the charges of illegal religion and inciting riot have a nexus and a common defense. The riots result principally from the issue of Gentile inclusion without circumcision into the faith of Abraham. Consequently the one defense which addresses both charges is that Jesus, the Messiah, has risen from the dead and called Paul to preach the faith of Abraham to the Gentiles (as Gentiles and not as converts to Judaism) in accordance with the Hebrew scriptures. The assertion of the Resurrection affirms both the Jewishness of the Way and that no desire to create civil unrest existed.

---

1 Acts 23:3 probably is such a charge

CHAPTER 5

DATING AND GENRE

In attempting to unlock the mysteries of *Acts*, New Testament scholarship in the twentieth century has searched for a crucial fact and been tormented by a usually reliable methodology which has proved inconclusive when applied to *Acts*. The fact besought is the date *Acts* was written. The pain-inducing methodology has been the attempt to discern the genre of *Acts*. Both dating and genre can inform our investigation. Both are considered in this chapter.

DATING

The time at which *Acts* was written can definitively determine if it was *not* composed as a legal defense. Many scholars date *Acts* to the mid 70s and later. Any date later than A.D. 63 means that *Acts* could not have been used to help Paul at his trial. Because *Acts* has not been dated within the text, three primary deductive approaches have been taken to determine when it was composed:

1. Internal evidence other than readership.

2. Readership.

3. Correlation with a principal source for the Gospel of Luke: the Gospel of Mark.

In weighing these approaches, the internal evidence merits the highest consideration because it is integral and not variable. For example, the ending of *Acts* at 28:30–31 speaks for itself. Although the meaning of the verses can be debated and placed in different contexts, all scholars agree that the "two years of Paul's imprisonment" was about A.D. 61–62.[1] In contrast, the reasonable argument which necessarily dates *Luke-Acts* after *Mark* because of the dependency of the Gospel of Luke on *Mark* itself depends on the additional questions of the dating of *Mark* and the particular oral and/or written versions of *Mark* on which Luke relied. The readership issue is also important because if *Acts* is written as a legal defense, it needed to be written around A.D. 62 to accommodate Paul's trial schedule. If it was written to Christians, then it could have been written in A.D. 62 or later. Thus, a legal readership precludes a later date for composition, but a Christian audience allows for one.

<u>Internal Evidence</u>—Within *Acts* four primary indicators point to a pre-A.D. 64 composition:

In A.D. 66 the Jewish nation exploded in widespread revolt against Rome. This revolt was suppressed, and Jerusalem and the temple destroyed in A.D. 70. Some of the most recurring themes of *Acts* are the spiritual, non-political, non-violent, and law-respecting nature of the followers of Jesus, in contrast to the allegedly subversive, illegal and anti-Rome machinations of many of their opponents. Question: Whether he was arguing the preceding points to Roman officials or to believers, would Luke have shunned mention of such a momentous war supportive of his accusations against the opposition? If he did so, as a lawyer it would be malpractice; as a historian or apologist he would be equally negligent. Likewise, why would Luke spend all of Acts 7 arguing that Jesus rather than the temple is now the focus of Judaism[2] if one need only point to its physical destruction in A.D. 70?

On July 19, A.D. 64, most of Rome went up in flames. Notoriously, Nero blamed the conflagration on the Christians, perhaps to exculpate himself. As a result, hundreds of believers in Jesus were executed by being hung on stakes throughout the city and burned alive. If Luke is writing to Christians after A.D. 64, is it reasonable to conclude that he would omit the severest persecution of the early church from his history, apology, or theology? Further, even if we theorize that Luke actually wrote after A.D. 64 and that Luke would have reached the events of A.D. 64 eventually but was interrupted for some reason, one cannot easily explain the relatively favorable light which *Acts* places on the expectations of justice from Nero: "if there is nothing in these things of which these men accuse me [against Caesar][3] . . . I appeal to Caesar."[4] Finally, *Acts* ends deliberately, not as an interrupted work.

Of course, the most obvious argument for the composition of *Acts* during Paul's imprisonment in Rome is that the narrative ends in Rome with Paul in prison. Paul has been the central character in the narrative since his conversion in Acts 9. If, by the time Luke writes *Acts*, Paul has had the opportunity to speak before an imperial tribunal or Nero, Luke, as author, to whatever audience, for whatever purpose he is writing, has no reason after pointing and leading his readership to a climactic trial to blithely omit the culminating event of the book. Proponents of later dating have attempted to explain the critical omission of the trial outcome by arguing that Theophilus must have already known the result. Such an explanation lacks persuasion when juxtaposed to the genre analysis which follows. In almost any of the hypothetical genres, such as *Acts* being a "biography of Paul," it would behoove Luke to *explain* the results of Paul's trial even though the results themselves would have been known to his reader.

Since we know *Acts* ends with Paul awaiting trial in Rome, it is logical that *Luke-Acts* could have been written during the period of Paul's imprisonment. If Paul ended up being held in prison in Rome for three years, five years, ten years, or longer and Luke had written at a time subsequent to Acts 28:30 (two years after Paul's imprisonment had begun), he most probably would have written in verse 30: For "three," "five" or "ten" whole years Paul stayed there.

Readership: In the commentary many details will be cited to show that Luke's Gentile Roman reader was not Christian and was, in fact, juridic. Let us consider some additional evidence. If Luke had written *Acts* in the late 70s to early 90s, he undoubtedly would have seen many of the epistles, particularly those written by Paul which would make their way into the New Testament canon. The large majority of those letters contain salutations explicitly reciting or commending the faith of the recipients. The salutation to Theophilus lacks any reference to his faith. Thus, Luke, if he is writing to a believer or believers, has broken a literary convention in his salutation. Although people on occasion ignore such conventions, the fact that conventions are usually or routinely followed is evidence that Luke's reader was not a Christian.

As I have argued, if Luke has written to a legal audience, *Acts* must have been written in A.D. 61–62 for use in Paul's trial. Of the four Gospel writers, *only* Luke mentions all four legal proceedings leading to the crucifixion of Jesus: The trial before Sanhedrin,[5] the "not guilty" hearing before Pilate,[6] the interrogation before Herod,[7] and the substitution of Barabbas for Jesus and sentencing of Jesus.[8] Luke alone tells of the severing of the ear of the servant of the High Priest when Jesus is arrested in the Garden of Gethsemane[9] and notes Jesus' healing of the ear to show that He did not want his people to be insurrectionists. These unique sections of *Luke* adumbrate the legal defense which Luke orchestrates to a crescendo in Acts 16–28. Surely Luke got many details for *Acts* from the recollections of Paul. Roughly one hundred individuals are identified in the narrative, most by name. Time references are sometimes included.[10] Geographic details abound. Such details are consistent with a legal brief which seeks to persuade the reader that the facts or legal decisions presented are *verifiable*.

If Paul contributed to *Acts*, as the close contacts between the men virtually assured, it also makes sense that his name not appear as author or coauthor. A legal brief to a tribunal or an investigator with an objective of freeing a prisoner carries less weight if written by the prisoner because of the self-interest and subjectivity which the reader will immediately presume of the writer.

Dependence on Mark: Probably the most often repeated argument for a later date for *Luke-Acts* is the dependence of the Gospel of Luke on *Mark*. Maddox who dates *Luke-Acts* from the late 70s to the early 90s, summarizes the principal argument:

Mark is a major source of the Gospel of Luke and Mark is definitely a second-generation Christian work: many scholars regard it as necessary to date Mark after the destruction of Jerusalem in 70 A.D., but in any case we have to allow time for the evident development of oral tradition which underlies Mark, and we have such signs as that Simon of Cyrene, who was young enough to be able to carry Jesus' cross, is now better known through his children (Mark 15:21). Then we have to allow time for the circulation of Mark and for Luke to develop his plan of using it as the basis of a larger work.[11]

Several points of scholarly consensus need to be noted before discussing the merits of the late date argument:

1. *Luke-Acts* is one work, so if the Gospel of Luke "depends" on *Mark* and *Mark* was written after the destruction of Jerusalem in A.D. 70, then so was *Acts*.

2. The "dependence on the *Mark* = late date for *Luke-Acts*" argument certainly conflicts with the internal evidence of much of *Acts*.

3. The Book of Luke does appear to be based in substantial part on *Mark* (see chapter on the Book of Luke where I point to numerous evident dependencies).

4. If *Acts* is written after A.D. 70, the argument that it is a legal brief disintegrates because of the timing of Paul's pretrial incarceration.

Having noted the points of agreement, I will now address what I see as the primary weakness of the *Luke/Mark* dependence = later date hypothesis.

1.   Mark 15:21 is a shaky foundation for a late date. Certainly, Simon could have been, say, twenty when he carried the cross of Jesus, about A.D. 30. His sons, Alexander and Rufus, could have been born about ten years later and may not have been well known in the church until they reached their 50s. This hypothesis would yield a date for *Luke* in the 90s. However, Simon could have been thirty-five or forty when he helped Jesus. At that time Alexander and Rufus could be in their late teens or early twenties. These men could have become well known in the church within a decade. Thus, Mark 15:21 leads to the possibility that *Mark* was written in the 40s, 50s, 60s, 70s, 80s, or 90s![12]

2.   It is not clear which *"Mark" Luke* depends on. Everyone agrees that the Gospel of Mark developed from oral sources, i.e., people told stories about Jesus and these stories were repeated, collected, and written. A simple and primitive example of this process is illustrated by Mark 16:6–7 where three of Jesus' female followers encounter a young man in a white robe in Jesus' tomb. He tells them, "He is risen! He is not here . . . But go, tell His disciples." These followers first told, later they wrote. What the proponents of a late date for the composition of *Luke* appear to understate is that the development of *Mark* from an oral gospel to its

final written form necessarily included many intermediate stages and forms. In other words, in writing his gospel, Luke could have relied upon:

A. The final written version of *Mark*.

B. An oral gospel similar to the final version which was routinely memorized by evangelists.

C. A prior, non-final, written version of *Mark*.

D. A combination of oral and written Markan sources.

Of course, *Luke* had other sources (Luke 1:1 indicates that the writer knew of *many* orderly accounts of the life of Jesus), but for the purposes of inquiry into dating it is only relevant to note that the shared passages with *Mark* in no way preclude a composition date of A.D. 61 to 62 for *Luke-Acts*.

Maddox, in the argument cited above, also argues for a later date because time was needed "for the circulation of Mark" and "for Luke to develop his plan of using it as a basis for larger work."[13] While such speculation is allowable, it advances our knowledge not a whit. If Luke, Paul, other companions, the church at Rome, Peter, or others had substantial portions of *Mark*, written or memorized, then it would be eminently sensible for Luke, as a brief writer, to utilize *Mark* as the background framework and then to engraft other sources, including the uniquely Lukan details which are discussed in the chapter on the Book of Luke.

DATING SUMMARY

The internal evidence of *Luke-Acts* is entitled to the greatest weight in dating the book and that evidence strongly, consistently, even overwhelmingly supports a date from A.D. 61 to 62. The internal evidence concerning the intended reader of *Acts,* such as being Roman, literate in Greek, and knowledgeable in Roman criminal law, also points to *Acts* being composed for the purposes of Paul's trial before Nero and thus written from A.D. 61 to 62. The argument for dating *Luke* after A.D. 70 because it has dependence on *Mark* is inconclusive. Thus all persuasive evidence supports a dating of A.D. 61 to 62.

GENRE

Biography, apology, scientific treatise, catechism, historical monograph (as distinguished from a universal history), historical romance, "N" document,[14] or conscious canonical creation? What is *Acts*? Many, if not innumerable, studies have been undertaken to identify the "genre" of *Acts* or of *Luke-Acts* with no consensus. The identification of a genre would certainly be helpful in understanding Luke's original intent. Examples from three scholars illustrate the *range of genre* suggested for *Acts*. Howard Marshall cautiously concludes: "Luke's work appears to be unique among Christian writings and to have no secular precedents in its combination of the stories of a religious leader and of his followers."[15]

Darryl Palmer summarizes his view of the genre of *Acts* by contrasting it with the conclusion of three other scholars:

> In modern study the phrase "historical monograph" is applied to ancient Greek and Roman writings which deal with a limited issue or period and which may also be limited in length . . . Acts is not a romance (Pervo), an "apologetic history" (Sterling) or a technical treatise (Alexander). In its length, scope, focus and internal features, Acts is a short historical monograph.[16]

Undoubtedly, in the broader sense, Palmer is right, that *Acts* is both a history and of limited scope but the conclusion that it is a "historical monograph" still does not help us understand much because it does not tell us *why* Luke selected the portions of history he included in *Acts* or the *occasion* for his work.

Likewise, Brian Rosner is clearly correct when he likens *Acts* to Hebrew scripture: "The Jewish Scriptures exerted a profound influence upon not only the theology of Acts, as is widely recognized, but also upon its character as a piece of literature."[17] And Rosner is correct when he finds the same "notion of God's control of human history [which] is basic to all of the Old Testament."[18]

Ultimately, the determination of genre is closely tied to the author's purpose, and the purpose dictates genre rather than genre dictating purpose. However, identifying a genre can give important insight into an author's purpose and meaning. When an item appears in the Chicago Tribune, for example, it can initially be assumed to be a "news report" designed to inform the reader of recent events of interest in the community, nation, or world. However, on closer reading, an identification of an article as an "obituary," "editorial," or "sports commentary" may help better understand its meaning. The identification of a broad genre may be initially useful in understanding purposes, but that utility diminishes significantly the more the writing is uniquely tailored to achieve a particular objective.

If we assume Luke's intention in *Acts*, for example, is primarily to write a biography of Paul to encourage Christians, then a study of other ancient biographies may provide insights into the meaning of his work. If Chevrolet makes a television ad to sell cars, it would only marginally contribute to an understanding of its meaning for a reader in the year 3000 to categorize its genre as "early twenty-first century American video production." Likewise, if *Acts* is written as a legal brief to defend Paul and Jewish Christianity and to inform, convince and convert Roman officials, then the "genre" is so *unique*, so removed from other writings that the "genre" approach will only help as a first step analysis and thereafter could lead to confusion or frustration. The many scholars who have attempted to identify a genre for *Acts*[19] more specific than "historical monograph" or Old Testament continuation have concluded:

1. *Acts* cannot be definitely said to fit any known genre; or

2. *Acts* contains many genres; or

3. *Acts* has a specific genre (though large majorities of other scholars have rejected their conclusion).

Through process of elimination, the effort to identify a genre has advanced scholarship significantly by telling us what *Acts* is not.

Of course, the absence of a clearly identifiable genre does not tell us what *Acts* is but it may open minds *to consider that rather than having a vague or unfathomable purpose, Luke had highly specific objectives in writing Acts.*

We now have established twelve distinct analytical frameworks for our investigation:

1. first-century Judaism and "Christianity."

2. the personal backgrounds of Luke and Paul.

3. the charges against Paul.

4. the Roman Emperors, particularly Nero and his advisers.

5. Roman substantive criminal law.

6. Roman criminal procedure.

7. the form and purpose of written legal advocacy.

8. a proposed identity of Theophilus.

9. questions of unique concern to a legal investigator.

10. fifty-nine arguments in defense of Paul.

11. the dating of *Acts*.

12. genre.

Let us now go deeper by examining the text proper. As we explore Luke's narrative, we will discuss whether and how *each passage* fits these frameworks, noting several additional paths to understanding Luke's purpose and audience. Early in our journey we will observe the frequent appearance of speeches on the literary landscape of *Acts*. We will ask whether the use of such discourses furthers a legal agenda. Shortly after we hear what the speeches tell us, we will encounter a chart of sixteen trials or investigatory proceedings in *Acts*. This experience will be an opportunity to ask whether those passages function, in the larger narrative, as a legal defense. Along the route we will pause to examine fascinating, and legally germane, social aspects of the first-century Roman Empire: the role of women, slaves, the military, and finances. Luke will introduce a number of interesting individuals of high and low estate and acquaint us with a unique company of people: the God fearers. Each encounter will speak, as it were, living words to guide us on our quest. Having journeyed through the text, we will then have a vantage from which to reflect and check the truth of what we have heard through six additional frameworks:

1. which witnesses would be called at a trial.

2. what written, relevant legal records are referenced in *Acts*.

3. why no New Testament letter of Paul is mentioned in *Acts*.

4. the events, people, and circumstances in *Acts* referenced in Paul's prison letters.

5. how the Book of Luke relates.

6. all of the alternative explanations for *Luke-Acts*.

We will see if the argument set forth in this book can withstand the cross-examination those paradigms provide.

---

1   Bruce, *New Testament History*, 346, places Festus as beginning his procuratorship in A.D. 59, which would put Paul after his appeal and long journey in Rome in the spring of A.D. 60. *Unger's Bible Dictionary* (Chicago: Moody Press, 1983), 383, dates the appointment of Festus to the fall of A.D. 60, which would put Paul in Rome in A.D. 61. Under either dating, the "two years" referenced in Acts 28:30 ends in A.D. 62 or 63.

2   Acts 7:48, 52.

3   Acts 25:8.

4   Acts 25:11.

5   Luke 22:66–71.

6   Luke 23:1–7.

7   Luke 23:8–12.

8   Luke 23:13–24.

9   Luke 22:50–5.

10   Acts 18:12; Luke 1:5.

11   Maddox, *Purpose of Luke-Acts*, 7–8

12   For discussion of the parallel passage, Luke 23:27–31, see Chapter 31.

13   Maddox, *Purpose of Luke-Acts*, 8.

14   In the later twentieth century, archaeologists discovered in Egypt and elsewhere a number of ancient Roman legal documents mostly from the second and third centuries which have been labeled "N" documents because they are headed by a singular capital "N." The N may be an abbreviation for the Latin *narratio*, meaning "narrative" or "story," or it may indicate preparation by a "paralegal" assistant. These documents contain 300–1,000–word summaries of legal presentations and were used by lawyers giving *oral* presentations of their cases. Based on these discoveries and the analysis by Bruce Winter of the components of N documents, "Official Proceedings," 308ff., it can be safely concluded that the speech of Tertullus in Acts 24:2–8 fits the N document format. However, *Acts* is *not* an N document, most importantly because it was not written for oral presentation but as an aid to gathering and confirming facts. Also *Acts* is far longer than any N document and does not fit at all into the rather formal pattern which that genre requires.

15   I. Howard Marshall, "Acts and the Former Treatise" in *Acts in Ancient Literary Setting*, 180.

16   Daryl W. Palmer, "Acts and the Ancient Historical Monograph," in *Acts in Ancient Literary Setting*, 1.

17   Brian S. Rosner, "Acts and Biblical History" in *Acts in Ancient Literary Setting*, 65.

18   Ibid., 78.

19   Palmer, "Acts and Ancient Monograph," 1–30, and I.C.A. Alexander, "Acts and Ancient Intellectual Biography," *Acts in Ancient Literary Setting*, 31–64.

CHAPTER 6

ACTS 1

BY MANY INFALLIBLE PROOFS
(ACTS 1:3)

Luke introduces the Book of Acts[1] with a reminder of his "first book."[2] This reminder serves as a transition because *Acts* will cover new ground. He summarizes his first book, *Luke,* as "all Jesus did and taught"[3] until he ascended to heaven. These opening sentences tell us several important things. First, a summary this short clearly indicates that his immediate reader, Theophilus, has already read the former book. Second, Luke discloses a chronological organization for *Luke-Acts*: first book = until ascension; this book = after ascension. Third, we have a hint that Luke is writing to an audience beyond Theophilus, because if someone other than Theophilus reads *Acts*, he is informed immediately that a great deal of background information is necessary in order to understand *Acts*.

Although *Luke* and *Acts* are one unified work from the viewpoint of authorship, subject matter, continuity, and purpose, they are separate "detachable" parts of a whole. The Book of Luke is completed even as *Acts* is commenced. Finally, Luke may be launching two legal arguments in the first sentence of *Acts*. He could have simply told the reader that this book and the former book were the before and after of the Resurrection, but Luke adds that the ascension of Jesus occurred *after* he gave the apostles instructions through the Holy Spirit. Each of these arguments will be expanded throughout *Acts* but they are introduced here:

Legal Argument One: The apostles have authority. In the words of John Belushi,[4] they are "on a mission from God." The source of their authority is Jesus and the Holy Spirit. The credentials of Jesus have been established in the Book of Luke. The power emanating from the Holy Spirit, which was adumbrated at the close of "part one" in Luke 24:49, will be more fully described in the next few verses. In saying the apostles have authority from Jesus, Luke also refutes two implicit charges against the apostles raised by their opponents. The first charge is that these men are self-proclaimed authorities operating on their own initiative. The second implicit charge is that the authority of the apostles has not been granted by the Jewish leaders in power over Israel. Roman officials would certainly have been concerned to know where these "apostles" came from, and where these men who were crisscrossing the empire got the right to spread this faith. Luke tells the reader from the beginning that those questions have an answer and will be addressed.

Legal Argument Two: Not only do the followers have authority, they have orders. They are "apostles," literally "sent out ones." Through most of *Luke* they have been called disciples but with the Resurrection and Ascension the terms "apostles" and "witnesses" are applied more often. In Luke 24:47–48, Jesus tells his disciples they will preach repentance and forgiveness and be filled with power. A similar message will be given in Acts 1:8. The Roman keeper of order would not only question the authority of this band of itinerate Jewish preachers and where they got their power to preach and perform miracles but what their objective was. Throughout history instances abound of those in power being afraid that preaching about Jesus was designed to subvert government. Indeed any strong religious movement is viewed with suspicion by authoritarian rulers because it is not under their control. Roman officials were no different in their fears. Due to the history of independent thinking and insurrection among Jewish subjects of Rome, movements arising from them would be singularly suspect. Accordingly, political issues are addressed in the first two verses of *Acts*.

Verses 3–6 also are a transition from *Luke*, striking in what they assert *and* omit. They assert:

1. Jesus gave the apostles many proofs that he was alive.

2. There were forty post-Resurrection days of direct contacts between Jesus and apostles.

3. Jesus taught about the kingdom of God.

4. The apostles were told to stay in Jerusalem until they received the Holy Spirit.

These affirmative statements further Luke's agenda to establish the authority of the ones Jesus is about to send out in three particulars:

1. Jesus has authority because he really is alive.

2. The apostles also have this authority because they spent considerable time with Jesus receiving instruction about the kingdom.

3. This authority will be reinforced by immersion into the Holy Spirit.

To any Roman official asking the question, "Where did these men get their authority?" an answer is being given. It might not be the expected answer and it might not satisfy him, but it is unflinching: "The men who are spreading this message across your empire have been sent on the authority of the God of the Jews, through his risen son, Jesus." As we read further in *Acts*, we learn that Paul and the other apostles are being accused of fomenting rebellion against the empire.[5] The Jews in general had a history of rebellion against Rome. As *Luke-Acts* was written, the forces which would boil over in A.D. 66 as a full-scale revolt were certainly simmering. Thus the accusations against Paul and the *Talmidei Yeshua* would, to a Roman official, have an immediate relevance and a *prima facie* (legally presumptive) credibility especially to the extent the followers chose to identify as Jews and not distance themselves from Israel. The accusations would also have credence because Jesus was crucified on orders of a Roman governor.

Accordingly, the next question which a Roman official would ask is: "Are these 'sent out ones' being sent out to incite revolt?" Luke has already answered this question partially in Luke 9:1–6: They are going out to heal and are unarmed; it is a spiritual mission. He answers the question again in Acts 1:4 and 1:6–7: The "kingdom" is a kingdom of God and not a competing political power structure or threat to Rome; this kingdom pertains to Israel and is not for "this time" but for a later time.

To fully appreciate the thrust of the affirmative statements in Acts 1:1–7, we must also consider its omissions. You are the jury. You weigh what each witness says. You also wonder about things *not* said during the trial. The Gospel of Luke gives detailed attention to Jesus' teaching, his last week before the crucifixion, his crucifixion and resurrection. In *Acts*, however, his forty days of teaching after the Resurrection are summed up in a few sentences! What follower of Jesus would not want to know about those teachings and accompanying events? What teacher whose primary goal was to edify or instruct believers would omit all but a few of the rabbi's words after he triumphed over the grave! What was it like to be dead prior to the Resurrection? What happened when he went back to the Father? How did the disciples react to his teaching? Would believers care more about the choosing of Mathias[6] than the teachings of the resurrected Messiah? From these *monumental* omissions one may deduce that Luke was not writing *Acts* to catechize believers. Luke's sources (which we will consider as we progress), especially Peter, would have known this information. In his introduction to his gospel, Luke emphasized his careful investigation of "everything."[7] He knew what happened but he apparently did not want to focus *Acts* on the needs or questions of believers.

Acts 1:8 has rightly been called both the introduction to and summation of the entire book: "But you shall receive power when the Holy Spirit has come upon you; and you shall be witnesses to Me in Jerusalem, in all Judea and Samaria, and to the ends of the earth." It explains the transformation of Jesus' followers from insecure fishermen to fearless apostles; it foretells and commands their ministry to expand from Jerusalem into all the earth. Luke may have fixed upon these particular words of Jesus as the outline and organizational structure for his writing. But, again, if we are to assume a skeptical investigatory or judicial readership, we can see important emphases:

1. The authority of the apostles comes from God (i.e., not from the priesthood, Sanhedrin, temple, or other Jewish leadership).

2. The apostles will be *witnesses*. Rosenblatt argues, persuasively in my opinion, that the theme of "witness" in *Acts* is used not just in today's evangelistic sense but also in the judicial sense; the apostles will give testimony about Jesus in legal proceedings: "Intensive forms of *witness* appear in several places and reinforce the juridical context of witness. . . . In classical usage [those forms] refer to what the witness says about one of the primary parties in a legal dispute"[8]

3. The "witness" will include the occasion upon which *Acts* was written: the forthcoming trial of Paul before Nero.

4. The reports then reaching the ears of Roman officials that followers of Jesus were multiplying among Jews and Gentiles throughout the empire will be explained.

In verses 9 to 11, Luke recounts Jesus' ascension to heaven and answers an obvious question: What happened to Jesus? The reason for Luke to include this passage could be to answer that question in the minds of Roman officials or of virtually any other assumed readership. Its inclusion neither serves to support nor weaken the understanding that *Acts* is written for legal purposes. It is also interesting to note that the taking up of Jesus is not final despite the dramatic nature of his departure and promised dramatic return. In Acts 23:11, Jesus stands before Paul and speaks specifically of the need for Paul to give (judicial) testimony in Rome. Thus, the message of the Ascension, by the time the reader gets to chapter 23 and which is greatly reinforced by intervening passages, I would characterize as: "Jesus has temporarily removed himself from being directly on the scene, but he is closely monitoring the situation. He has been fully involved in the work of the apostles and will be present at the trial in Rome in spirit, if not in person. The outcome of the trial is in his hands, and the witnesses before you, most respected Roman official, are there on his authority." While such a claim may be bold and, to a Roman official, even considered arrogant, the claim is made by implication and never with disrespect to Roman authority.[9]

The Ascension account would also be of particular interest to an educated Roman. Romulus, the legendary first king of Rome, is said to have founded Rome in 753 B.C. At his death, he is also said to have disappeared in a thick cloud during a thunderstorm and become a god. Certainly, Luke knew the similarities which would be perceived between the Romulus account and the ascension of Jesus. By calling attention to these similarities, Luke invites consideration of their differences. In contrast to Romulus, Jesus has first died and then risen from the grave. The accounts of the "ascension" of Romulus are from a distant past, while the ascension of Jesus is recent (thirty years) and, in all probability, will be attested to by Peter or other witnesses at Paul's trial. Romulus, presumably, has not been heard from since he disappeared. Jesus, however, will reappear as *Acts* unfolds. Thus, if Luke is writing for

Roman officials, the inclusion of the Ascension reinforces the assertion of Judaism that its God is the only true God and the assertion already made in the Gospel of Luke that Jesus is the God of all humanity.[10]

After describing the Ascension, Luke names the apostles and tells the reader of the replacement of the betrayer, Judas. In the choosing of Matthias,[11] Luke continues to deal with one of the big *legal obstacles* to Paul's defense: authority. If faith in Jesus is Jewish, *ergo* legal, then why do all the Jewish leaders want Paul killed? A Gentile Roman official would see Judaism in terms of ethnicity, a one God religion, the Sanhedrin, Jerusalem, the temple, the priesthood, adherence to Jewish Scripture, circumcision, and observance of dietary and other ritual practices. By any of these measures a case can be argued that some or all of the followers of Jesus were *not* following Judaism. Luke, especially in the earlier parts of *Acts*, addresses each of these "indicators" of Jewishness and argues that the followers of Jesus are faithful to the teachings of Moses and the Prophets, are proven correct by the presence of the resurrected and ascended Messiah, and are continually vindicated by the presence of the Holy Spirit operating in their midst. His battle is uphill because of all the distinctive marks of Jewishness, his audience is probably least familiar with the Hebrew Scriptures and they certainly are skeptical about the Resurrection.[12]

The reintroduction of the apostles by name[13] thus establishes a counterpoint to the presumed authority of the priests and the Sanhedrin. The emphasis upon their being twelve in number with a multiple of twelve (120)[14] as followers may echo the number of tribes of Israel and thus be a claim to the mantle of authority to lead Israel. It may also be a legal assertion to Roman authorities that the apostles were entitled to self-governance under *Jewish* law and were not under the authority of the Jerusalem Sanhedrin because the Romans allowed the Jews and other subject peoples a measure of self-governance. Indigenous laws were respected if Roman interests were not compromised. One passage in the Talmud suggests that 120 was the minimum number for a town to have its own Sanhedrin: "What must be the population of a town to make it eligible for a [small] Sanhedrin?—one hundred and twenty."[15]

The reader is also told that apostles have authority because:

1. Jesus, the resurrected Messiah, has chosen, taught, and sent them out.

2. The Lord has kept the group intact and shown who is to be the successor to Judas.

3. The proceedings to replace Judas have been in accordance with the Scriptures.[16]

4. The Holy Spirit will confirm this authority through the events in chapter 2.

As a brief writer, Luke has given himself a tough sell. After reading his introduction and his legal argument in verses 1:12–26, Theophilus could be forgiven for chortling, "Who are these guys? The only thing Jewish about them is their chutzpah!" Nevertheless, Luke has a few points in his favor: First, hopefully, the reader has read the customized background for *Acts,* the "former book," the Gospel of Luke, and sees a consistency and continuity. Second, Luke should have the reader's interest. If the reader is not convinced, at least he is intrigued. Third, Luke would surely be counting on his unseen ally, the Holy Spirit, to help with the convincing. It would be strange indeed if the writer who so assuredly proclaims the working of the Spirit in the lives of the apostles was not also counting on the Spirit to reveal truth to the heart of the reader.

---

1   The title "Acts of the Apostles" is not part of the original book but rather dates to the end of the second century; Fitzmyer, *Acts of the Apostles,* 47–49.
2   Acts 1:1.
3   Acts 1:1.
4   In *The Blues Brothers.*
5   E.g., Acts 17:6, Acts 24:5.
6   Acts 1:20–26.
7   Luke 1:2–3.
8   Rosenblatt, *Paul the Accused,* 4.
9   Acts 27:23–24.
10 This passage is thus an interesting parallel to Exodus which shows that the God of the Jews is the one true God over all the mighty deities of Egypt. But I digress.
11 Acts 1:12–26.
12 See Acts 25:19.
13 Acts 1:11–13.
14 Acts 1:15.
15 Sanh. 1.1.
16 Acts 1:16, 20.

CHAPTER 7

ACTS 2

PETER'S FIRST SPEECH:
"*JEWS . . . FROM EVERY NATION*"
(ACTS 2:5)

The Pentecost "explosion" is the natural progression from the points made in Acts 1. The first apostles got their authority directly from Jesus; now they, and all subsequent followers, will get their power from the Holy Spirit. In addition to explaining the source of power, Luke takes the first step in explaining the universality of the witnessing which was adumbrated in Acts 1:8. Universally available salvation is an important *legal* point because Luke is arguing that the faith of the apostles is true to Judaism and not an illegal religion. "Tongues" and "nations" are the two themes he uses to show universality in chapter 2. Tongues enable the hearers to understand the wonders of God in their own language. The nations listed in verses 8–11 are a roster of the known world as seen from Jerusalem,[1] including but extending beyond the Roman Empire and its client states. As Luke writes *Acts*, "Christianity" had spread rapidly throughout the empire. Officials in Rome might not have understood it, but they were aware of it. As already noted, typical questions of a Roman observer would be:

1. Why is this faith suddenly appearing all over the empire?
2. Why does it involve Gentiles as well as Jews?
3. Is it from Jews in a certain region, tribe, political viewpoint, or religious predisposition?

Luke answers the third question by explaining that all Israel is included. To paraphrase from modern vocabulary: "Although Jesus' original followers were all Sabras, the faith quickly spread throughout the Diaspora." While Luke does not yet answer the second question regarding Gentiles, he lays the foundation for an answer when he addresses the first question by explaining how the faith spread so quickly from Galilean Jews to Jews from so many nations. He also hints at the coming inclusion of Gentiles in mentioning that the *Roman* contingent contained both Jews and "converts to Judaism." The assembled crowd was at least 3,000.[2] Presumably, converts to Judaism were present from other nations also. Luke may be making this point only for Romans because he is writing to a Gentile Roman who would sense a personal connection with these converts.

WOMEN IN ACTS

The discerning reader of *Acts* will notice the relative prominence of women in the narrative. At a time when the ancient world and Rome, in particular, saw women as property, Luke introduces them as significant participants in the plan of God due to the outpouring of the Holy Spirit. His first mention of women in *Acts* is in 1:14 when he recounts that the disciples were constantly in prayer "along with the women and Mary the mother of Jesus . . ." Next in Acts 2:17–18, Peter's speech to the Pentecost crowd includes this significant passage from the prophet Joel: "And it shall come to pass in the last days, says God, That I will pour out My Spirit on *all flesh*, your sons and your *daughters* shall prophecy . . . And on My menservants, *and on My maidservants*, I will pour out my Spirit in those days, . . ." (emphasis added)

Later we learn that the first convert in Philippi is Lydia, a dealer in purple cloth.[3] The Philippian church first meets in her home. Then Luke introduces the reader to Priscilla, a Jewish evangelist![4] Together with her husband, Aquila, she is mentioned four times in Acts, always being first mentioned after the couple's initial introduction. When Paul, on his final journey to Jerusalem, visits the home of the evangelist Philip in Caesarea, Luke adds the detail that Philip had "four unmarried daughters who prophesied."[5]

Why so many references to women? Certainly the universality theme is one good legal reason, however the particular inclusions of Acts 1:14 (women and Mary joining in prayer), Acts 2:18 (*both* men and women), and Acts 21:8–9 (daughters of Philip) do not advance the narrative; they are deliberate but parenthetical inclusions. Consequently, one may reasonably surmise that Luke wanted Theophilus to take particular note of the role of women among the believers. Why? To me, the most plausible reason for such emphasis is that women were participating significantly in the spread of the gospel. Theophilus had probably noticed and needed an explanation. As a departure from both Roman and non-Christian Jewish norms, it could be used by opponents as further evidence of faith in Jesus being socially subversive to Roman social order, in this case to patriarchy. The Judaism practiced by the leaders who rejected Jesus also severely restricted the role of women. With the early believers including female evangelists and prophets, Luke had to show that the Way was not a new religion. He does this by quoting the Hebrew prophet Joel.

BEYOND UNIVERSALITY

Luke's account of the speech of Peter[6] and its reference to Joel also serve a legal/evangelistic agenda in multiple ways beyond the legal argument made by universality:

1. It continues the explanation of the explosion of faith as not being "new", "this is what was spoken by the prophet Joel."[7]

2. It proclaims the resurrected Messiah.[8]

3. Almost half of the speech is Hebrew scripture, reminding a Roman judicial reader that faith in Jesus is *not* a new religion, but anchored in Judaism and the authority of its writings.

4. It does not blame Jesus' crucifixion on the Romans or the Jews, but on "God's set purpose and foreknowledge."[9]

5. It shows a *broad-based* response to the preaching.[10] Luke says 3,000 believed. By the time *Acts* is written, substantial majorities of Jews and Jewish leaders had not accepted the messiahship of Jesus. Luke's point here, reiterated throughout *Acts*, is not the modern conceit of "proof of truth by majority vote," but rather that a substantial number of Jews did believe that following Jesus was fully Jewish and, contrary to the accusation by some opponents, the Christians had not left Judaism.

6. The description of the confidence and fervor which Peter and the Eleven exhibit in the proclamation of Jesus[11] introduces the theme of boldness which will typify the preaching of the apostles, and particularly of Paul, throughout *Acts*.[12] This description contrasts with the fearful attitude of the believers before Pentecost and functions in a purely legal framework to explain:

   A. The rapid spread of the faith.

   B. The opposition against the faith.

The theme of fearlessness functions in a compound legal and evangelistic agenda to explain:

   A. The deliverance through the immersion into God's Spirit from the universal human experience of bondage to fear.

   B. Paul's (and Luke's) boldness in proclaiming the Messiah of the Jews to Nero and Roman officialdom through his writing of *Acts*.[13]

7. Finally, Peter's strong emphasis on the Resurrection[14] not only explains the apostles' enthusiasm but is also the type of assertion we would expect from a legal advocate: *Fifty days* after the crucifixion, 3,000 God-fearing Jews from all over the empire, including Rome, believed in the Resurrection of Jesus. If the body of Jesus were available or the explana-

tion of the Jewish or Roman leaders as to its disappearance were credible, why, *in the face of the universal human experience that dead people stay dead*, would so many people believe and respond so radically?[15]

If Luke is writing a legal brief, why does he include so much of the gospel in Peter's speech and later in the sermons of Paul?

> Men of Israel, listen to this: Jesus of Nazareth was a man accredited by God to you by miracles, wonders and signs, which God did among you through him, as you yourselves know. This man was handed over to you by God's set purpose and foreknowledge; and you, with the help of wicked men, put him to death by nailing him to the cross. But God raised him from the dead, freeing him from the agony of death, because it was impossible for death to keep its hold on him.[16]

Perhaps an example from American history is pertinent: "that the government of the people, by the people and for the people shall not perish from the earth." Lincoln's Gettysburg Address was formally a dedicatory speech by him for a cemetery but was used to impart a vision for the survival of democracy. Likewise, even as Luke was writing a legal brief, he used the opportunity to tell his readers of Jesus and salvation as often as the legal objectives comfortably allowed.

Verses 37 to 41 recount the baptism of those who accepted Peter's message. Would not this passage be an admission to Rome that a new religion was being created? No, not from a first-century perspective. Baptism, as noted in the glossary, was in ancient times a ritual of conversion *to* Judaism. However, because those accepting *mikva* in Acts 2 were already Jews, their immersion was neither a conversion to nor from Judaism, but an action required by God within Judaism, (albeit an obvious echo of the action of converts to Judaism) a public acknowledgement of repentance and cleansing from sin through Jesus the Messiah of Israel which would bring the "gift of the Spirit."

Verses 42–47 which close Acts 2 affirm that the decision to believe and be baptized was not fleeting but transforming, that the same fervor which had gripped the apostles was now moving powerfully in the new believers. Luke's comment in verse 47 about the believers enjoying favor "of all the people" is added to indicate that the true causes of their rejection, and of the turmoil which would occur throughout the empire, had not yet arisen. Luke will subsequently articulate those causes:

1. Fear by Jewish leaders of being blamed for Jesus' death.

2. The jealousy and threat to the power, prestige, and financial interest of the Jewish leaders.

3. The widespread and relatively easy incorporation of Gentiles into the faith of Abraham.

At this early point in the narrative Luke is saying the Resurrection is not an issue dividing the followers of Jesus from other Jews because the Resurrection so strongly emphasized in Peter's Pentecost speech evidently had been widely believed. This acceptance will be explained further in *Acts* when Luke informs Theophilus that the Pharisees believed in the resurrection of the dead.[17]

---

1   Richard Bauckham, "James and the Jerusalem Church," in *Acts in Palestinian Setting*, 420.
2   Acts 2:41.
3   Acts 16:11.
4   Acts 18:2.
5   Acts 21:8–9.
6   Acts 2:14–41.
7   Acts 2:16.
8   E.g., Acts 2:31–32.
9   Acts 2:23.
10 Acts 2:41.
11 Acts 2:14, 29.
12 Acts 4:13, 29, 31; 9:27; 13:46; 14:3; 18:26; 19:8; 26:26; 28:31. See Rapske, *Paul in Roman Custody*, 310–11, where he concludes that boldness and fearlessness are thematic to Acts.
13 Acts 20:24.
14 Acts 2:24, 27, 29, 31–32.
15 See Acts 2:44.
16 Acts 2:22–24.
17 Acts 23:6.

CHAPTER 8

ACTS 3

PETER'S SECOND SPEECH: *ALL THE KINDREDS OF THE EARTH* (ACTS 3:25)

Peter's second speech echoes the first. Like the first, which is preceded by the out-pouring of the Spirit, the second speech is preceded by a miracle, in this case the healing of a beggar. Luke tells us many miracles were then occurring,[1] so why does he recount this particular one? Probably the highly *public* nature and location of the miracle rather than the imparting of the ability to walk is Luke's agenda.

Similar to the tongues on Pentecost, the healing of the beggar crippled from birth became known to thousands. The beggar was already known to all Jews who frequented the temple because he was put there "every day."[2] The miracle itself was immediately and widely known because the newly healed man made a pub-lic display[3] by "walking, jumping and praising God in the temple courts." The identity of the beggar as a former cripple who was fully healed could not be refuted,[4] or the family of the high priest[5] would have done so.

Not only does the miracle reconfirm Peter's authority, but the public nature of it is a bold assertion by Luke that it really happened. Even if the healing could not be verified easily because of the passage of thirty years until the writing of *Acts,* and the distance between Rome and Jerusalem, Luke has weaved the miracle and Peter's sec-ond evangelistic speech into a cogent explanation of the beginnings of the persecu-tion of the *Talmidei Yeshua* in Acts 4, which is first articulated as motivated by fear by the leadership in Acts 5:28 of being held accountable for Jesus' death.

The second speech,[6] as did the first, explicitly absolves the Jewish people from the unjust execution of Jesus both by stating their ignorance[7] (lack of intention) in actions which contributed to the crucifixion of Jesus and by repeating the fore-knowledge and intention of God that Jesus would suffer.[8] The second speech, how-ever, goes further *by also including the Jewish leaders among the innocent!*[9] When Luke wrote *Acts* thirty years later, the persecution of believers had intensified and Paul was on trial for his life. The temptation for Luke to edit the exoneration of the Jewish leadership out of Peter's speech must have been great. Its inclusion was deliberate and underscores the integrity and reliability of the writer. The speech concludes with a repetition of the ancient scriptural promise to the Jews that through their offspring all the peoples of the earth would be blessed.[10] Luke is noting another major fault line which will cause the believers in Jesus to be rejected by their fellow Jews: the widespread inclusion of the Gentiles, while he segues into the first confrontation with the leadership. In addition to the explicit legal relevance of each speech in *Acts*, it is significant how frequently Luke employs them to further his presentation.

SPEECHES

Scholars have rightly observed that Luke's quotation of speeches is a literary technique that unifies the narrative. Defining a "speech" as an "address to a group or an individual in a non-private setting, usually involving the attention of a number of people," Joseph Fitzmyer identifies twenty-eight speeches in *Acts* and concludes that they comprise about one-third of the text (295 verses out of 1,000!).[11] I have added one additional speech to his list. Given the overwhelming importance of this literary form to the narrative, we must ask, "Can Luke's extensive use of speeches be squared with the conclusion that *Acts* was written to a Roman pretrial investigator as an aid to gathering facts in defense against the charges facing Paul?" To answer the question I will address it on two levels:

1. Form; and 2. Content

If both square with the hypothesis, we can fairly conclude that the use of speeches is, by virtue of compatability, evidence that *Acts* is a pretrial "brief."

THE SPEECH AS FORENSIC FORM:

Drama: When Luke, for example, wants to make the legal point to Theophilus that the rejection of Messiah by most of the Jews was foreknown and foretold by the prophets, he persuades more effectively than by just asserting Scripture. Instead, he quotes Stephen: "Was there ever a prophet your fathers did not persecute?"[12] and illustrates the history of prophet rejection by referring to Moses: "This is the same Moses whom they had rejected . . ."[13]

Testimony: A speech can be a form of evidence. It is testimony. It is witness. In contrast to general assertions, quotation of a speech pins down the matter to a *specific* speaker who spoke *certain* words at a *particular* place in front of *identified* witnesses at an *ascertainable* time. Credibility is enhanced significantly.

Verifiability: Closely related to the credibility gained from quoting a speaker is the verifiability afforded to the legal writer. An investigator then can decide whom to question or depose to establish veracity. An innocent person being investigated or a lawyer defending him will usually lay out facts to the investigator, confident that inquiry will confirm the truth. Fitzmyer's observation that the *particular* speeches quoted in *Acts* involved a "*number* of people" in a "*non-private* setting" is further evidence of forensic purpose in Luke's composition: he does not assert things that could not be widely confirmed.

Thus the speech as "form" is not only consistent with the hypothesis that *Acts* is a pretrial brief but can be seen as an effective enhancement of such a document. The use of speech as form, however, is only effectual if the *content* furthers one or more of the legal defenses which I believe Luke is presenting.

Content of the Speeches in *Acts*:

To analyze content I have listed the twenty-eight speeches identified by Fitzmyer and one noted by me. Then, as in the Chart of Fifty-nine Arguments in Defense of Paul, I have simplified, to two, the legal defenses:

1. Christianity is not an illegal new religion, it is authentic Judaism made universal through Jesus.

2. Paul and the Christians are not a threat to Roman order, they are peaceful proclaimers of the Resurrection.

Next, I asked the question: "Would the original reader have understood this particular speech as supportive of either of the above legal defenses?" As will be seen, *every* speech supports at least one, and most support both, by focusing on the *witness of the Resurrection*. Fitzmyer has well labeled the speeches by speaker, place, and occasion. I have added a phrase or sentence from each speech which I believe illustrates Luke's forensic objective:

		TWENTY-NINE SPEECHES		
	Passage	Fitzmyer's Summary and *One Key Phrase from Speech*	Christianity is authentically Jewish	Paul and the Christians are evangelists not subversives
1.	1:4–5, 7–8	Risen Christ to apostles and disciples; *you will be my witnesses*		X
2.	1:16–22	Peter at the choosing of Matthias; *one of these must become a witness with us*	X	X
3.	2:14b-36, 38–39	Peter to Jews gathered in Jerusalem on Pentecost; *God has raised him . . . we are witnesses*	X	X
4.	3:12b-26	Peter in temple after cure of the lame man; *but God raised him . . . we are witnesses*	X	X

	Passage	Fitzmyer's Summary and *One Key Phrase from Speech*	Christianity is authentically Jewish	Paul and the Christians are evangelists not subversives
5.	4:8b-12, 19b-20	Peter before the Sanhedrin, I; *God raised him . . . we cannot help but speak*	X (v. 8b-12)	X (v. 19b-20)
6.	5:29b-32	Peter before the Sanhedrin, II; *We must obey God rather than man*	X	X
7.	5:35b-39	Gamaliel before the Sanhedrin; *If their purpose is from God . . .*	X	
8.	6:2b-4	The Twelve before the assembled disciples; *We will give our attention to prayer and to . . . the word*	X	X
9.	7:2–53	Stephen before the Sanhedrin; *Lord, do not hold their sin against them*	X	X
10.	10:34b-43	Peter at Cornelius's conversion; *We are witnesses . . . God raised him*	X	X
11.	11:5–17	Peter to the apostles and brothers in Jerusalem; *the Holy Spirit came on them as he had on us*	X	X
12.	13:16b-41	Paul at Antioch in Pisidia; *But God raised him . . . [his disciples] are now his witnesses*	X	X
13.	14:15–17	Barnabas and Paul to the crowd in Lystra; *. . . telling you to turn . . . to the Living God*	X	X
14,	15:7b-11	Peter at the "Council" in Jerusalem; *through the grace of Jesus we are saved just as they are*	X	
15.	15:13b-21	James to the assembly in Jerusalem; *we should not make it difficult for the Gentiles*	X	
16.	17:22–31	Paul to the Athenians at the Areopagus; *God . . . does not live in temples built by hands*	X	X
17.	18:14b-15	Gallio to the Jews of Corinth; *it involves questions . . . of your own law*	X	X
18.	19:25b-27	Demetrius to fellow silversmiths; *our trade is in danger*		X (discrediting accuser)
19.	19:35b-40	Town clerk to the Ephesians; *There is no reason for this commotion*		X

TWENTY-NINE SPEECHES

		TWENTY-NINE SPEECHES		
	Passage	Fitzmyer's Summary and *One Key Phrase from Speech*	Christianity is authentically Jewish	Paul and the Christians are evangelists not subversives
20.	20:18b-35	Paul to Ephesian presbyters at Miletus; *I have declared repentance to both Jews and Greeks*	X	X
21.	22:1, 3–21	Paul to the Jerusalem crowd at his arrest; *I am a Jew . . . a light from heaven flashed around me*	X	X
22.	23:6[14]	Paul before the Sanhedrin; *I am a Pharisee on trial because of my hope in the resurrection*	X	X
23.	24:2b-8	Tertullus before Governor Felix; *by examining him yourself you will learn the truth*		X
24.	24:10b-21	Paul before Governor Felix; *they cannot prove the charges . . . I admit I worship the God of our fathers*	X	
25.	25:8b, 10b-11	Paul's appeal to Caesar; *I have done nothing wrong against . . . the temple or Caesar*	X	X
26.	25:14c-21, 24–27	Festus before King Agrippa; *they had some dispute about their own religion and sent to the Gentiles a dead man who Paul claimed was alive*	X	X
27.	26:2–23, 25–27, 29	Paul before King Agrippa; *I appoint you as a witness [to the Gentiles]*	X	X
28.	27:21–26	Paul to fellow travelers aboard ship; *You must stand trial before Caesar*	X	X
29.	28:17c-20, 25b-28	Paul to Jewish leaders of Rome; *I have done nothing against our people . . . God's salvation has been sent to the Gentiles*	X	X

1   See Acts 2:43, 5:12.
2   Acts 3:2.
3   Acts 3:7–10.
4   Acts 4:14.
5   Acts 4:5.
6   Acts 3:12–26.
7   Acts 3:17.
8   Acts 3:18.
9   Acts 3:17.
10 Acts 3:25–26.
11 Fitzmyer, *Acts of the Apostles*, 103–4.
12 Acts 7:52.
13 Acts 7:35.
14 Fitzmyer omits 23:6, probably inadvertently.

CHAPTER 9

ACTS 4–5:11

THE FIRST SANHEDRIN TRIAL: *THE THINGS WHICH WE HAVE SEEN AND HEARD* (ACTS 4:20)

As the apostles confront the temple officials, Luke returns to the legal problem of the church leadership directly affecting the charges against Paul: where do the evangelists get their authority? In this encounter, Luke mentions six overlapping authority groups which stand in opposition to Peter and John:

1. Temple priests.
2. Captain of the temple guard.
3. Sadducees.
4. Annas, the high priest, and several men of his family, Caiaphas, John, Alexander, and others.
5. Rulers, elders, and teachers of the law.
6. The Sanhedrin.

At this point, the temple officials' consternation is about the preaching of the "resurrection of the dead in Jesus."[1] While the resurrection teaching alone might have somewhat bothered this group because of their Sadducean tilt (direct reference to Pharisees is conspicuously absent from the passage), the real concern is that the teaching was not theoretical but centered explicitly on Jesus. Their response was the same as oppressive governments anywhere: censor or silence. Luke records this encounter not because the Romans would recoil at heavy-handed use of authority, but because he wants:

1. To show that leadership of the temple had a direct and timely opportunity to refute both the Resurrection and the healing of the cripple but was unable to do so.

2. To show that the authority of the apostles surpassed the authority of the Jewish leadership, because of the Holy Spirit[2] and because of the healing of the cripple,[3] despite the educational and political inferiority of the apostles.

Remember that Luke wants to prove a legal point to Rome: the apostles and followers of Jesus are Jews, therefore practicing a lawful religion. However, this line of defense has an inherent weak point: "If you are Jews, why do you not submit to the Sanhedrin which we Romans have determined to be the lawful authority over the people of Israel?" Both to make his point and avoid rebuttal, Luke must discredit the authority (presumed in the minds of Roman officials) of the existing leadership to define who is and is not a Jew. Verses 1–21 function as a mini-trial, an "administrative hearing" if you will. Ostensibly, Peter and John are on trial and are enjoined from teaching in the name of Jesus. The apostles, however, emphatically reject the authority of the court to enter such a judgment: "Then they called them in again and commanded them not to speak or teach at all in the name of Jesus. But Peter and John replied, 'Judge for yourselves whether it is right in God's sight to obey you rather than God. For we cannot help speaking about what we have seen and heard.'"[4]

Legally, Luke is asserting that the apostles *never* submitted to the jurisdiction of the Jewish leadership. Otherwise, the *Talmidei Yeshua* can be seen as rebels rather than the self-governing sect of Judaism which he contends they are. (Remember also that under Roman law *collegia*, or "associations," were illegal for all *except* Jews). In Luke's presentation, in fact, the high priest, his family, and the other leaders are as much on trial as the apostles. Peter accuses them of being responsible for the crucifixion of the Messiah,[5] and the rulers, elders, and teachers do not contest his accusation.

An important objective in legal advocacy is to "frame the issue." I do a lot of zoning litigation on behalf of churches. I try to frame the issue as whether the zoning regulations in question infringe upon the rights of my clients to free exercise of religion or freedom of assembly. The attorney representing the municipality will generally claim the case is about the authority of the municipality to protect its residents through the regulation of land use. These competing frameworks will be sounded in the initial complaint and answer and echo through motions, briefs, the trial, and appeals. Inevitably, the court decision will adopt one of the competing viewpoints. If the court begins its opinion, "This case is about free exercise of religion," I know I have won without reading further because a court which adopts my analytical framework will agree with my conclusions.

Luke appears to be engaged in a similar rhetorical wrestle. For the most part the opposition is presenting the issues as:

"Have Paul and the Christians broken Roman law? Are they a threat to society?"

Luke, however, is framing the question as:

"Do law-abiding Jews have a right to believe that Jesus is the Messiah and to tell others about him?"

Luke's tireless restatement of his framework permeates *Acts*. In his refutations, the issue statement of the opposition echoes throughout *Acts*.

When Peter and John are freed and return to the other believers,[6] the struggle is immediately placed in a biblical context. Luke selects Psalm 2, "Why do the nations rage . . . [a]gainst the LORD and against His Anointed?" and the particular portions of the disciples' prayers quoted to show that the battle is not "us versus them" but "the world versus God and his Messiah." The conspirators are Herod, Pilate and Gentiles and Jews in Jerusalem. By naming two Roman officials and both Gentiles and Jews, Luke is telling the reader that his "clients" are not in an ethnic struggle, nor is the "power struggle" which occupies Acts 3–7 the usual sort in which each vies to occupy positions of control. The opposition's objectives, in Luke's view, are typical of a power struggle to control:

1. The temple.
2. The priesthood.
3. The flow of money to the temple.
4. The right to define to Roman authorities who is a Jew.

The believers in Jesus, however, are not seeking those objectives, but rather:

1. To define only themselves; they do not call the opposition non-Jews.
2. To understand and teach the scriptures as they see them.
3. To control their own finances.

Nowhere in *Acts* (or other New Testament writings or in non-biblical sources) is there any hint of believers wanting to control the temple. While Luke certainly criticizes the high priest and his family, he does not suggest that the believers are trying to replace him or overthrow the priesthood.

HANDLING OF MONEY

In the charts outlining charges both against Paul and against other Christians, we see that their opponents may have attributed a financial motive to them. Apparently, Paul and the leaders of the Way are accused of "being in it for the money." While one cannot conclude absolutely that this charge was made, Luke certainly seems to be refuting it throughout *Acts*. Further, extensive discussions of money in *Acts* differ markedly from Paul's teachings on finances in the Epistles when addressed to Christians.

Consider first that most of Paul's accusers regarded him as a scurrilous liar, not a respected opponent, or a misguided protagonist, but a LIAR. As he crisscrossed the diaspora[7] and spoke to groups of non-Christian Jews in Jerusalem,[8] Paul recounted that he had met the resurrected Jesus on the Damascus Road and been told to preach to the Gentiles.[9] *This personal testimony required the hearer to conclude that the evangelist was telling the truth or lying.* Paul's intelligence and erudition probably would have discounted the "insanity" conclusion. Those who believed him would have either embraced the faith or have been particularly hardened against the implications of that truth, perhaps due to self-interest such as retention of the high priesthood.

Those who did not believe Paul must, for the large majority, not only have thought him a liar but a destructive deceiver, a threat to Israel and Judaism. As such, they would have a duty to strenuously oppose him, exactly as Paul himself had opposed the first believers. Conclusion: "If Paul is a liar and not going through these enormous efforts to further the truth, he must be trying to get rich. Not only Paul, but the rest of the leaders must have hit upon a real money maker. He has not been content with fleecing gullible Jews but now he is milking the goyim!"

For about ten years I was the attorney for a group of Christians in Chicago called the Jesus People. They pattern their community on Acts 4:32–35 and own everything in common. Much of their ministry involves helping the poor in the Uptown area of Chicago. As their attorney, I was privy to their lack of money. Thus, I was amused on one occasion when a community leader assured me, in a whisper, that the Jesus People were secretly wealthy and that Denny (an older elder of the group) who, with the rest of the community, subsisted on very little income, was "the one with the money." When people cannot understand the motives of another group because these motives are foreign to their experience, they will often attribute the action of those people to motives with which they are familiar.

In Acts 4:32–36 and in Acts 5:1–11, Luke recounts the grace of God and presence of the Holy Spirit among the believers which created such generosity and the intense opposition from Satan which such holiness engendered.[10] Yet he is also providing a legal defense by showing why the believers give so much and what is done with the money.[11] In his epistles, Paul writes to believers about how they are to handle their finances,[12] always impressing on them the duty to support God's work financially. One would expect Luke, as a disciple of Paul, if he was writing to believers, to be equally directive. However, such a tone confounds a legal defense of Christian leaders against charges of financial exploitation. The depictions found in *Acts* are exactly what one would expect in a legal defense: hospitality and voluntariness of giving rather than duty.[13] The Ananias and Sapphira account, particularly because it could be construed as a warning against not giving, is accompanied by Peter's full disclaimer in verse 4: "While it remained, was it not your own? And after it was sold, was it not in your own control?"

One scholar has observed "the status which granted the [Roman] citizen the right of appeal never implied the means to carry it out."[14] Paul's eventual appeal to Rome,[15] the prison support,[16] housing needs,[17] the support of his companions and witnesses, and the writing of *Luke-Acts* were certainly expensive. As a man of no apparent wealth who on occasion supported himself as a tentmaker[18] and was suspected as a charlatan religious profiteer, Paul needed to explain his finances and the financing of the church. In Acts 4:33–5:11 Luke begins that explanation/defense which he expands throughout *Acts*.

---

1   Acts 4:2.
2   Acts 4:8.
3   Acts 4:9.
4   Acts 4:18–20.
5   Acts 4:10–11.
6   Acts 4:23–31
7   Acts, various passages.
8   Acts 9:27–30; 22;6–18 and probably during the confrontation at Acts 23:1–9.
9   Acts 22:21.
10   Acts 5:3, 9.
11   See Acts 11:29–30; 16:15b; 18:3; 20:33–35; 21:7–8, 16; 24:17, 26; 27:3; 28:14.
12   E.g., 1 Cor. 16: 1–4, 2 Cor. 9:1–15; Phil. 4:10–19; Gal. 6:6.
13   Certainly Paul teaches a voluntary spirit in giving (2 Cor. 9:7). The lessons from Acts are not contradictory to Paul's teaching in the Epistles but complementary. Paul tells the believer what he or she should do, Luke describes what the believers are doing.
14   Rapske, *Paul in Roman Custody*, 55.
15   Acts 25:11.
16   Acts 24:27.
17   Acts 28:30 and Rapske, *Paul in Roman Custody*, 228–36.
18   Acts 18:13.

CHAPTER 10

ACTS 5:12–42

THE SECOND SANHEDRIN TRIAL: *OBEYING GOD RATHER THAN MEN* (ACTS 5:29)

Luke intersperses his accounts of healings and miracles with frequent parenthetical comments such as Acts 5:14: "Nevertheless, more and more men and women believed in the Lord and were added to their number."' This particular growth spurt occurred as a result of healing miracles and the fear of God that resulted from the deaths of Annanias and Sapphira. Previously, the church is reported as growing enormously when Peter preaches on the Day of Pentecost.[1] The church grows when the believers break bread and praise God.[2] The number increases again when Peter and John are arrested.[3] We will see the word spread when major persecutions begin.[4] It will continue as the missionaries are sent forth. While those asides are certainly a literary device to provide transitions, they also further the legal goals of Luke, the brief writer:

1. They clearly show that the dramatic growth of believers in Jesus throughout the empire in the thirty years since his resurrection is **not the work of just Paul** but of many people empowered by the Holy Spirit.

2. They continually **answer a major question** in the minds of Roman officials: "Where did all these people come from?"

3. Any experienced litigator realizes that the attention his case gets and possibly the outcome will be a function of the perceived public importance of the case. By constant mention of the growth of the church, Luke subtly reminds the reader that Paul's upcoming trial is very **important to many subjects of the emperor** and highly deserving of careful investigation and deliberation.

4. To the extent that Luke is concerned that nonlegal factors may influence the outcome, he is also hinting that the Christians are a **growing political constituency** which expects fair treatment.

Luke's mention of the great healings at Solomon's Colonnade obviously furthers an evangelistic purpose but that purpose is woven around the legal framework in which Luke is explaining the *motivation of the opposition* to the followers of Jesus. In Acts 5:17 he states flatly that the high priest and his associates, all Sadducees, were *jealous*. Verses 12 to 16 have prepared the reader for this conclusion:

1. Many miraculous signs and wonders, verse 12.
2. [Apostles] highly regarded by the people, verse 13.
3. More men and women believed, verse 14.
4. Peter's shadow becomes a means of healing, verse 15.
5. Crowds from neighboring towns, sick and demonized, were healed, verse 16.

Thus even though Luke is always trying to spark the reader's interest in Jesus, his evangelistic efforts are built into the legal framework foundational to *Acts*.

When the Sadducees became jealous, they decided to arrest the apostles.[5] Luke is making a none-too-subtle legal point: Creating jealousy through healing sick people is no crime and the "trial" by the Sadducees was a farce. No tribunal, however out of control, will acknowledge it is motivated by impulses such as jealousy, greed, or whim. Rather, a corrupt court will always find some pretext for an unjust decision. Luke later explains the reason given by the Sadducees for the arrests:[6] they felt that the violation of their order to Peter and John not to speak or teach in the name of Jesus,[7] issued in their capacity as the Roman recognized high court over the Jews, was "contempt of court" meriting arrest. Having previously contested the right of Sanhedrin to punish them, Peter and John, as well as the other apostles, assert the order not to teach in the name of Jesus was illegal as inherently beyond the scope of governmental authority. "We must obey God rather than men."[8]

PRISON DELIVERANCES

The imprisonment of the Twelve in the "public jail" due to jealousy and the subsequent dialogue recounted by Luke bears directly on whether the opponents of Paul and Christianity were following the law, or abusing it for their own purposes. In setting forth a counbercharge to discredit the accusers, Luke cites the miraculous angelic release[9] as the first of three miraculous escapes or releases from prison[10] attesting that God is strongly with the apostles. The angel's orders to them, "Go, stand in the temple courts and speak to the people all the words of this life,"[11] are forensic (i.e., legal) assertions of innocence. Breaking out of jail, especially a mass jailbreak, would be seen by a Roman tribunal as a *serious threat to civil order,* something even innocent people are not supposed to do. It may be that the charges against Paul and other Christians included jail breaking. If so, the inclusion of the three prison deliverance accounts and the great detail given to each account make sense. But even if no such allegations are being countered in *Acts*, the inclusion of these episodes furthers the legal defense:

1. All deliverances are without any violence or force by the prisoner(s).

2. In the deliverance in Acts 5 and the deliverance for Paul and Barnabas in Acts 16:25, no attempt is made to run. Instead, the opportunity is taken to preach further in public places. Nothing is hidden. These are actions of innocent men. The escape of Peter in Acts 12 is different because Herod intended to execute Peter, so Peter hid out.

3. All the imprisonments were illegal.

4. All incidents involved secure imprisonment and, in the Jerusalem cases, many guards.

5. All deliverances were clearly supernatural: Two angels and an earthquake.

6. All, or portions of all, deliverances were currently verifiable (or were verifiable at sometime in the past) through the Roman record keeping system or eyewitnesses.

Luke, the lawyer, is asserting that the law-abiding believers submitted to authority except when forbidden to teach of Jesus and that the deliverances were fully known to the public and verifiable. Rapske notes that all Roman prisons were required to keep written records of prisoners:

> These records would have been kept by clerical personnel known as *scribae* or *commentarienses*, and contained the name, homeland, date of entry and time in jail, as well as other personal data of the prisoner together with the outcome of the case. Each month the record was reviewed by the prison overseer or other competent authority. The records were updated on the basis of daily reports from assistants. [12]

Thus, the assertions made by Luke are bold because if they were contradicted by the official records his entire defense could collapse due to lack of credibility.

The dialogue with the Sanhedrin which the Sadducees convened is notable because the exchange is markedly rougher. First, the high priest accuses the apostles of attempting to make him and other leaders "guilty of this man's blood."[13] Luke apparently doubts the charge of the high priest or that the high priest even believes his own charge because Luke has just told his reader that jealousy is the motive for the persecution. Nevertheless, Luke quotes Peter two sentences later saying to the Sanhedrin "[Jesus] whom you had killed by hanging him on a tree."[14] Although the gospel writers all agree that Jewish leaders conspired to have Jesus executed, Luke, two chapters earlier, has quoted Peter as exonerating the men of Israel and their leaders: "Now, brothers, I know that *you acted in ignorance as did your leaders*"[15] (emphasis added).

Thus the forensic sense of Luke's quotation of Peter in Acts 5:30 is that the Jewish leaders initially were innocent because of ignorance but are now deliberately fighting God by ignoring the numerous miracles occurring in their midst (e.g., a cripple walking, the healing effect of Peter's shadow, and twelve men being freed from prison by an angel) and by ignoring the teaching in their midst (temple courts). Now, the defense of ignorance is no longer valid. Because they now have strong evidence of who Jesus is, they are responsible for attempting to keep the people from hearing about Messiah through their orders and arrests.

Naturally the Sanhedrin did not appreciate being confronted, but their response is extreme: they want to kill the apostles. This juncture allows Luke to insert, at 5:34, another teaching from a third party. Gamaliel, a teacher of the law (a rabbi in the first-century sense of the word), stands up. Although he was well known to his contemporary Jews (and remains a famous and honored person in Jewish history),[16] the Roman reader needed an introduction which Luke provides in several particulars:

1. By name.

2. As a teacher of the law.

3. As a Pharisee (i.e., a minority voice in the presence of a Sadducean Sanhedrin).

4. As honored by all the people.

5. Of sufficient authority to stand up and order the apostles removed from the meeting.

Luke emphasizes Gamaliel's credentials as a highly honored Jewish teacher who was not following Jesus for several reasons:

1. As a non-follower of Jesus, Gamaliel has greater credibility when he essentially sides with what Americans would call the free speech position of the apostles. Establishing free speech rights as a defense to the charges against Paul and the believers is a major objective in Luke's legal agenda.

2. Gamaliel demonstrates that the opposition against the apostles was not monolithic; if those Jews who didn't follow Jesus had different opinions about the apostles, *among themselves*, why should a Roman court blindly adopt the charges of the most vehement opponents?

3. Gamaliel's argument, from a presumption that God ultimately controls in the affairs of men, is persuasive:

Men of Israel, take heed to yourselves what you intend to do regarding these men. For some time ago Theudas rose up, claiming to be somebody. A number of men, about four hundred, joined him. He was slain, and all who obeyed him were scattered and came to nothing. After this man, Judas of Galilee rose up in the days of the census, and drew away many people after him. He also perished, and all who obeyed him were dispersed. And now I say to you, keep away from these men and let them alone; for if this plan or this work is of men, it will come to nothing; but if it is of God, you cannot overthrow it—lest you even be found to fight against God.[17]

Thus Luke contrasts Gamaliel with the high priest and his Sadducean followers to show that those in control lack the same presumption about God's immanence as this respected teacher. Whether the Roman reader believes in the God of the Jews as sovereignly governing humanity is immaterial because Luke is showing that the actions of the high priest and his followers, the one group who should most trust in God's hand over the nation of Israel, are inconsistent if not hypocritical in wanting to put the apostles to death.

4. The subject matter of Gamaliel's discourse, both the armed revolt by Theudas, "Some time ago,"[18] and by Judas the Galilean, indicates that Theophilus may have the security interests of Rome on his mind. He may be asking, "Are these Christians fomenting revolt?" If so, Luke's answer from the mouth of Gamaliel is that these followers of Jesus are different.

Gamaliel's intervention enables the apostles to be set free after a flogging and to go forth praising God and proclaiming Jesus as Messiah. The resulting growth in the church also leads to further explanation of the handling of money and the introduction of the first martyr, Stephen.

---

1   Acts 2:41.
2   Acts 2:46–7.
3   Acts 4:4.
4   Acts 5:41–2, 8:1–4.
5   Acts 5:17–18.
6   Acts 5:27.
7   Acts 4:18.
8   Acts 5:29.
9   Ibid.
10   See Acts 12:1–18 and 16:23–29.
11   Acts 5:20.
12   Rapske, *Paul in Roman Custody,* 250.
13   Acts 5:28.
14   Acts 5:30.
15   Acts 3:17.
16   See generally *Encyclopedia Judaica* (Jerusalem: Keter Publishing, 1971) under "Gamaliel."
17   Acts 5:35b-39.
18   Acts 5:3b.

CHAPTER 11

ACTS 6—7

STEPHEN'S TRIAL: *MEN OF HONEST REPORT* (ACTS 6:3)

STEPHEN INTRODUCED

The community of believers had begun to experience cross-cultural growing pains. Grecian Jews complain their widows are overlooked as food from the common pantry is distributed. Certainly, this conflict is an interesting episode, but what part does it play in *Acts*? How does Luke feel it will help Paul and the followers of Jesus in the minds of Roman officials? Actually, I believe it furthers nine legal points, five of which have already been introduced. Four are new and will be elaborated throughout *Acts*.

Reemphasized legal defenses:

1. The believers are organized, **a government unto themselves** as shown in Acts 6 by the selection of deacons and the assumption of the governmental function of food distribution. The Romans considered grain supply and safeguarding it a highly important *governmental* function.[1]

2. The faith is intended to be and is becoming **universal** as shown by the segue from Hebraic Jews to Hellenistic Jews.

3. The **leadership is not being monopolized** by the founding Hebraic Jews as shown by the names of deacons all being recognizably Greek and the selection process being entrusted to the general congregation.

4. The **use of money** is accounted for.

5. **Growth of the fellowship** is reemphasized.[2]

New legal arguments:

1. **Stephen, the first martyr,** who takes center stage in Acts 7 is introduced.

2. **Opposition is shown to expand** beyond the original Aramaic-speaking leaders who were connected with the crucifixion of Jesus to Jews in Jerusalem who were Greek speakers from other countries; as the evangel goes forth the opposition will likewise increase.

3. The **opposition begins to falsify evidence.**[3]

4. The **charge of blaspheming the temple is addressed.**[4]

STEPHEN'S DEFENSE

Stephen's speech to the Sanhedrin is a masterful summation of Israel's history, but some of its most moving points do not become clear until considered from the vantage of a Roman official. Although this speech is only one of twenty-nine noted in Acts, Luke gave it extraordinary attention: it is by far the longest. Therefore, let us carefully consider why that attention was given by analyzing three components of the speech:

I. Principals

II. Form

III. Content

Stephen's defense abounds in forensic and evangelistic purposes, so those will be analytical subcategories of both form and content.

I. **Principals**: Stephen has been introduced in detail as a deacon (i.e., a food distributor and table waiter),[5] full of the Spirit and wisdom,[6] full of faith,[7] full of grace and power, a miracle worker,[8] an apologist/evangelist,[9] and as described at his trial, having an angelic facial appearance.[10] Not a bad introduction for a star witness, who due to his death, will be unable to appear at Paul's trial but will hush the courtroom when his dramatic video deposition, made just prior to his murder, is played!

Annas, the high priest likewise has been previously introduced but in less complimentary terms.[11] He is jealous and dishonest.

The prosecution witnesses and their sponsors in modern legal terms are described as perjurers or suborners (those who assist others to perjure). The Sanhedrin, the tribunal, is described as "stirred up." From prior encounters the reader recognizes them as strongly opposed to the followers of Jesus but capable of tempering their opposition when presented by logic from one of their own members.[12]

The overall sense which Luke conveys to his readership as the scene opens is one of a show trial.

II. **Form**: The speech is explicitly a *rebuttal to legal charges*. The high priest asks: "Are these *charges* true?"[13] Stephen's speech is quite simply his legal defense. He is before a tribunal,[14] his accusers are present, charges have been made, witnesses have testified against him,[15] the prosecution has apparently rested, and the judge, the high priest, asks him to present his defense.[16] Thus, in the immediate context, Stephen speaking to the Sanhedrin, the speech is a legal argument. *It is also a legal argument on the primary level*, Luke writing to Theophilus. Almost all legal briefs of any length quote depositions (testimony given before a court reporter), testimony given in other courts and other court decisions.

The logic of Luke defending Paul the evangelist by using a trial defense of another evangelist is the same as that of any lawyer who pores over depositions or prior court opinions looking for a good passage to quote: "Where can I find someone else who said what I want to say?" A lawyer realizes that different witnesses who make the same point from other contexts cumulate the persuasiveness of an argument and are often more convincing because they are removed from the passion and subjectivity of the immediate controversy. Thus, Acts 7 is most helpfully understood as a legal argument within a legal argument. Luke summons Stephen to testify just as Stephen calls Abraham, Joseph, and Moses to the stand.

The form of Stephen's speech helps the legal case in another way: by its forum. It is apparent from *Acts* and other Jewish sources, that the Jews of the first century were heterogeneous religiously and politically. They were dispersed geographically. The charges against Paul and the other evangelists were varied in source, seriousness, and specificity. To get a handle on this cluster of charges and accusers and to set the agenda in the reader's mind, Luke can more persuasively argue the "official" position of Paul's opponents by quoting an argument made before the recognized governing body of Israel. In other words, Stephen probably gave similar speeches in the synagogues of Greek-speaking Jews.[17] However, by quoting the one given to the Sanhedrin, Luke makes it impossible for the accusers of Paul to argue that the pervasive persecution and violence against the apostles in other cities of the empire is aberrational or anything other than the reflection of an official leadership policy emanating from Annas, the high priest, his family,[18] and the Sanhedrin.

Also, two scribes were present at every session of the Sanhedrin to make a written record of the proceedings.[19] Certainly some, and possibly all, these records were available as *Acts* was written. Consequently, Luke's mention of hearings before the Sanhedrin in chapters 4, 5, 7, and 23 all are assertions of the verifiability of his accounts, or, possibly, are refutations of records brought to Rome by Paul's opponents.

Finally, the form of Acts 7 sets forth both the evangelistic and legal message stylistically. Stephen's legal argument is a *speech* before a hostile forum, and a confrontational setting that creates interest through dramatic tension. The visual image created of Stephen standing in front of a sitting audience which is looking "intently" while his face glows[20] certainly captures and helps focus the reader's attention on the substance of the speech, as does Luke's evangelistic technique (for reaching his Roman readership) of overhead conversation rather than direct confrontation with the evangel (see Acts 10:34–43).

III. **Content**: The charges have been set forth in Acts 6:13:

1. speaking against this "holy place" (the temple).

2. speaking against the law.

The two charges are more specifically embodied in the witnesses' quoting Stephen as allegedly saying that Jesus would destroy the temple and change the customs Moses had given the Jewish people.

As a brief writer quoting another legal proceeding, Luke is not limited to citation of that proceeding just to answer the charges against Stephen or those which were common to Paul and Stephen. Rather, Luke appears to understand that his reader cares about Stephen's case *primarily as it affects Paul's case*, the one Theophilus is investigating. Thus Luke selects portions of Stephen's argument uniquely suited to Paul's defense, such as the meaning of circumcision in determining faithfulness to the God of Israel or whether the dispute with the "Nazarene sect"[21] was intra or extramural to Judaism. Nor is Luke limited to answering the charges as framed by the opposition. For example, the charges against Stephen are that he said certain things that Jesus would do. Instead of answering those charges directly, the response of Stephen is to explain who Jesus is by establishing a context in the history of Israel. Luke, as a good lawyer, appears to be constantly informing his legal and evangelistic arguments through greater contextualization for the Roman official who has little knowledge of Judaism or Jesus:

1. Fuller history of Israel (Acts 7).

2. Filling in of historical gaps (Acts 13:17–22).

3. Life of Jesus (Book of Luke).

The four substantive *legal* arguments made in Stephen's speech can be outlined as:

A. **Internal Controversy**—The dispute between the followers of Jesus and the leadership establishment is an internal Jewish theological controversy.

B. **God's Presence** is not, and throughout the history of Israel has never been, limited to the temple or the land of Israel.

C. **Circumcision**—Physical circumcision without circumcision of the heart does not please God.

D. **Prophets Rejected**—Jesus is the prophet spoken of by Moses as evidenced by the fact that the true prophets of Israel have always been rejected by majorities of their brethren.

Each of these substantive points furthers both the legal and evangelistic objectives of Luke.

A. Internal Controversy. Luke makes sure to record Stephen's respectful address to the Sanhedrin, "Brothers and Fathers," to show that he, and by extension Paul and the other evangelists, do not purpose to divide themselves from the other Jews. The entire speech deals with the events and personalities of Israel's history. The issue is not whether those events or men are exclusively Jewish, but how they are to be seen in the light of Jesus' presence. Of course, by showing that the controversy is internal, Luke is buttressing his argument that Paul is preaching a legal religion.

The evangelistic thrust of the "internal controversy" point is subtle, yet implicit, to the Roman reader: Jesus cannot be "another God" added to the Roman pantheon. To believe in him will require the reader to identify with the God of the Jews, the history, scriptures, and faith of a people generally disliked[22] or at least not admired by the majority of Roman officialdom.[23]

B. <u>God's Presence</u>. The charge against Stephen concerning the temple that he "never stops speaking against it" is similar to at least one charge for which Paul is on trial in Rome.[24] Consequently, Stephen's refutation of the charges against him functions, in Luke's narrative, as a refutation of the charges against Paul. To make his case, Stephen cites *five* instances of God's presence with Israel, each occurring outside its national boundaries:

1. God appears to Abraham in *Mesopotamia*, the land of the Chaldeans (Acts 7:2–4) and sends him to Haran.

2. While Abraham is in *Haran*, God then sends him to the land which Israel will eventually possess although, at the time, he does not get "even a foot of ground there" (Acts 7:5).

3. In Acts 7:9, Stephen begins an account of Israel in *Egypt*.

4. In Acts 7:30, God meets Moses in *Midian* near Mt. Sinai.

5. Then in verse 44, the Tabernacle of testimony is with them in the *desert*.

These examples are tied together in Acts 7:48 as Stephen concludes "...the Most High does not live in houses made by men." In other words, Stephen says he has nothing against the temple *per se*,[25] but he disputes the opposition position that God is headquartered in the temple; he denies the place controlled by the high priest and the Sanhedrin was the "home of God." Thus, Luke's legal defense is that Paul's teaching and the teachings of Jesus and his other disciples had been twisted or distorted to make them seem to be an "anti-temple" rather than "anti-temple exclusivity" theology.

The second prong of the legal argument regarding the temple and the presence of God relates to the question of authority[26] and whether the Sanhedrin can define the believers in Jesus out of Judaism and thus make the spreading of the evangel illegal. In *Acts*, Luke is arguing that the Sanhedrin cannot do so because God has the last word, in that Jewish history has shown that control of the temple is not equivalent to authentic Judaism, and because the Sanhedrin itself evidenced no regard for law whatsoever when it was confronted by Stephen. The evangelistic message which Luke is sliding in with the legal defense about the presence of God and the temple is simple. Theophilus is encouraged that he can receive salvation from the God of Israel through faith in Jesus outside the temple setting.

As a sidebar to the temple focus in this chapter, the reader should note that if *Acts* were written after the temple destruction in A.D. 70, then all of Stephen's argument on this point would be superfluous.

C. **Circumcision**. Controversy about circumcision reverberates throughout *Acts*. One of the charges, that Jesus of Nazareth will "change the customs Moses handed down to us," appears to refer to circumcision[27] because Stephen mentions it twice.[28] While no evidence of any circumcision issues exist during the early church era prior to the admission of Gentiles, it was certainly raised later to discredit the Nazarenes in the eyes of their fellow Jews.[29] By the time *Acts* was written, circumcision, or, more precisely, non-circumcision of Gentile believers in Jesus, had become a major issue dividing the Messianic and non-Messianic branches of Judaism and was also divisive within the Jewish church. For that reason, Luke may be reaching back into Stephen's speech to grab some points that were of lesser or tangential importance to Stephen and giving them more prominence in his defense of Paul in A.D. 61–62. Again, the point is simple. Stephen and by extension Paul and the Apostles approve of circumcision for Jewish followers of Jesus: circumcision was established by God as a covenant.[30] However, circumcision of heart is paramount in God's economy.[31] The evangelistic message of the circumcision discussion is even more simple: if you want to follow God you must allow Him to circumcise your heart.

D. Prophets Rejected. One reason Luke's account of Stephen's speech is effective in grabbing attention is that he does not tell the reader where he is going. The reader must think, as Stephen mentions:

1. **Abraham separated** from his country and people.[32]
2. **Joseph rejected** by his brothers because of jealousy.[33]
3. **Moses rejected** by the two Israelites he is trying to help.[34]
4. **Moses rejected again** by the Israelites in the desert.[35]

The reader is prompted to ask, "What do these episodes have to do with the charges against Stephen and how do those charges relate to the charges against Paul?" For the Roman unfamiliar with the history of Israel, Luke recounts Stephen's cutting summation: "Which of the prophets did your fathers not persecute? And they killed those who foretold the coming of the Just One, of whom you have now become the betrayers and murderers."[36]

The evangelistic point of this theme of prophet rejection is that Jesus is the Righteous One,[37] the prophet foretold by Moses.[38] Two related legal arguments are that Paul is also a rejected prophet and that Paul is preaching Judaism, not some illegal religion.

THE STONING OF STEPHEN

The speech ends abruptly when Stephen implicates the Sanhedrin. As their anger boils, Stephen sees the luminescence (glory) of God and sees Jesus standing at God's right hand. His description of this vision causes their anger to overflow into murder by stoning. Luke had to include this stoning to complete the story of the speech but in so doing he is also able to insinuate that the very opposition which is seeking Paul's execution by Rome had no regard for Roman order when it was itself confronted with the serious charge of murdering Jesus.

Because factual accuracy is essential to legal advocacy, let us pause to consider the source of Stephen's speech. Paul is the obvious first choice because he is introduced in the closing verses of chapter 7. He may have heard the speech and been greatly impressed by it. Yet the text implies Paul was not present during the speech. Other possible sources include believers who were with Stephen or opponents of Stephen who repented and became believers in Jesus or who just repented of their murderous complicity and recounted the speech to believers. Logically, Stephen's speech, because of his martyrdom, the forum in which he spoke, and the leadership position which he held, would be memorialized in writing and circulated within the church. This hypothesis is consistent with the text which is remarkably precise if it is only first recorded about twenty-five years later when *Acts* is written. It is also consistent with the lawyer's craft evidenced by Luke elsewhere in *Acts* of utilizing written records whenever possible.

A YOUNG MAN NAMED SAUL (ACTS 7:58)

Luke now introduces the defendant and chief protagonist of *Acts*, Saul of Tarsus (Paul). Heretofore, *Acts* has been what modern lawyers refer to as a "statement of facts" (or what a reporter would call "deep background") necessary to understand the context of the charges against Paul. Extensive background is often supplied to the judge or jury in a criminal proceeding. One need only consider the many spectacular trials of the twentieth century to realize how broad a scope of inquiry and proof most courts will allow and consider relevant, for a prosecutor or defendant, when a man's life or important social issues are at stake.

The trial Paul faced, however, was much broader than those of any other accused criminal because his innocence or guilt depended on the legality of the "Way" itself. Further, because his trial was occurring at the "Supreme Court" level, the legality of the Way in turn depended on whether Paul would be acquitted or convicted! Not only was Paul's life in the balance but, potentially, the lives of others and certainly the right of believers to tell the Jews of the diaspora and the Gentiles of the empire about the eternal life God had made available to all in Jesus. Accordingly, *Acts* is not a brief with a lot of fluff. Even details that seem tangential can, on closer reading, be seen to further the legal agenda.

For instance, why does Luke introduce Saul in 7:58 and 8:1 as an accomplice to the death of Stephen? Probably Luke is giving his *yekas*, his credentials, as an opponent of the Way. Consider what Luke tells his intended reader about Paul in his introduction. First that he was a "young man." This simple observation is necessary because Paul is probably in his mid-forties as *Acts* is written in A.D. 62. Positing a date of A.D. 35 for the stoning of Stephen and an age of eighteen for Paul as a "young man," Paul is forty-five as *Acts* is written. Luke's two points in noting that Paul was a "young man" are:

1. Paul's adult life has spanned the time during which the faith in Jesus has existed.

2. The reader should focus on Paul as the central protagonist as the narrative continues.

Luke also tells Theophilus of Saul's participation in the stoning of Stephen in two parts: the laying of the witnesses' garments at his feet[39] and Paul's "approval" of Stephen's death. Why would someone defending Paul against serious criminal charges volunteer evidence of his criminal conduct? Six good reasons, mostly legal, are apparent or implied:

1. <u>Credibility</u>. By strengthening his credentials as a former persecutor, Paul's credibility as a witness to the resurrection of Jesus is enhanced. It's small news when a radical political group claims FBI persecution, but when a former FBI supervisor says the FBI lab has been fabricating evidence, people listen.

2. <u>Preemptive defense</u>. Even though the event occurred thirty years before *Acts* was written, a reasonable possibility remains that his presence, if not his intent of heart, at the stoning, will be recalled and used against him by opponents. Only a foolhardy lawyer fails to explain facts that could be used against his client hoping that his opponents will omit them. In the context that Luke puts Paul's involvement (see reasons 4 to 6) no real harm is done to his legal case in Rome. If first raised by the prosecution, however, a possible spin of the incident would be, "This fellow Paul has always been a gangster and lover of violence. He perpetrated violence when he was originally in Jerusalem and he just graduated to being a top gangster when he found this cult of Christians to lead."

3. <u>Evangelism</u>. The account has a clear evangelistic thrust. Paul had a murderous intent in his heart, yet he will find forgiveness and a new life on the Damascus Road. The verses about Paul bracket and highlight the great declaration of Stephen in 7:59 and 60. Remember that we are considering not only whether Luke is a brief writer, but whether he is a lawyer/evangelist. A judicial reader knows that the intent of Paul's heart at an event twenty-eight years earlier and several weeks distant from Rome cannot be proved. Thus Luke volunteers this information (undoubtedly after talking to Paul) to let the reader know of Paul's sincere admission of sin in order to help convince the reader of the sincerity of his conversion.

4. Accountability. Paul was "young" when the stoning occurred, not as fully aware of or accountable for his action as an older person.

5. Innocence. Paul's involvement was tangential. The garments of the witnesses were "laid at his feet." I.e., Paul only watched.

6. Disdain of Rome. The participation and approval of Paul are in the context of a judicial lynching. The high priest[40] and Sanhedrin[41] are the court that allowed Stephen to be stoned. Although Stephen did have a "trial" of sorts, the court operated illegally in that Stephen had not been accused of a capital crime, had committed no crime, and it had no right under Roman policy to execute him. The Sanhedrin is portrayed as disdaining Roman authority. Luke links his introduction of Paul, the persecutor, with the first widespread persecution of the church and the growth which results, ironically, because of that persecution.

A best defense, in law, as in a sport or other trial of life, requires a good offense. In addition to telling the reader of the charges against Paul and the Christians, Luke also alludes to or accuses their opponents or accuses Roman officials of a number of crimes. The primary function of the countercharges in *Acts* is to diminish the credibility of the charges against Paul.

	Chart of Thirteen Countercharges Against the Opponents of Paul and the Christians			
	Acts	Accused	Charge[42]	Alleged Crime Location
1.	5:40	Sanhedrin	flogging innocent men	Jerusalem
2.	6:11	members of the synagogue of the freedmen	persuading men to perjure	Jerusalem
3.	7:58	Sanhedrin	murder; violation of Roman law not allowing capital punishment by the Sanhedrin	Jerusalem
4.	9:23	Jews of Damascus	conspiracy to murder Paul	Damascus
5.	21:31	Rioters	conspiracy to murder Paul	Jerusalem
6.	23:12–14	Jewish leaders including chief priest and elders	conspiracy to murder Paul	road to Caesarea
7.	12:1–3	Herod Agrippa I	murder of James, brother of John; attempted murder of Peter; *maiestas* suggested in execution of guards at 12:19	Jerusalem

		Chart of Thirteen Countercharges Against the Opponents of Paul and the Christians		
	Acts	Accused	Charge[42]	Alleged Crime Location
8.	13:50, 14:5, 14:19, 17:5, 21:27–28	Jewish opponents of Paul in various cities	*Vis*, inciting riot; murder of Paul attempted in Iconium and Lystra	Pisidian Antioch, Iconium, Lystra/Derbe, Thessalonica, Jerusalem
9.	16:37	slave owners	making false criminal charges, *calumnia*	Philippi
10.	16:37	Roman Magistrates	*Vis*, flogging a Roman citizen without trial	Philippi
11.	23:2	high priest Ananias	causing a physical attack (slap) against Paul	Sanhedrin in Jerusalem
12.	24:26–7	Felix	*Res Repetundae*, official corruption	Caesarea
13.	25:9	Festus	*Res Repetundae*, official corruption	Caesarea

Acts is a book of trials. Sixteen formal and informal, investigative and quasi-judicial trials occur. The first four are of church leaders before Jewish authorities or Herod Agrippa I. One is of Paul before the leaders of the church and the last eleven are of Paul, ten before Roman officials and one before the Sanhedrin. Certainly, *Acts* is not just about trials, but rather a tapestry of many threads. However, just as he uses speeches, Luke uses arrests, investigations, and trials to unify the narrative.

The presence of so many legal and quasi-legal proceedings in the framework of *Acts* suggests a forensic purpose for its composition. The fact that the last twelve of these sixteen proceedings involve Paul suggests that legal defense of Paul is the particular forensic purpose. Thus as Paul is introduced to the narrative the reader should note the many ways in which Luke not only parries the accusations against his friend and mentor but counterpunches the accusers.

	Acts	Forum	Accused	Charge	Result
			Chart of Sixteen Trials in Acts		
1.	4:1–21	Sanhedrin	Peter/John — Also Sanhedrin on trial	Probably proclaiming resurrection of dead through Jesus v. 2	Enjoined from using name of Jesus/defi-ance by defendants
2.	5:17	Sanhedrin	Apostles	Violating previous injunction	Flogging, injunction continued, probation, defiance continued
3.	7:1–60	Sanhedrin	Stephen	Blasphemy against Moses, God, temple. Changing Moses' cus-toms. Believing in Jesus	Stoning, death
4.	12:6	Herod Agrippa I	Peter	None stated	Divine *habeas corpus*[43] successful
5.	15	Jerusalem Council	Paul and Barnabas	Breaking law of Moses—not circumcising disciples	Charges dismissed, Gentiles need not be circumcised
6.	16:19	Phillipian magistrates	Paul/Silas	Inciting civil unrest—advocating "unlawful customs"	Jail and second divine *habeas corpus*
7.	17:6–9	City Officials of Thessalonica	Paul, Jason et al.	Promoting civil unrest, illegal religion, pro-moting Jesus as king	Bond posted
8.	17:18b -34	*Areopagus* in Athens	Paul	Illegal religion	No conviction
9.	18:12	Proconsul Gallio	Paul	Un-Jewish worship	Dismissed for lack of jurisdiction
10.	19	Ephesus city clerk	Paul, et al.	Slandering or discred-iting Artemis	Dismissed for lack of jurisdiction
11.	21:33–4	Jerusalem temple Roman commander	Paul	Bringing a Gentile into temple	Riot/protective cus-tody
12.	23:1–10	Sanhedrin	Paul	Preaching resurrection of dead	Inconclusive, protective custody continued

Chart of Sixteen Trials in Acts					
	Acts	Forum	Accused	Charge	Result
13.	23/24	Felix	Paul	Breaking Jewish law; troublemaking; desecrating temple	No decision, Paul left in prison two years
14.	25:1–12	Festus	Paul	Same case as above	Appeal to Rome
15.	25:13–27	Agrippa/ Festus	Paul	Same case as above	"Acquitted" but sent to Rome
16.	28	Rome/Nero	Paul	Same case as above	Pending as Acts ends

1 Robinson, *Criminal Law*, 89.
2 Acts 6:1, 7.
3 Acts 6:11; see Acts 24:6.
4 Acts 6:13; see Acts 24:6 and Rosenblatt, *Paul the Accused*, 22
5 Acts 6:2.
6 Acts 6:3.
7 Acts 6:5.
8 Acts 6:8.
9 Acts 6:9–10.
10 probably luminous, see Acts 7:2.
11 E.g., Acts 5:17.
12 Acts 5:33–40.
13 Acts 7:1.
14 Acts 6:12.
15 Acts 6:13.
16 Acts 7:1.
17 See Acts 6:9–10.
18 See Acts 4:6.
19 Rapske, *Paul in Roman Custody*, 105.
20 Acts 6:15.
21 See Acts 24:5.
22 See Acts 18:2.
23 See 2 Kings 5, esp. vv. 11–12.
24 See Acts 24:6, 25:8.
25 See Acts 7:46–7.
26 See discussion of Acts 1.
27 Although circumcision antedated Moses, he "handed it down" through the Pentateuch.
28 Acts 7:8–9.
29 See Acts 16:1–3.
30 Acts 7:8.
31 Acts 7:51.
32 Acts 7:3.
33 Acts 7:9.
34 Acts 7:27, 35.
35 Acts 7:39–41.
36 Acts 7:52.
37 Ibid.
38 Acts 7:37.
39 Acts 7:58.
40 Acts 7:1.
41 Acts 6:15.
42 These are not formal legal charges, which would have required separate proceedings, but countercharges to show Paul's innocence.
43 *Habeas corpus* is a legal petition asserting a person is illegally in jail.

CHAPTER 12

ACTS 8—9:31

"A LIGHT FROM HEAVEN" (ACTS 9:3)

Remember the mind of the judicial reader. He wonders how this sect/cult/religion spread all over the empire in just thirty years. Obviously, Luke cannot follow every evangelist, recount every conversion or chronicle each miracle. He has to choose his events. So why does he choose to further his purposes by citing the persecution at Jerusalem,[1] Philip in Samaria,[2] Simon the Sorcerer,[3] and Philip with the Ethiopian eunuch?[4] to further his purposes?

To explain the spread of the faith, Luke has chosen an organizational framework of progressions:

1. **Geographic** –Jerusalem to Judea, to Samaria, to Asia Minor, to Rome.

2. **People groups**—Galilean Jews to Aramaic-speaking Jews to Greek-speaking Jews, to Samaritans, to Greeks, to Romans.

3. **Religious groups**—Jews to Samaritans, to God fearers, to pagans and philosophers.

4. **Legal**—Sanhedrin to Roman proconsuls, to Roman governors, to the Roman emperor.

5. **Personalities**—From Peter as evangelist to Hebraic Jews, to Stephen as evangelist to Grecian Jews, to Philip as evangelist to Samaritans, to Paul as evangelist to Jews and Gentiles.

These progressions give the original reader one message and allow the modern reader to deduce a second. For Theophilus, the point is that this gospel, this faith, is growing and progressing inexorably as God moves it. Paul is only an instrument. To us it speaks much deliberation in composition. The organizational precision suggests *Acts* was thought through and rewritten at least once. Rewriting is a hallmark of a legal brief (at least in my firm!). In fiction or casual history the accuracy of details is usually not crucial. In a legal work, the scrutiny of the judge and the cross-examination of the opposition, whether written in a brief or verbal at trial, puts a premium on precision. Imprecision, even as to seemingly inconsequential matters, can undermine the tribunal's confidence in the entire case of the sloppy litigator. The practice of rewriting legal "briefs" for accused criminals imprisoned by Rome is recounted by Brian Rapske: "the prisoner, intent upon sending a petition, would call for a professional scribe near the prison. For a fee, the scribe took down in rough draft the relevant details, returned to his office, and rendered a finished copy. It was then reviewed and signed by the prisoner and delivered by the scribe to the appropriate official."[5]

Thus, if *Acts* does show signs of being redrafted, especially if the redrafts appear to be extensive, it is a point of consistency with the hypothesis that *Acts* is a legal brief rather than, say, an epistle.[6]

Luke is the master of many agendas. Consider the account of Simon the sorcerer who tries to purchase the Holy Spirit's power.[7] Luke may be refuting the charge that Paul and other evangelists were cynics whose true motive for evangelism was financial gain. By selecting the Ethiopian eunuch episode,[8] he also reiterates three important legal points:

1. "Christianity" is **thoroughly Jewish** as evidenced by baptism.[9]

2. The followers of Jesus remained thoroughly committed to the **Hebrew scriptures.**

3. **Judaism has become available universally** through the Messiah Jesus to a man thoroughly different from Jews due to his nationality, skin color, and complete inability to approach God through the Jerusalem temple (as a Gentile and eunuch[10]).

While Luke is making legal arguments, he is again inserting the gospel message. No verse better illustrates this point than the Isaiah 53 passage the eunuch was reading, as noted in Acts 8:32–33: "He was led as a sheep to the slaughter; And as a lamb before its shearer is silent, So He opened not His mouth. In His humiliation His justice was taken away, And who will declare His generation? For His life is taken from the earth."

The Roman reader would not know that Jewish teachers considered Isaiah 53 to point to the Messiah,[11] but having read *Luke*, Theophilus would certainly wonder whether it could refer to Jesus. Luke wants his reader to become a believer in Jesus even as he sifts through the evidence for Paul's defense and is introduced to his dramatic conversion.

PAUL MEETS JESUS

Bracketed by the early Samaritan and Gentile conversions in Acts 8 and 9:35–45 is the Damascus Road encounter of Paul. Although Luke is telling his reader that many changed their thinking about Jesus, the story of Paul's conversion is special to the narrative. As the chief persecutor of the Way, Paul had no motive to believe in Jesus. His credentials as a persecutor of the *Talmidei Yeshua*, which from a forensic view are enhanced by to his ability to obtain *written authorization* from the high priest, serve to promote the credibility of his testimony. Luke is emphasizing that Paul was law-abiding in a way the modern reader may find curious but the Roman authorities would find proper: his persecution of the believers in Jesus was pursuant to due authorization and letters of introduction from the high priest.

Further, Paul's conversion is not a matter of study or thought (those come later) but a matter of direct intervention from God. The Jesus whom Paul meets is not an impersonal Roman or Gentile God, but is the God of the very Jews Paul is persecuting, who appears dramatically, speaks audibly, and questions personally with tenderness (Saul, Saul) and emotionally (Why do you persecute me?). He commands with authority and knowledge of the future ("Now get up and go . . . and you will be told.").

Luke the lawyer is ever conscious of his agenda in this account. Immediately after telling of the light and voice, he adds that the witnesses, the men traveling with Paul, only "heard the sound but did not see anyone."[12] This detail is of importance to anyone questioning or investigating facts concerning the conversion of Paul, the accused, because it provides the most immediate source of corroboration or discreditation. Under other theories of why *Acts* was written, such as the catechistic or purely evangelistic, such details are not easily explained.

Against the legal charge that Paul has started a new religion, Luke is asserting that Jesus is the God of Israel ("Who are you, Lord?" . . . "I am Jesus"). The response of Saul to this revelation and accompanying blindness is a fast from food and water. Luke tells the reader this detail to show that Paul, after his conversion, only intensified his fervency in his Jewish way. A Roman even minimally familiar with Judaism would know that fasting was a Jewish practice. Luke's intended reader certainly was aware of the connection between Judaism and fasting, because in Acts 27:9 Luke refers to *Yom Kippur* simply as "the Fast." Thus, Luke's two other mentions of fasting in *Acts*[13] appear to function as reinforcement of the continued Jewishness of the faith in Jesus.

The Lord had revealed himself to Paul, had told Paul part of what would be the rest of his life,[14] and that details would be forthcoming,[15] but Paul does not wait passively. Rather, he goes on an extreme fast, lacking even water, evidently to draw closer to God. Luke is emphasizing to Theophilus that Paul's break with his prior understanding of God and his life as a persecutor of believers in Jesus is not a break from his understanding of himself as a Jew or his dedication to serving Israel's God. The legal issue reiterated is that Paul did not start a new religion but followed Peter and the other apostles in recognizing the divinity of Jesus.

The encounter with Ananias, who delivers God's message and restores Paul's sight, functions on many levels. First, one objective of all good legal writing is to be engaging and dramatic. A good story makes a point better than an abstract argument. The reader already knows from verse 6 that God is going to send a message, so the prayer of Ananias, his vision, and resistance to God are humorous and reassuringly human. Both Paul and Ananias struggle with God on different levels, which makes the point to a judicial skeptic: the ultimate yielding by each man is not a matter of personal predisposition but rather a clear indication of God's direction, because the results were contrary to where each man would have gone if left to himself.

The miracles, the blindness of Paul, the vision of Ananias, and the healing of Paul's eyes all reinforce the point: God has sovereignly intervened and set the agenda: "This man is my chosen instrument to carry my name before the Gentiles and their kings and before the people of Israel. I will show him how much he must suffer for my name."[16] As the declaration of Jesus in Acts 1:8 serves as a summary of the entire book, so the words of Jesus in Acts 9:15–16 summarize the second half of *Acts*, certainly alerting the Roman reader that:

1. The inclusion of Gentiles into the faith of Israel is by the foreknowledge and set purpose of the God of Israel.

2. The people of Israel will also need to hear the message.

3. The suffering and persecution of Paul are also foreknown and within God's plan in order to spread the news about Jesus.

If one were to argue that Luke is not making the most focused of legal arguments in this passage, I would agree. He sometimes makes his legal points subtly and often is as concerned with bringing the reader to faith in Messiah as he is in winning a legal battle.

The healing of Paul and impartation of the Holy Spirit by Ananias, who is only introduced to the reader as a disciple (i.e., not a leader, an apostle, a deacon, or a member of the Jerusalem church) also counterbalances Luke's previous stress on the leadership/authority structure established among the believers: Peter does not lead the church, Paul does not lead the believers, Jesus does. Consequently, the Roman in authority cannot dispense with the church by eliminating the leadership. Luke will make this point again as he recounts Herod's attempt to destroy the church through murdering its leaders.[17] While a personal sense of divine leadership certainly would be a difficult concept to grasp for anyone not believing in a God who is involved in the lives of his people, Luke has no option but to face the issue squarely. If he avoids or equivocates on this issue, his case will fall apart. The Roman official reading *Acts* is led to conclude:

1. The God of Israel is in charge.

2. Paul is his servant, under orders.

3. God's plan is good and true, but suffering may be part of the package.

Luke lets the presumably dubious reader know that Paul's change of heart is evidenced immediately not just by the cessation of his persecuting Christians but by his preaching in the synagogues that Jesus is the Son of God.[18] These show that Paul's first and urgent impulse was to share the message with his fellow Jews in a completely Jewish context. Thus Luke reiterates that faith in Jesus is Jewish, *ergo* legal.

The concept of personal conversion and its effectual inner working on the heart of a man was probably difficult for Theophilus to comprehend, apart from a personal encounter with Jesus. Rather than explain what happens to people who become believers, as Paul does in his epistle to the Roman church in Romans 5–8, Luke illustrates the transformation through the life of Paul, because he knows that a non-believer would be virtually unable to comprehend that theological explanation unconnected to a personal encounter with Jesus. And so, we have yet another indication that Luke was writing to the unconvinced rather than the converted.

Luke then recounts Paul's first brush with death and fulfillment of the prophecy of his suffering. Jews who have not believed in Jesus, who believed as Paul had believed a few days earlier, now plot to kill him and Paul barely escapes. Upon his return to Jerusalem he now seeks succor among the believers only to find they doubt his conversion.[19] Apparently only Barnabas and the apostles are sufficiently fearless or mature to risk befriending him. Nevertheless, Paul does not stop preaching. He again is the object of a murder plot, so he is sent to his home in Tarsus for his own safety.

Luke is now introducing a variation on a theme: As Jesus and Peter and John were persecuted, so now is Paul. A pattern is to characterize Paul's life as a missionary throughout *Acts*: first preaching, then many or a few accept; those who reject become vehement and persecution follows. A good lawyer needs themes to tie his argument together and Luke, the brief writer, expertly weaves this and other themes throughout his narrative to explain to Roman officials the true causes of the civil unrest accompanying Paul and thus his innocence of the charge of inciting unrest.

Acts 9:31 provides an excellent transition: "The churches throughout all Judea, Galilee, and Samaria had peace and were edified. And walking in the fear of the Lord and in the comfort of the Holy Spirit, they were multiplied." One of Luke's tasks is to explain the rapid spread of the faith. So far it has not reached Gentiles in any appreciable numbers but that is about to change. Before moving into that dynamic, Luke reminds his readers that the church is still growing rapidly among the Jews and Samaritans within the national borders of Israel.

---

1   Acts 8:1–3.
2   Acts 8:4–8.
3   Acts 8:9–25.
4   Acts 8:26–40.
5   Rapske, *Paul in Roman Custody,* 327.
6   See the "stream of consciousness" in some of Paul's letters.

7   Acts 8:9–24.

8   Acts 8:26–40.

9   "... proselyte baptism in Pharisaic Judaism signified the end of the process of purification from the sinful Gentile world and its impurities; thus it eventually became a definitive mark of entrance into the Jewish community. When baptism was used for proselyte conversion it also signified the rebirth of the convert, commencing a new identity in Israel." Segal, *Paul the Convert*, 135.

10 See Deut. 23:1.

11 See comment on Isaiah 53 in *Encyclopedia Judaica* (Jerusalem: Keter Publishing, 1971) under "Isaiah" which cites Targum Jonathon Isaiah 42:1 and 52:13 as referring to the "destined redeemer, the Messiah" but also points out that subsequent to the time of Jesus most Jewish commentators have held that the suffering servant in Isaiah is Israel.

12 Acts 9:7.

13 Acts 13:2, 14:23.

14 See Acts 26:15–18.

15 Acts 9:6.

16 Acts 9:15–16.

17 Acts 12:1–3.

18 Acts 9:20.

19 Acts 9:23–25.

CHAPTER 13

ACTS 9:32—11:30

CALL NO MAN UNCLEAN
(ACTS 10:28)

After describing the continued growth of the church, Luke recounts two mir-acles which brought many to faith in Jesus in the Jewish towns of Lydda, Sharon, and Joppa. Peter is the instrument of God as he speaks healing to a crip-pled man named Aeneas in Lydda and resurrection to a disciple named Tabitha in Joppa. Many miracles were occurring as the faith spread, so why did Luke include these *particular* miracles in a brief defending Paul and the Way? Perhaps:

1. to show the continued authority of Peter because these accounts parallel so closely healings by Jesus in Luke 5:24 and 8:54;

2. Luke is positioning these accounts to show why Peter was able to convince the leaders in Acts 11 to allow Gentiles into the faith without their first being circumcised;

3. the miracles were *per se* notable because of the many conversions which followed. Other miracles may have resulted in only a few believing, but the raising of Tabitha may have been an unusual miracle that could still be verified by Roman investigators twenty-five years later; or

4. to further the defense to the accusation against Paul of being the primary contaminator of Judaism by bringing in Gentiles. Luke refutes that charge by showing that it was in the process of reaching Jewish people with the message of Jesus that the Jewish church and Peter the apostle to the Jews first reached Gentiles, not through Paul the "apostle to the Gentiles."

Luke does not tell us why he includes these particular miracles, but because he so adeptly furthers several agendas at once, perhaps all of the foregoing reasons influenced his selection process.

Even as Acts 9:31 is a transition to 9:32–43, so those verses explain how Peter, the Jerusalem-based Jew and former fisherman, ends up sharing the Jewish faith with a Roman centurion and his family in the Roman provincial capital of Caesarea. The account of their conversion and its importance to both the legal and evangelistic agenda of *Acts* cannot be overstated. We have already seen that Luke wants to detail the introduction of the first group of Gentile converts to the reader because he must explain how the Messianics could claim at the time *Acts* was written, about twenty-five years later, to be Jews and how Paul could be innocent of breaking Roman law concerning new religions when so many Gentiles were joining the faith. Also, Luke had to ease Roman *political fears* concerning the impact of an acquittal of Paul on the integrity of the Roman military. Remember that Nero's military adviser, Sextus Afranius Burrus, was a potential, if not intended, secondary reader of *Acts*. Also, a massive revolt against Roman rule had broken out in Britain only two years before *Acts* was finished. Join me on an interesting and highly relevant digression:

Jews, Rome, and the Military: Jews had a special exemption from Roman military service and, as any Roman subjects would, desired that exemption for good reasons:

1. Hardship and low pay.
2. Risk of death.

As Jews, they also wanted exemption for special reasons:

1. The manifold ritual uncleanness of the Roman military life.
2. The inability to follow dietary laws.
3. The inability to worship or observe the Sabbath.
4. The possibility of being ordered to kill fellow Jews.

The Romans had some good reasons to grant the exemption:

1. Jewish loyalty was suspect due to their refusals to offer sacrifices to the emperor as a God.
2. The exemption brought with it an extra tax on the Jews which fattened the Roman treasury.
3. Because the Jews had a history of revolt, it seemed unwise to equip a cadre of officers and fighting men with the knowledge of Roman weaponry, discipline, and tactics.

A backdrop to both the Jewish and Roman self-interest in the exemption was the Maccabean Revolt of 167 to 165 B.C. in which the Jews had, after a long and bloody war with their Greek rulers, won religious freedom. The Romans certainly knew that the supposed benefit to Roman society of enforced religious conformity on the Jews would be outweighed by the costs in terms of war. *Unless, of course, Judaism spread to the Gentiles.* What would become of the détente on military service? What would happen to the military draft if Paul (and Christianity) were acquitted and all believers in Jesus were found by the Romans to be another sect of Judaism alongside the Sadducees, Essenes, and Pharisees and if Gentiles could become Jews without circumcision? If conversion to Judaism became painless and simple, might not young Gentile men all over the empire declare their faith in this Jesus to avoid the rigors of military service? And would Roman soldiers seek discharge upon becoming Jews? While such a worry might seem distant to a modern reader, Nero and his followers, who held power by the sword, would have looked closely at the implications of the spread of Messianic Judaism upon the military security of the empire. And to bring us back to the point of digression, would not Luke, the defender of Paul, have heard these concerns and anticipated them in his defense?

Cornelius. Next, we must note that the inclusion of the story of the conversion of Cornelius and his family was highly significant aside from his status as a Roman centurion for at least four reasons:

1. The dramatic revelation of God's will through the vision and angel.[1]

2. Apparently the first group Gentile conversion.

3. The Holy Spirit gift of tongues.[2]

4. The inquiry into the precedent-setting circumstances of the conversion.[3]

The preceding four factors correspond quite well to parts of Luke's agenda:

1. This faith in Jesus is from God.

2. Judaism becomes universal through faith in Jesus.

3. The place of Gentiles in the Jewish faith is divinely confirmed.

4. The admission of Gentiles is not by Paul but through Jacob (James) and the Jerusalem authority structure.

Perhaps the conversion account would have been included even if Cornelius had been a merchant or farmer and a non-Roman. The fact that he was a centurion, however, dramatically impacts a Roman official considering the political impact of an acquittal of Paul. Cornelius is specifically identified as a member of the Italian regiment in Caesarea. Consequently, the Roman official reading *Acts* can check his service record: did Cornelius seek exemption from service after his conversion? Did he remain loyal to Rome? Throughout *Luke* and *Acts*, Roman military men are portrayed sympathetically. We can only imagine how the Luke of many agendas delighted to explain Gentile inclusion into the faith through a man who would also illustrate that faith in Jesus would not undermine the Roman military.

GOD-FEARERS

As is his family, Cornelius is identified as "devout and God fearing," generous, and a regular prayer.[4] God-fearers abounded throughout the empire at this time

95

in history: Gentiles who had rejected Greco-Roman pantheism and had come to believe in the God of Israel. Not having converted to Judaism due to unwillingness to undergo circumcision, unwillingness to live according to Torah, or other reasons, God-fearers would nevertheless attend synagogue services, hear the reading of scripture, pray, and emulate other Jewish practices. God-fearers and Gentile converts to Judaism, especially women, were common in Rome. Thus, Cornelius, the God-fearer, would have been a familiar, if not sympathetic, character to Theophilus.

MEANING OF THE VISIONS

However, the dual visions of Cornelius and Peter function to show that the subsequent conversions are not a matter of Gentile affinity for Judaism or persuasive eloquence of Peter but a sovereign act of the God of Israel. The vision of Cornelius is straightforward because the angel instructs him to go directly to Peter, yet the vision of Peter may have seemed strange to Theophilus. Therefore, Luke records Peter's puzzlement[5] and explains his realization that the vision was an instruction to accept Gentiles into the church: "In truth I perceive that God shows no partiality. But in every nation whoever fears Him and works righteousness is accepted by Him.[6] . . . To Him all the prophets witness that, through His name, whoever believes in Him will receive remission of sins."[7]

Luke's evangelistic goal is to present the gospel again to his readers through overheard conversation in Acts 10–11:18. His legal agenda is to reemphasize the universality of the gospel and to answer the big questions any first-century Roman official would have: how did all of these Gentiles come to be a part of this Jewish sect and how can they be considered Jewish? Although the converts are Gentiles, Luke reinforces the Jewish continuity of the encounter with God by numerous details:

1. God is mentioned ten times from Acts 10:28 to 43.

2. The Holy Spirit is a key actor in giving Jesus power and giving the gift of tongues to the Gentiles. (The Holy Spirit would be seen strictly in a Jewish context by non-Jewish Roman readers).

3. Baptism is the culmination.[8] *Mikva* likewise would be perceived strictly in the context of a Jewish ceremony and/or of the Jewish prophet John the Baptist (see discussion of Acts 19).

4. The encounter is not only witnessed by Peter but by six "circumcised" believers.[9]

5. The results, after explanation, are endorsed by other "circumcised" believers.[10]

The overall impression which Luke, the lawyer, is conveying is that the Gentile conversions at Caesarea are a Jewish affair completely, not a break with Judaism but a fuller understanding of how the God of Israel seeks to be known by all through Jesus. This understanding leads naturally to an explanation of the origin of the word "Christian."

"The Disciples Were Called Christians."
(Acts 11:26)

Verses 19–29 of Chapter 11 describing the church at Antioch are a digression in the sense that Luke interrupts his recounting of Peter's ministry. However, the common thread between those verses and the preceding account of Peter and Cornelius is the progression of faith among the Gentiles. In a brief segment, Luke manages to further his legal agenda in seven particulars:

1. Explanation of how the **faith spread** among Gentiles at Antioch.[11]

2. Emphasis on how **quickly** Gentiles were turning to Jesus. "Great numbers" used thrice.;[12]

3. Emphasis that the movement of faith in Jesus among Gentiles did not create a new religion or reject Judaism, noting examples of the **connection** of new Gentile believers with existing Jewish believers:

   (a) Spreaders of the news were Jewish.[13]

   (b) Jerusalem leaders heard and supervised.[14]

   (c) Barnabas superintended.[15]

   (d) Prophets came from Jerusalem.[16]

4. Explanation of the first use of the **word "Christian."**[17] In writing a brief, a lawyer must be extremely careful to explain his terminology lest it be used against him. Accordingly, Luke gives the origin of an important word. He does not say that the Christians ("ones in Christ" or "Messianics") used that word to describe themselves. Rather, they "were called" the name apparently by others who needed a word to describe a group of Jews who remained Jews, yet shared a faith in the Jewish God and his Messiah with a group of Gentiles who did not become Jews but remained Gentiles. E. A. Judge concludes that the suffix "-ianus" used in the Latin *christianus* "constitutes a political comment. It is not used of the followers of a god. It . . . is mildly contemptuous."[18] Rather than call themselves Christians, the believers in Jesus referred to themselves most often as the church, "the Way," or as disciples.[19] The term "Jews"[20] or "circumcised believers"[21] could no longer be used to describe all of the Jesus people but only a subset. It is of great significance to an understanding of who the original intended reader of *Acts* was to note that, unlike Paul in several New Testament Epistles, Luke does not explain the theology or

mystery of how the Gentiles can be included into the Israel of God without becoming Jews.[22] Instead, Luke answers the questions that would occur to a mind most interested in judicial matters, rather than the questions most believers would ask.

5. The inclusion of verses 28 to 30, the **prophecy of Agabus** of famine throughout the world during the reign of Claudius, does not at first consideration appear to directly further the legal agenda. However, no greater internal threat to Roman power existed than the civil unrest which famine could cause. Bruce Winter notes the importance of grain to the stability of Roman power, citing the words of Nero's adviser, the philosopher Seneca, "Hungry people do not listen to reason."[23] Just as modern politicians fear recession may put them out of office, so Roman emperors feared famine. Luke may be adding to the legal equation a political argument for the acceptance of Messianic Judaism.[24] Luke's assertion that the Holy Spirit of the God of Israel gave warning in the past certainly implies that He could give warning in the future. If Roman leaders believed Luke's account of the prophecy, then Luke would have made a strong argument, appealing to Roman self-interest, for the toleration of Messianic Judaism.

6. When we consider that **financial accusations** were being hurled against Paul and the other leaders, possibly for exploiting the Gentile believers,[25] a judicial explanation for the inclusion of the famine prophecy can also be seen because the prophecy results in a large sum of money being given to Paul and Barnabas as a benevolence offering for Judea. As discussed earlier, those Jews who disbelieved Paul's eyewitness testimony of an encounter with the resurrected Jesus had little option but to conclude that Paul and the other leaders were essentially selling the right to become Jews cheaply (no circumcision or law observance), and falsely, to an easy market: God-fearing Gentiles. Luke is explaining church finances for some reason. It is a fair inference that the rebuttal of charges of financial exploitation is that reason.

7. **Paul is reintroduced** to the narrative[26] as the reader is about to say farewell to Peter.

---

1 Acts 10:19–22.

2 Acts 10:44.

3 Act 11:1–18.

4 Acts 10:2.

5 Acts 10:17, 19.

6 Acts 10:34–5; Peter's interpretation of the vision belies certain church teachings that the vision was intended to repeal the dietary laws of Torah.

7 Acts 10:43.

8 Acts 10:48.

9 Acts 10:23, 45; 11:12.
10 Acts 11:2, 18.
11 Acts 11:20.
12 Acts 11:21, 24, 25.
13 Acts 11:19–20.
14 Acts 11:22.
15 Acts 11:22–26.
16 Acts 11:27.
17 Acts 11:26.
18 E.A. Judge, "Judaism and the Rise of Christianity: A Roman Perspective," *Australian Journal of Jewish Studies* 7:2 (1993): 89, quoted by Gill and Winter in "Acts and Roman Religion," *Acts in Graeco-Roman Setting*, 102.
19 For a self-understanding of the people of Yahweh being "called out ones," see Gen. 12:1–3, Ex. 3:14–17, Ex. 33:1, Hos. 11:1, Matt. 2:14–15).
20 Acts 11:19.
21 Acts 11:2.
22 Contrast this passage with Paul's theological explanation of how Gentile believers relate to Judaism in Romans 9–11.
23 Seneca, "On the Shortness of Life, xviii 5 and Pharsalia, iii. 55–58," quoted by Winter in "Acts and Food Shortages," *Acts in Graeco-Roman Setting*, 71.
24 See Genesis 41.
25 See Acts 20:34–35.
26 Acts 11:25–26, 30.

CHAPTER 14

ACTS 12

"HIS CHAINS FELL OFF" (ACTS 12:7)

Acts 12 marks the end of the focus on Peter. Except for Acts 15:7 in the Jerusalem Council, he is not mentioned again. The placement of the preceding passage on Antioch, which does not mention Peter, indicates Luke is now more concerned with explaining the spread of the faith to the Gentiles than with chronologizing Peter's ministry. Nevertheless, second only to Paul, Peter is the most significant personality in *Acts*. Let us pause to consider how his roles function in the larger narrative. Do his roles as an original disciple of Jesus, leader of the apostles, and bridge to the conversion of the family of Cornelius fully account for his prominence in *Acts* as background for the defense of Paul before Nero? In particular, do those roles account for the inclusion of this episode of his imprisonment by Herod and miraculous escape? No. Chapter 12 becomes a part of *Acts* for different reasons.

While *Acts* was being written, Paul and the believers in Rome had two years to gather facts and prepare for trial. Trial preparation does not, however, consist just of writing a brief and gathering documents. Witnesses must be located, summoned to Rome, and prepared! Although Rosenblatt has written a convincing book based upon the thesis that the theme of "witness" permeates and unifies *Acts*,[1] left open in her analysis is the identity of the witnesses who would be called in Paul's defense before Nero. Paul's life was at stake. Even without the hindsight of two thousand years, the church in A.D. 62 certainly would have concluded that he was its leading missionary. Beyond the importance of Paul's life and work, the outcome of his trial would directly and dramatically affect the work of every missionary and Christian. O. F. Robinson, in her treatise on Roman criminal law, states that the personal testimony of witnesses was by far the most important aspect of a Roman trial. Event witnesses are, of course, essential, but character witnesses for the defense were of particular importance in Roman practice.[2]

No defense lawyer would fail to consider Peter at the top of his witness list. Accordingly, it is hard to imagine that Peter would not have been dispatched to Rome to testify on behalf of Paul.[3] As a key witness, Peter would also be subject to cross-examination and impeachment. One of the obvious grounds for discrediting Peter's testimony would be his "rap sheet," his arrest record before Jewish and Roman authorities. Luke has already explained the charges leveled against Peter by the Sanhedrin and Sadducees in chapter [4] but the arrest by King Herod Agrippa I was more recent and more plausibly discrediting. As a Roman client ruler, Herod Agrippa's actions were ostensibly more objective than the actions of Peter's theological opposition: hence protection of Peter's credibility is the first reason chapter 12 is put in the brief.

In line with the need to protect Peter as a witness, Luke takes dead aim at Herod's character, labeling him as a persecutor[4] and a murderer.[5] These charges, in themselves, attract the reader's attention because they allege patent violation of Roman law. Luke, as he was living in Rome and writing, however, would have been becoming aware of Nero's increasingly tyrannical behavior,[6] realizing the charges against Herod Agrippa to be insufficient if Nero (or a loyal subordinate) is within the intended readership of *Acts*. Nero would not necessarily condemn behavior in which he, himself, routinely engaged. Therefore, Luke must go further: he must show that Herod acted tyrannically *and contrary to the interests of Rome*.

Luke does so in three ways. First, he alleges that Herod is motivated by the desire to please a special interest group, the Jews,[7] implying that this may not be in the interest of the empire. Second, he recounts that Herod executed sixteen innocent Roman soldiers,[8] which is obviously a detail included by Luke to discredit Herod in the eyes of Roman officials. (Again, this is hardly the type of detail which would be of great interest if Luke were writing to believers.) Luke completes his impeachment of Herod by describing his death.[9] Although the manner of death[10] is unclear (Herod may have had what resembled a stroke followed by a fatal parasitic infection, or he may have died on the spot, with the reference to worms in verse 23 referring to the grave), the reason for death is flatly stated: Herod allowed himself to be worshiped as a god.

While the account of Herod's death does seem, as I have said, to serve a specific forensic purpose, its second function appears to be a direct challenge to the religious authority of Rome. Since the reign of Caligula (Gaius), the emperors had allowed themselves to be worshiped as living gods. Nero, the emperor while *Acts* was written, actively encouraged this worship. If *Acts* was written to Theophilus as a fact gatherer, other Roman officials would subsequently read it. Nero himself was one of the potential readers. Because this audience would immediately recognize that the cause of Herod's death could, as assuredly, become the cause of Nero's, it was bound to provoke a strong but varied reaction. Historians believe that much of the Roman aristocracy was disgusted and embarrassed by Nero but were too fearful to stop him.[11] To the extent that any reader fell within that group, Luke's account of Herod's death was bound to evoke admiration and tacit approval. To the extent the readership included Nero, his loyalists, or hangers-on, the assertion that God would send an angel to kill a king who allowed himself to be worshiped would immediately arouse anger and perhaps would seal Paul's death.

Would Luke take such a risk? As Rosenblatt and others have noted, the "witness" theme of *Acts* includes not just the primary meaning of giving court testimony but also the martyr implication.[12] Luke's primary goal as an advocate and the goal of his "client," Paul, was not to win Paul's freedom, but to be a witness and thus to win freedom from the bonds of sin and death for as many people as possible through faith in the Messiah. While Luke obviously hoped he could help gain Paul's freedom *and* faithfully proclaim the gospel, he would have been painfully aware of the potential inconsistency of those goals.

The second and third centuries abound with accounts of martyrs (literally, "witnesses" in Greek) who chose agonizing deaths rather than offer a pinch of salt at the base of an emperor's statue. Jews in the centuries preceding *Acts*, under the Maccabees, died by the thousands in revolt against Greek rulers who had erected a statue of Antiochus Epiphanes in the Jerusalem temple. Why should we think that Luke or Paul, *in nonviolent opposition to emperor deification*, were any less willing to risk death than their spiritual forbearers or descendants?

Further, Luke and Paul believed repentance and conversion were possible for anyone, no matter how determinedly opposed to Jesus,[13] if only the good news could be proclaimed to him clearly.[14] Reactions other than anger or repentance could also be anticipated. Twenty years earlier when Caligula was told that Jews were offering incense for, rather than to him, he stated that he pitied them. "These fellows are not criminals," said the emperor, "they are pitiable fools, or else they would have recognized my divine nature."[15] Whatever reactions Luke may have anticipated or hoped for, he did not allow possible disapproval, reprisal, or even his legal objectives to muzzle the confrontational aspects of his evangelistic agenda.

In addition to neutralizing the probable negative perception which Peter's arrest by Herod Agrippa may have created in the eyes of Roman officials, Luke also shows Peter in a positive light as a man directly protected by God. The record of his arrest, his escape, and the execution of the sixteen prison guards (although certainly not the angelic intervention) would probably have been verifiable from Roman prison or diplomatic records, or from eyewitnesses, to enhance Peter's credibility as a key witness and, consequently, to further Luke's legal agenda.

The details of the angelic deliverance make high drama and, by intriguing and entertaining the reader, enhance both Luke's legal and evangelistic agendas. These dramatic aspects of *Acts* consistently serve those objectives rather than the other way around. However, chapter 12 is unusual in that the evangelistic objective appears to transcend the continuing legal argumentation. Reread verses 1 and 2 of chapter 12. Luke, as he prepares Theophilus to understand the reason for missionary journeys on which Paul is about to embark, is informing or reminding him that whether the apostles die (verse 2) or live (verse 1), God is in charge.[16]

1   Rosenblatt, *Paul the Accused*, various references.

2   Robinson, *Criminal Law*, 5.

3   It is also possible that Peter may have been charged and brought to Rome to face trial or could have been charged once he arrived to testify in Paul's behalf, but the evidence for such a conclusion is not patent in Acts.

4   Acts 12:1.

5   Acts 12:2.

6   See previous chapter on the emperors.

7   Acts 12:3.

8   Acts 12:4, 19.

9   Acts 12:19–23.

10 Acts 12:23.

11 See e.g., Rudich, *Dissidence Under Nero*, 84; Arthur Boak, *A History of Rome to 565 A.D.*, 3rd ed. (New York: The Macmillan Company, 1943), 297.

12 Rosenblatt, *Paul the Accused*, various references.

13 See Acts 9:5.

14 See Col 4:3–4.

15 Bruce, *New Testament History*, 253, quoting Philo, "Legation to Gaius," 367.

16 See Acts 21:13.

CHAPTER 15

ACTS 13

THE FIRST MISSIONARY JOURNEY
"*WITNESSES*" (ACTS 13:31)

Having made important evangelistic and legal points in chapter 12, Luke now explains the origin of Paul's missionary expeditions which will comprise the middle one-third of the narrative. Barnabas, Saul (Paul), John Mark, and the church at Antioch have all been introduced to the reader. Luke now links them together in Acts 12:24–13:2 with the continued spread of the word of God.

Let us reflect for a moment on Luke's use of transitions and introduction of characters. Certainly, any form of writing, whether evangelistic presentation, epic, fiction, or "pure history," can benefit from clear transitions and careful character identification. However, in legal writing, they are crucial because failure to link accounts and track characters can at best result in an irritated judge and at worst loss of credibility. Given that Luke certainly had credibility concerns due to the stature of the opposition and the frequency of supernatural intervention in his presentation (which would probably seem unusual even to a Roman who had a spiritual or spiritist worldview), one would expect to see great care given to subject transitions and character introduction.

Acts 12:24–13:2 illustrates that great care. This careful usage also supports the conclusion that *Acts*, as legal briefs usually are, was rewritten. Luke's organization of themes, characters, chronology, geography, and transitions suggests a lawyer's craft. The assistance of Paul and proofreading of others also are consistent with its refinement.

Theophilus is given the names of Barnabas and Saul and three other prophets and teachers at Antioch. Why does Luke give the names and certain fascinating details about the three who have yet to be introduced? Simeon's name, deriving from one of the twelve tribes, marks him as a Jew. His identification as "Black" probably is given to distinguish him from other Simeons and could imply he was a black African. The prophet or teacher Lucius is identified as being from Cyrene.

In an age when clan and city loyalties usually predominated over national identities, the note that Lucius was a leader but "not a hometown boy" from Antioch also underscores the substantive reality of the universality of the faith. For the purposes of legal argumentation, however, the most important introduction to an elder is given to Manaen as a man "who had been raised with Herod the tetrarch" (Herod Antipas). This Herod ruled Galilee from 4 B.C. to A.D. 39. We know from *Luke* and the other gospels[1] that he beheaded John the Baptizer and concurred in the execution of Jesus. As a Roman surrogate, Herod's actions against the believers in Jesus would carry some presumptive credibility as being justified. Consequently, Herod is discredited and the legitimacy of the Jewish sect enhanced to a Roman official when a close childhood companion of Herod has chosen to identify with the persecuted and become a leader among them. In identifying the leadership, Luke is also making three points to his reader which may be less obvious to the twenty-first century reader:

1. There remains a plurality and depth to the church's leadership as the Gentile bricks are laid with the Jewish bricks on the Jewish foundation.

2. This is not a case of a secret cult with a membership explosion fueled by a charismatic Peter and Paul. The leaders are public figures unafraid to be identified.

3. The identities are verifiable; Theophilus can check the facts if he wishes.

The description of John Mark as a helper (he was previously introduced[2] via his mother who lived in Jerusalem) may seem extraneous. He leaves Paul and Barnabas shortly after they begin their mission[3] but he is a necessary character to explain why Barnabas and Paul eventually split[4] and why Paul teams with Silas. Further, he is an eyewitness who can corroborate part of Paul's defense. Consider the epistle to the Colossians which was written during Paul's imprisonment in Rome.[5] Col. 4:10 indicates that Mark is now with Paul and perhaps about to travel to parts of Asia Minor. In addition to being an obvious witness when Paul is brought to trial, he may be on that journey intending to gather evidence for Paul's defense.[6] Thus, if Theophilus is also gathering evidence for Paul's trial, we can see why Luke gives Mark such a detailed introduction.

Cyprus (Acts 13:4–6)

Paul and Barnabas journey first to Cyprus. After mentioning the presence of John Mark, Luke adds three important details in verse 4:

1. "[T]hey preached the word of God in the *synagogues of the Jews*," signaling that the inclusion of Gentiles has not changed the understanding that the "sent out ones," the apostles, were to share their message with fellow Jews and, evidently, share it with them first. The inclusion of Gentiles into

faith in the God of Abraham and the Messiah promised by Jewish scriptures had not transformed that faith into a non-Jewish religion.

2. These apostles did not proclaim their experiences or theology but "the word of God." The apostles were not a new authority but men under the existing authority which defined Judaism: Tanakh, the Hebrew scriptures.

3. God's Holy Spirit impelled the journey. It was not initiated or carried out by men based upon their own conceptions.[7]

The overall impression Luke intends in Acts 13:4–6 is that the essential Jewishness of the faith is absolutely constant even as the *method and object of its spread* changes from Jew to Jew and becomes from Jew to Jew and Gentile and as the *locus shifts* from Judea/Samaria to the diaspora. Luke could have written that they went to the "Jews" or to the "synagogues" but because he combines the words with some redundancy in verse 4, we can see he is once more stressing the Jewish nature of the expedition.

SERGIUS PAULUS (ACTS 13:7–12)

Although the evangelists travel "through the whole island," Luke mentions only two cities by name: Salamis and Paphos. Because those cities were the former and current Roman provincial capitals, they would be well known to Luke's reader if he is a Roman official.

Luke details an encounter at Paphos[8] for four reasons:

1. The main character, Sergius Paulus, is a Roman proconsul. Luke may well have had scores and possibly hundreds of dramatic or miraculous events in the ministry of Paul to choose from in telling *Acts*. Why do so many of them involve Roman officials? Did miracles mainly occur only in their presence? If Luke is writing to believers do they care more about miracles among Roman officials? Unlikely. The more plausible explanation for so many encounters with Roman officials is that Luke thought them the most:

    A. **Exculpatory**. Although Paul appears in the narrative before Roman magistrates, proconsuls, governors, and a client king, rightly none finds Paul guilty of any crime;

    B. **Empathetic** and interesting to a readership of Roman officials;

    C. **Credible;** and

    D. **Verifiable.**

So, by defending Paul and the Christian faith through interactions with Roman officials, Luke supports his legal agenda. We also see that he is not writing to Christians as a primary intended audience.

2. One scholar notes that this Sergius Paulus "is quite feasibly" the same Roman senator who held the important position of river commissioner in Rome a few years earlier (sometime between A.D. 41 and 47).[9] If so he, and probably his family, would have been especially well known to an official Roman readership, including Nero. By giving Sergius Paulus such prominence, Luke probably is appealing to Paul's political connections, which is wise for a lawyer in any high-profile trial, particularly one that may be decided as much on political as legal grounds.

3. The antagonist, Bar-Jesus, is a Jew, albeit a sorcerer and false prophet. Part of Luke's legal agenda is to demonstrate that Paul and the other evangelists are preaching Judaism and not some new, unauthorized, and illegal religion. Certainly, Luke hopes and intends that the reader come to believe in Jesus, but having a dual legal/evangelistic agenda is totally consistent internally. If Luke wins the reader over to faith in Jesus, certainly the reader will adopt Paul's view of Christianity as being truly Jewish and realize that Paul has not broken Roman law. Even if he fails to convert the reader, he may at least persuade him that the controversy is between Jews rather than between warring religions. Thus the detail about Bar-Jesus being Jewish adds to Luke's defense.

4. Luke is also, without theological elaboration, informing his reader that some of the opposition to Paul is traceable to the devil.[10] The message he seeks to convey: "God wants you Roman officials to believe in the Messiah of Israel; however, the devil wants to keep you from the truth and is even using people such as this Jewish sorcerer to that end. Nevertheless, God is demonstrating the truth about Jesus (and innocence of Paul) through miraculous signs, and some, such as your fellow official Sergius Paulus, have come to believe after seeing a sign and considering the teaching."[11]

PISIDIAN ANTIOCH (ACTS 13:13–49)

Luke continues to assert that the ministry of Paul and Barnabas in Pisidian Antioch was emphatically Jewish in several ways:

1. It begins on a **Sabbath**.[12]

2. Takes place in the **synagogue**.

3. Where the **Law and Prophets** are read there.[13]

4. **Synagogue rulers** invite Paul and Barnabas to speak.

While Paul may have remembered this sermon well and the several texts he cited (Ps. 2:7; Is. 55:3; Ps. 16:10; and Hab. 1:5), the sermon recorded in *Acts*[14] and those four scriptures were certainly not all that Paul preached. Later in *Acts*,[15] Luke informs the reader that Paul could speak for many hours. Given Paul's excellent opportunity to present his message, Luke obviously does not give his readers

Paul's entire sermon, just an edited portion. Why then does he select the portion which gives a synopsis of Exodus,[16] Joshua, Judges, and Samuel,[17] and the rule of Saul and David?[18] Evidently, this historical digression is chosen as a "Chapter Two" to supply background which a Gentile lacks about Israel. It complements Acts 7 where Luke gives a "Chapter One" introduction to the history of Israel focusing on Moses. Such fill-ins of knowledge gaps are consistent with the hypothesis of a readership of Roman officials.

Luke also wants to connect Jesus to David[19] and to the Scriptures to show that the link between Paul's message and Judaism was seamless. He makes this link also in five phrases which Paul uses to address the congregation:

1. "**Men of Israel** and you Gentiles who worship God."[20]

2. "**Our fathers.**"[21]

3. "**Brothers, children of Abraham** and you God-fearing Gentiles."[22]

4. "**Our fathers.**"[23]

5. "**My brothers.**"[24]

This manner of address reminds the reader *relentlessly* that Paul identified with the hearers as a Jew, expected the hearers to react to the message and Scripture as faithful Jews, and to remain Jews. To the extent Paul was addressing Gentiles, he expected them to come to or maintain their belief in the "God of the people of Israel."[25]

JOHN THE BAPTIZER AS WITNESS

Luke's mention of John the Baptizer is also significant. To understand its import, the modern reader must free his or her mind from vague conceptions of John as a "Christian" and instead consider how he might have been perceived by various groups in the early 60s, some thirty years after his execution. While the writers of the gospels all feature John as the proclaimer of Jesus as Messiah, the majority of the Roman world did not see him as such in A.D. 62. To Jews who were not followers of Jesus, he was widely known as a preacher of repentance and baptism. Repentance was integral to Judaism.[26] The duty of ceremonial washing to be right before God was set forth in Torah[27] and practiced in *mikvas* throughout Jerusalem, Judea, and the diaspora.

By emphasizing the connection between repentance and *mikva* and by powerful preaching, John gained a large following among Jews *independent* of the growth of the *Talmidei Yeshua*. Note Luke's mention of John as turning the focus to Jesus as he, John, "was *completing* his work."[28] Also, like Jesus, John had disciples.[29] Apparently, they spread John's teaching about repentance and baptism.[30]

To Roman officials, John could have been known in many ways: perhaps through the eyes of their Jewish acquaintances in Rome, as a leader of another

Jewish sect, from Roman political history as an agitator executed by Herod the tetrach, from Luke as the man described in the Book of Luke (see chapter on Book of Luke), or John would have been unknown. Thus because *Acts* has a readership who could have a widely varied understanding of John the Baptizer but would probably recognize him as an important *Jewish* figure, Luke includes Acts 13:24–25 in Paul's sermon to reinforce his legal point that the faith being preached was Jewish.

More Witnesses

Having given the Gentile Roman some more Jewish biblical history[31] and recent history concerning the Baptizer, Luke then records those portions of Paul's evangelistic message which further his agenda. Since Luke is writing *Acts* as a lawyer/evangelist, all of Acts 13:26–42 easily fits his evangelistic purposes. One particular element of the sermon which also fits the legal agenda is the "witnesses."[32] The many who had traveled with Jesus are now traveling about confirming that they saw him resurrected "for many days." Luke is explaining why the faith is spreading all over the empire and, in so doing, makes a dangerous point: the *religio illicita* charge against Paul is not against just him. Paul is only one of many. If Paul is guilty of breaking Roman law, so are the others. A guilty verdict for Paul may mean an arrest warrant for every evangelist in the empire. In essence Luke asserts that if Jesus has risen, the evangelists are just telling the truth. He quotes only four of the scriptures from Tanakh used by Paul in his sermon. They all allude to Jesus or the Resurrection.

The reaction to the preaching of Jesus as Messiah in Pisidian Antioch is both strong and typical of most missionary encounters Paul will have. It is strong because "many Jews and devout converts to Judaism" were deeply affected and wanted to hear Paul more.[33] The news spreads and the next Sabbath most of the city comes to hear. It is also strong because Jewish opposition arises. Although they could have disagreed with Paul's message, Luke attributes their opposition to "jealousy."[34] The reaction is typical because the pattern of preaching, curiosity, faith by some Jews and Gentiles, rejection by other Jews and Gentiles, and persecution of the evangelists[35] will repeat often.

This episode fits Luke's legal defense plan in three ways:

1. The message is Jewish and continues to go to Jews first.

2. The expansion of the faith from the tribe of Israel to all humanity is foretold in the Hebrew scripture.

3. The Gentiles hear and believe.

Thus, Luke the lawyer asserts that Paul is not breaking Roman law, he is just spreading the Jewish faith. Further, the opposition to Paul is not based upon the non-Jewishness of his teaching but upon the resistance of some Jews to the repeated message of the Prophets that Gentiles would be included into their religion.[36] Put another way, the opponents in Pisidian Antioch are saying that Paul has no authority to admit people into the faith. Luke is saying that Paul's authority comes from Scripture, the Resurrection, and the Holy Spirit. This authority continues to be demonstrated as Paul and Barnabas travel to the synagogue in Iconium.

1 Matt. 14:1, 3; Mark 6:14, 8:15; Luke 3:1, 19; 9:7; 13:31; 23:7–14.
2 Acts 12:12.
3 Acts 13:13.
4 Acts 15:36–40.
5 Acts 28:30.
6 See Col 4:10b.
7 Acts 13:4, echoing 13:2.
8 Acts 13:6–12.
9 Alanna Nobbs, "Cyprus," in *Acts in Graeco-Roman Setting*, 282–7.
10 See Acts 13:6, 10.
11 Acts 13:12.
12 Acts 13:14.
13 Acts 13:15.
14 Acts 13:16–41.
15 Acts 20:7, 9.
16 Acts 13:17.
17 Acts 13:20.
18 Acts 13:21–22.
19 Acts 13:21.
20 Acts 13:16.
21 Acts 13:17.
22 Acts 13:26.
23 Acts 13:32.
24 Acts 13:38.
25 Acts 13:17.
26 2 Kings 7:13; Ezek. 18:30–31; Joel 2:12.
27 Ex. 19:10; Lev. 14:8, 16:26.
28 Acts 13:25. Also see comments on Acts 19 later in the text.
29 Luke 7:18.
30 Acts 19:3–4.
31 Tyson, *Images of Judaism*, 33, confirms the conclusion that Acts 7 and Acts 13:16–22 are written to inform a reader ignorant of the history recorded in Hebrew Scripture.
32 Acts 13:31.
33 Acts 13:42–43.
34 Acts 13:45.
35 Acts 13:50.
36 E.g. Is. 49:6 at Acts 13:47.

CHAPTER 16

ACTS 14

"*FAITH UNTO THE GENTILES*" (ACTS 14:27)

ICONIUM (ACTS 14:1–7)

Luke begins the account of the missionary journey to Iconium by stating explicitly a point which is repeated implicitly throughout *Acts*: Paul and Barnabas went *as usual* into the Jewish synagogue. Such repetition makes it obvious that Luke wants to implant that understanding in his reader. Although "a great number" of Jews and Gentiles believed, Luke tells the reader nothing of the message presented. Luke loves to tell the good news and does so in many ways. In this passage however, his editing instincts caused him to refrain. Luke tells about each city Paul visited and the resulting riots, persecutions or legal proceedings, but he does not explain the gospel at each stop. If Luke is teaching believers, the instruction in this section comes up short. From what he actually writes, one may deduce that the forensic structure of *Acts* is primary in chapter 14 and the evangelistic message secondary: he is writing to a pretrial fact gatherer.

Although Luke omits any portion of the gospel message at Iconium, he does explain the interaction between the opposition and Paul and Barnabas. *Because* Gentiles were having their minds "poisoned," Paul and Barnabas stayed quite awhile. Positions were hardening. Initial openness is followed by conversions and reactions to those conversions. As the reactors become, in Luke's view, less and less honest, Paul and Barnabas stiffen their resolve, saying in essence, "Then we'll stay, we'll preach, and the signs and wonders from God will do some of our arguing for us!" As the rift widens,[1] the third murder plot against Paul is conceived.[2] The believers presumably could have defended the apostles by force but instead they flee when they discover the plot.[3] Luke notes an important and legally relevant fact in Acts 14:1–7. Although vigorous debate and sharp disagreement occur, he asserts that the apostles do not breach the peace, and when they could lawfully defend themselves, they do not fight back. Rather, they flee but continue to evangelize elsewhere.

LYSTRA (ACTS 14:8–19)

Whereas in Pisidian Antioch, Luke records a sermon very focused to a Jewish audience and in Iconium the narrative is primarily forensic in purpose, the Lystra narrative starts with a miracle. Preaching occurs in all three cities, miracles and persecutions as well. From his abundance of sources, Luke varies his presentation to make *Acts* readable and interesting. The Lystra miracle is probably selected because:

1. It was **spectacular** (the crippled man was lame from birth).

2. It **echoes** a miracle of Jesus,[4] illustrating that the same Spirit of God in Jesus[5] is present in Paul and Barnabas.

3. The reaction of the crowd was intense. The local pagan religious leader tried to make them an object of worship. These details add to the **verifiability** of the account.

4. Luke is selecting an incident from Paul's travels which will "connect" with an **educated** Roman reader. Not only would Zeus and Hermes be well known, but also the Lyconian legend that the two deities once visited the region but were refused hospitality by everyone except an elderly couple, Philemon and Baucis, would be familiar to someone with the social standing of a high-ranking Roman official. The well known Roman poet Ovid had memorialized the legend.[6]

5. Paul and Barnabas strenuously resist worship, tearing their clothes and rushing into the crowd. Luke may be **refuting charges** that Paul was making himself the object of a cult following.

A MESSAGE TO EVERY RELIGION.

The healing miracle, as often occurs in *Acts*, creates the opportunity to point the hearers to the "living God,"[7] Luke covers a broad base of potential readers in the theological discourses he chooses to record. Here Paul addresses the beliefs of rustic worshipers of Zeus. Elsewhere in *Acts*, Luke selects sermons of Paul and words of others which were crafted to reach Jews,[8] God-fearing Gentiles,[9] followers of John the Baptist,[10] Gentiles presumably ignorant of Judaism,[11] followers of Greek philosophical teachings,[12] exorcists and sorcerers,[13] worshipers of the Goddess Artemis,[14] and just plain pragmatic, agnostic Roman officials.[15]

Luke would want to reach each group with his message while saying something persuasive to Roman officials of all religious persuasions, yet **three strong legal**

arguments also are present as Luke recounts Paul's interactions with these various religious groups:

1. <u>Free Exercise of Religion</u>. Although Rome did not think in the American "free exercise" paradigm, government was as unequipped then as it is now to make theological distinctions. If Rome convicts Paul for promoting a non-Jewish religion, all Christians are lawbreakers. If all Christians are lawbreakers, then other sects of Judaism are probably illegal unless officially sanctioned by the temple hierarchy. The Talmud says that twenty-four sects of Judaism existed at this time although they are not named. Pagan sects would probably be safe so long as they incorporated emperor worship and did not otherwise pose a civil threat.

2. <u>Other Faiths</u>. Luke needed to answer a question that would occur to any judge, the same question that occurs to any student of a particular religion: "What about the other religions? Aren't they all ultimately the same?" Although Luke devotes far more ink to the truth of biblical Judaism, the scriptures and faith in Jesus, he does to an extent address the various alternative belief systems to offer reasons why they are not fully true. If he failed to do so, Roman officials could legitimately ask why Paul needed to be preaching at all.

3. <u>Universality</u>. Along with the two preceding points, Luke supports his theme of Judaism made universal through faith in Jesus the Messiah of Israel.[16] Universality is described throughout *Acts* on manifold levels.[17] Salvation being made available to all people through Jesus is yet one more level. *To the legal listener, the universality theme explains how the Messianics can be faithful Jews and not starting a new, illegal religion.*

While Luke's point, universality of the Gospel = authentic Judaism = *religio licita*, might seem to contradict his implicit argument that Rome really rules an Empire of many faiths, it is actually quite consistent. The apparent contradiction is this:

A. Many religions are allowed in the Roman Empire; *ergo* Jewish Christianity should be permitted.

B. We know that only Judaism and the Roman umbrella pantheism/emperor worship are legal and Luke is arguing that the Nazarenes are Jewish to the core.

A legal advocate, however, does not see these arguments as necessarily contradictory for two reasons:

1. Many religions are <u>allowed</u> (*de facto*) but only two are <u>formally legal</u> (*de jure*). In other words, the formal law should be read expansively to accommodate the true state of the world.

113

2. Arguments are often made <u>in the alternative</u>. While non-lawyers assume that legal decisions are made by taking law and applying it to a situation, lawyers know that in complex, novel, or tightly contested cases, the law often proceeds in the other direction. The facts are established and the emotions of the court are appealed to concerning the rightness of a particular result. The attorney then argues what the law *should* be. Because the court always reserves to itself the right to say what the law is, the attorney can offer more than one legal theory to obtain his desired result. For example, to defeat the effect of a will, a lawyer may argue, "Janet Warren was not in her right mind when she signed it." Alternatively, he can argue, "Even if Ms. Warren was sane, the document was not properly witnessed, it is a letter not a will." Luke's primary argument in *Acts* is that the apostles are spreading the legal Jewish faith. His alternative implicit argument seems to be, "Even if you judges reject the argument that the Nazarenes are Jews, so many other religions are allowed, *de facto*, that you should find Paul not guilty."

After Luke completes the joint "speech" of Paul and Barnabas,[18] he notes that opponents from Pisidian Antioch and Iconium turned the crowd against Paul. What they said is not recorded probably because Luke wants to focus on their murderous intentions which result in Paul being stoned and left for dead. No hint of a violent response by the believers is given. Instead Luke tantalizes the reader with the implication that Paul himself was resurrected at the hands of the other believers.

If Luke indeed believed Paul had been resurrected, he had good legal reason to avoid digressing into it. His case for Paul and for Christianity rested on the physical resurrection of Jesus. To have presented the chief defendant as resurrected would clearly have shifted the focus away from Jesus. Also Paul's resurrection would be far more debatable from a physical point of view. Paul, if he did die, was only dead for perhaps ten minutes (enough time for the stoners to leave). Nevertheless, Paul's recovery is miraculous in itself because the day after being left for dead he goes to Derbe to preach. Primarily, Luke wants Theophilus to see Paul as a man so fully convinced of the truth and urgency of his message that, to reach his people and the Gentiles, he will risk death repeatedly but will not use violence himself.

The intrepidness of Paul and Barnabas is reinforced and their love, even for their opponents, is underscored further in the next few verses.[19] Instead of returning to Antioch in Syria by another route, they retrace their steps through Lystra, Iconium, and Antioch in Pisidia! These latter two cities are the homes of the men who had orchestrated Paul's stoning. Luke is certainly letting Theophilus know that Paul was not afraid and was showing himself to his persecutors in part so that they could have another chance to believe. Fittingly, Paul and Barnabas now deliver a message to the believers in each city which is summarized in one sentence: "We must through many tribulations enter the kingdom of God."[20] The stated purpose of Paul and Barnabas for the return trip was to strengthen and encourage the disciples in regard to the persecution they were encountering. Luke includes these return stops and details about appointment of elders to:

1. **Explain** the growth and endurance of the church.

2. **Harmonize** the peaceful message of the gospel with the persecutions erupting in its wake.

3. Show that the facts in his narrative are **verifiable.**

4. **Account** for Paul's whereabouts.

Luke then relates that Barnabas and Paul return to Antioch, report to the believers how God was reaching the Gentiles, and stay in Antioch "a long time." This transition prepares the reader for the theologically momentous decision about to issue from Jerusalem and around which Luke will center his legal defense.

---

1   Acts 14:4.
2   See Acts 9:23–4 and Acts 9:29.
3   Acts 14:6.
4   Luke 5:24.
5   See Luke 5:17, Acts 10:38.
6   Gill and Winter, "Acts and Roman Religion," 82.
7   Acts 14:15.
8   Acts 2:14–39.
9   Acts 10:34–43.
10 Acts 19:1–6.
11 Acts 16:30–31.
12 Acts 17:18.
13 Acts 19:13–19.
14 Acts 19:25–27.
15 Acts 27:21–26.
16 Acts 1:8.
17 See discussion of Acts 1 and 2.
18 Acts 14:15–17.
19 Acts 14:21–22.
20 Acts 14:22b.

CHAPTER 17

ACTS 15:1–35

"*CIRCUMCISED . . . HEARTS*"
(ACTS 15:1, 9)

Questions. Investigators and judges are full of them. Sometimes they are asked, sometimes unspoken, even unformulated. The good brief writer anticipates the thinking of his reader and gives answers before or as the questions arise. What would Theophilus wonder as he read about *Gentiles*, without becoming Jews, believing in Jesus and joining Jews in the worship of Israel's God? How could he conclude that the faith was Jewish and therefore legal, when Gentile converts were are not being circumcised? After all, one need not have been a professor of comparative theology to know that circumcision was a special mark of the Jew.

Luke, the legal apologist, has the serious issue of Gentile circumcision to anticipate and address lest it undercut his case. Luke, the "theologian," also has a task: "Keep it simple: you are not writing to believers!" The theological task is handled well. The characters already familiar to the reader, Peter, Barnabas, Paul, and Jacob (James), express their thoughts. Peter's observation is practical:[1] "[God gave the Gentiles] the Holy Spirit, just as He did for us … purifying their hearts by faith," making unnecessary the "yoke" of circumcision. Jacob's judgment,[2] prefaced by Scripture, is equally pragmatic: "we should not trouble those from among the Gentiles who are turning to God."

Clearly the issue of circumcision for Gentiles and the question of Gentiles becoming Jewish was a big issue within the primitive church and is discussed extensively by Paul in his letters to the Romans and the Galatians. However, Luke's pragmatic approach stands in contrast to Paul's theological analysis. Perhaps the difference in approach stems from the viewpoints and personalities of the writers, but a difference in readership also is a possibility. Luke's treatment of circumcision seems more like a trial summary written by a lawyer to a legal audience, rather than a missionary explaining a theological point to an audience of believers:

1. The subject is framed as a controversy, succinctly repeated:

   A. Unless you are circumcised according to the custom taught by Moses, you cannot be saved.[3]

   B. The Gentiles must be circumcised and required to obey the law of Moses.[4]

2. The parties to the controversy are clearly identified: men from Judea and Antioch[5] and "some of the sect of the Pharisees who believed"[6] versus Paul and Barnabas.

3. Luke notes a sharp disagreement existed (verse 2), his otherwise respectful reference to the circumcision groups contrasts markedly with Paul's trenchant comment about the Jewish Christians who were advocating the requirement of Gentile circumcision in Galatians 5:12: "I could wish that those who trouble you would even cut themselves off!" This different treatment is consistent with a desire by Luke not to hang the church's "dirty laundry" before Roman officials.

4. The debate proceeds in the nature of a trial, with arguments from both sides presented and the judges Peter and Jacob commenting.

5. Facts are presented from which a legal argument can be made.

6. A "judgment" is rendered.[7]

7. The judgment is explained as a judge would customarily do.[8]

8. The judgment is reduced to a written "opinion"[9] to communicate, memorialize (i.e., make official), and avoid ambiguity.

Thus even a subject which would invite the most theological of expositions[10] is put in a legal framework in *Acts*. If Luke is intending to address readers who think in terms of trial as a means to arrive at truth, he has done a good job in shaping his narrative to their paradigm.

In addition to the trial framework in which Luke treats the circumcision controversy, many other details fit the Lukan legal plan:

1. **Jewishness of the controversy:**

   A. "Pharisees" are believers.[11]

   B. Scripture informs the argument and decision.[12] Acts 15:17, a part of Jacob's interpretation of the prophet Amos, is particularly important: "that the rest of mankind may seek the Lord, Even all the Gentiles who are called by My name." It tells the Roman reader that the Hebrew prophets had foreseen that not all Jews would remain faithful to God, while Gentiles would become followers of Israel's God without becoming Jews. The Messianics were not inventing a new faith, but following a plan of God unfolding from ancient times.[13]

    C. Decisions are tied to the teaching of Moses.[14]

2. Legitimate authority of the decision makers:

    A. Apostles and elders in Jerusalem make the decisions.[15]

    B. Paul and Barnabas submit to the other leaders,[16] therefore Paul is not a rogue teacher or cult leader.

    C. Peter, likewise, is depicted as sharing authority with the other apostles and elders and subject to the leadership of Jacob.

    D. Judas and Silas are sent as confirmatory witnesses to the authenticity of the letter;[17] the authority of Paul and Barnabas is not sufficient on its own to convey this important message to the congregations.

3. Verifiability/documentation:

    A. **Letter quoted apparently verbatim**[18] (note "Greetings" v. 23 and "Farewell" v. 28 which suggest the entire letter is included).

    B. A **physical copy of the letter** itself may have been available for evidence at Paul's trial in Rome.[19] In modern legal terminology: Exhibit A to defendant's brief.

    C. The **general applicability of the letter** to all Gentile believers and the fact that it was addressed to three communities[20] assures that copies were circulating and that the asserted facts were verifiable.

    D. Because Judas[21] **is further identified as "Barsabas,"** it seems that Luke is going into detail to enhance the credibility or verifiability of his account.

By carefully setting forth the controversy, summarizing the arguments of the disputants, recounting the decision-making procedure, and memorializing the decision and reasons for it, Acts 15:1–35 exemplifies how a legal brief addressing a theological subject should be written to a secular reader.

CONTENTS OF THE LETTER

Instead of the far more extensive law of Moses which the Jewish Christians were following,[22] the Gentiles who are now going to be included in the people of God have been given four laws to obey:

1. Abstain from food sacrificed to idols.

2. Abstain from blood.

3. Abstain from the meat of strangled animals.

4. Abstain from sexual immorality.

Dan Gruber has shown how the Jerusalem Council never changed the requirements of Torah[23] but rather took portions of Torah which applied to Gentiles living among the Jews[24] and informed the Gentiles of those requirements. The theological basis for this decision would be lost on a Roman official reading Luke's brief except that Luke records Jacob's pronouncement that his decision is based upon the teaching of Moses,[25] which accords with Luke's legal agenda to show that "the Way" is authentically Jewish. However, if Luke were writing to Gentile or Jewish Messianics, it seems to me that a more comprehensive or edifying explanation for these rules would be forthcoming than simply, "Do it because Moses said so!" (The actual letter did not explain the Jerusalem Council's ruling either, but it explicitly was to be accompanied by Barnabas, Paul, Judas, and Silas[26] who would be able to explain and teach on the basis for the ruling). Thus, Acts 15:19–29 especially appears to convey what a good defense lawyer would want a judicial investigator or a judge to know, rather than the teachings which a Christian audience would want or need to understand about Gentiles and Torah observance.

LUKE'S USE OF CHRONOLOGY AND DATING

Verses 35 and 36 provide a transition from the decision concerning circumcision to the second missionary journey. After the completion of the first journey, Paul and Barnabas had stayed in Antioch "a long time." Then the circumcision controversy arises. Once it is settled, they return to Antioch and Luke picks up the narrative "some time later."[27] Although Luke's precision with geography is apparent even to the modern reader, his precision with dating is also notable. *Acts* is almost totally chronological and a serious effort is made to relate events in *Acts* to various Roman events.

To begin, Luke specifies that the birth of Jesus took place immediately after the first census when Quirinius was governor of Syria.[28] Similarly in Acts 18, he effectively dates Paul's missionary journey to Corinth to the Jews' expulsion from Rome by Claudius.[29] The contemporary historian Josephus used the same dating technique, often relating events in his *Antiquities of the Jews* to corresponding Roman consulships. It appears that as a "lawyer," Luke needed to tie his chronology to important events so that Theophilus could relate *Acts* to other occurrences already in mind.

In contrast, the other gospel writers, Matthew, John, and Mark, make little effort to date events. They fail even to tie particular events to more widely known occurrences in Israel or the Roman Empire. They may not have not dated their events because they saw no need for their audience to have dates. Luke may have supplied his chronology through Paul's (and/or possibly Peter's) recollection.

As *Acts* is written, Paul is in his mid-forties. Having been that age, I can confirm the predations of time on human memory. My wife and I remember most events from twenty years earlier, not by year but in relation to events: "We sold that car before we moved to Evanston" or "She was Allyson's friend when Allyson was in second grade at Washington School." Luke's chronology is similar or more precise. Given the absence of daily newspapers or CNN and that some events took place more than twenty years before *Acts* was written, Luke does as good a job dating as can be reasonably expected. As *Acts* progresses, the dating becomes more precise because events are tied to the governorships of Felix and Festus. In summation, Luke's attention to dating and chronology in *Acts* and *Luke*, particularly when contrasted with the other gospel writers, is a solid piece of evidence that he is writing to someone who has the intention *and* capacity to verify events.

---

1 Acts 15:7–9.
2 Acts 15:19–21.
3 Acts 15:16.
4 Acts 15:56.
5 Acts 15:1.
6 Acts 15:5.
7 Acts 15:19.
8 Acts 15:19–21.
9 Acts 15:22–29.
10 See Col. 2:11: the circumcision controversy is raging in the early church.
11 Acts 15:5.
12 Acts 15:5, 15–18.
13 Bauckham, "James and the Church," 452–8.
14 Acts 15:21.
15 Acts 5:2, 22.
16 Acts 15:2.
17 Acts 15:22, 27.
18 Acts 15:23–29.
19 See discussion of Acts 23:27–30.
20 Acts 15:23.
21 Acts 15:22.
22 Acts 21:20–25.
23 Dan Gruber, *Torah and the New Covenant* (Hanover, N.H.: Elijah Publishers, 1998), 26–7 and other references; see Bauckham, "James and the Church," 459–62.
24 Lev. 17:8, 10, 12, 13, 15; 18:26.
25 Acts 15:21.
26 Acts 15.
27 Acts 15:36.
28 Luke 2:1–2.
29 The date of expulsion itself is uncertain. See Leon, *Jews of Ancient Rome,* 24–5; Bruce, *New Testament History,* 299, more confidently attributes the date to A.D. 49. In any event, the date or at least the chronology would have been known to Luke's readers.

CHAPTER 18

ACTS 15:36—18:22

THE SECOND MISSIONARY JOURNEY:
"*THE WORLD UPSIDE DOWN*"
(ACTS 17:6)

Chapter 15 closes with a description of the separation of Paul and Barnabas and the beginning of Silas' work with Paul on the second missionary journey. In addition to the dating and chronology noted in the previous chapter, Paul's *whereabouts* and *companions* are carefully identified throughout *Acts*. Why? Would a readership of believers be concerned with the level of detail Luke provides?

Judging by the lesser degree of precision in geography and persons (especially minor participants) in the rest of the New Testament, I suggest such detail was not of great interest to believers. However, perhaps because so many charges were thrown against Paul, it behooved Luke to make a careful record of Paul's journeys. If a riot had occurred among Jews in Alexandria, Egypt (a city that Paul apparently never visited), or between Jews and Gentiles consequent to the preaching of another evangelist, say, Apollos,[1] Paul might have gotten some of the blame by the time the charges reached Rome. Likewise, if trouble on account of the gospel arose before or after Paul was in a city, he could well be charged with precipitating it.

Paul is not the only evangelist mentioned in *Acts*. He and eight others, Silas, Apollos, Barnabas, Priscilla, Aquila, Mark, Peter and Phillip, all are Jews. All except Philip went to Jews first or exclusively. Presumably, they too encountered, on occasion, opposition. Although Paul had a confrontational personality, it is unlikely *any* first-century evangelist would be conflict-avoidance-oriented. The Jews in Thessalonica shout, "The *men* who turned the world upside down have come here." The gospel in its first-century context was not just revolutionary spiritually; it also had emphatic social and political implications. In other words, civil unrest did accompany the gospel and was almost certain to have occurred on occasions other than the preaching of Paul.

However, Paul could only be legally responsible for his own actions. Major incidents of civil unrest in provinces or colonies were always reported to Rome.

And if reported, is it not reasonable to assume that those incidents would be kept track of by date, by cause (e.g., bread riot, revolt, religious disturbances) and by location? After all, the Romans built their empire on the ability to conquer, subjugate, administer, pacify, and assimilate the peoples they conquered. In the detail which he provides throughout the three missionary journeys of the places, time, and people involved and sometimes even of the particular route Paul followed, Luke may be intending, in part, to protect Paul from charges arising from places where or times when he was not present.

The passage regarding the dispute between Paul and Barnabas[2] advances the narrative first by informing Theophilus that the church continued to grow.[3] Then Silas, having been introduced as a leader in Jerusalem, joins Paul. Would not a careful judicial investigator ask, "What happened to Barnabas after he departed with Mark to Cyprus?"[4] After reaching Acts 16:1, would he not also ask, "Who is Timothy?"

<u>Barnabas:</u> Acts 15:40 is the next mention of Barnabas in *Acts*. From his introduction in Acts 4:36 and explanation of his Hebrew moniker "son of encouragement" through his departure with Mark in chapter 15, apparently on yet another mission, Barnabas is assigned an important supporting role. He is first portrayed as the protector of Paul.[5] Then he is sent by the Jerusalem leadership officially to investigate, in Antioch, the first wave of Gentile conversions.[6] Next Barnabas seeks Paul out in Tarsus and brings him to Antioch to help teach the rapidly growing congregation of Gentiles and Jews.[7]

Finally Barnabas is a co-missionary on Paul's "first missionary excursion." Actually, he is more than a co-missionary because the prior context, and the coupling of him with Paul in Acts 13:2 and 13:7 where Barnabas is named first, suggests to the reader that Barnabas began as mentor and leader. He is called an "apostle"[8] and is the first mentioned reporter to the Jerusalem assembly in Acts 15:12. Clearly Barnabas was an important leader in his own right.

Yet from chapters 13 through 15, although Barnabas is mentioned eighteen times by name and, depending on how you count, approximately seventeen times is referred to by pronoun (e.g., "When *they* finished"[9]), in *every* instance he is coupled with Paul or included among Paul's companions. Paul, however, is named several times in those chapters without reference to Barnabas.[10] We discern, therefore, that Luke includes Barnabas in the narrative to tell Theophilus about Paul rather than about Barnabas. Luke also uses Barnabas to reinforce the argument that Paul was not a rogue evangelist who "invented" Gentile Christianity. When Paul and Barnabas part ways, the relevance of Barnabas to the narrative ceases and he is no longer mentioned. Consequently, we can further deduce that the original reader was not interested in a general history of the church, but rather in the history of Paul and the spread of the faith to Gentiles seemingly as it pertained to the particular charges pending against Paul.

<u>Timothy:</u> In contrast to the abrupt departure of Barnabas from the narrative, Luke's introduction of Timothy provides some important facts which would

be of interest to Roman officials because Timothy is a frequent companion of Paul throughout much of the rest of *Acts* (he is mentioned in each of chapters 16 through 20). Timothy could certainly have been called as a witness at the trial in Rome to refute some of the charges against Paul. We see that Timothy is introduced as:

1. A disciple.[11]
2. A resident of Lystra.[12]
3. Son of a Jewish mother.[13]
4. Son of a Greek father.[14]
5. Well-spoken of by the brothers in Lystra and Iconium.[15]
6. Circumcised by Paul.[16]
7. Known by local Jews as the son of a Greek father.[17]

The detail of this introduction suggests that Timothy matters to Theophilus not only within the narrative of *Acts* but, in contrast to Barnabas, beyond. Whether that importance is his relevance to legal proceedings (and thus an assumed judicial readership) or to giving him credibility in the eyes of believers (and thus an assumed church readership) cannot be asserted absolutely. Nevertheless, it seems that the scant introductions of Timothy in Paul's letters to the Romans ("my fellow worker")[18] and 1 Corinthians ("my son whom I love who is faithful in the Lord")[19] and his coauthorship of 2 Corinthians,[20] Philippians,[21] Colossians,[22] 1 Thessalonians,[23] and 2 Thessalonians[24] (in which he is referred to only as a brother, fellow servant or not introduced at all) reflect a man who needs little introduction to believers anywhere. The concluding paragraphs of Hebrews state simply that "our brother Timothy has been released"[25] as if every reader would certainly know him. Thus the weight of evidence suggests that the detailed introduction in Acts 16 is intended for a non-Christian because Timothy was so well known to believers everywhere.

Also, the inclusion of Paul's circumcision of Timothy is quite consistent with the conclusion Theophilus is a Roman investigatory official because apparently Luke wants him to realize that Paul was making every effort to follow the practices of Judaism and did so in the sight of fellow Jews. Luke thus refutes charges that Paul and the Messianics were changing "customs handed down from Moses."[26] After introducing Timothy, Luke reports the rapid growth of the churches yet again[27] before recounting Paul's foray into Phrygia and Galatia. In contrast to his more detailed accounts of other missionary stops, Luke makes no mention of where, what, or to whom Paul preached or of any response to his preaching.

If Luke is writing to believers, the comments about Phrygia and Galatia have little import but if written to a judicial investigator, they at least account for Paul's presence and communicate that civil unrest did not always accompany him.

PAUL'S VISION (ACTS 16:6–10)

The mention of the Holy Spirit's direction which kept the missionary band from going in certain directions and then a dream pointing them to Macedonia certainly could fit the "*Acts*-is-written-to-believers" paradigm, but it also furthers legal themes:

1. The apostles are not self-annointed but under God's authority.

2. Paul, although clearly a leader, moves in harmony with the other believers: "*they* tried to enter Bithynia;[28] "*we* got ready . . . concluding that God had called *us* to preach."[29] (emphasis added)

The famous shift of Luke's narrative from the third person to the first person in Acts 16:10 is *prima facie* evidence[30] that he was on or joined the missionary team at this juncture.[31] Legally, the shift matters because it enhances the reliability of the narrative. Everyone knows that although hearsay can be true, it is less reliable than direct evidence. An investigator, such as the holder of the office of *a cognitionibus*, would be acutely sensitive to these distinctions, having had much experience with hearsay proving to be exaggerated or false.[32] Luke has been at pains to stress how carefully he has investigated matters he has reported based on hearsay and that many of the events he has recorded in *Acts* are in various written records.[33] Now that Luke can report events as an eyewitness, the judicial reader will adjust his credibility meter up at least one notch. Archaeology suggests that the modern reader can adjust his own credibility meter up a notch also.

LUKE AND ARCHAEOLOGY

If Luke was writing to a Roman official who could be expected to check his accounts of Paul's travels, then his geographic references had to be accurate. New Testament scholars Norman Geisler and Thomas Howe report the accuracy of Luke's references to all thirty-two countries, fifty-four cities, and nine islands has been confirmed by archaeology without a single error.[34] Of course, one would expect Luke to be generally accurate no matter what the reason for writing *Acts*. However, if he were writing a letter for catechistic or social purposes, the accuracy or thoroughness of his geographic references would be a secondary consideration. Thus the precision and ubiquity of his geography is significantly consistent with the hypothesis he was writing a legal defense.

PHILIPPI (ACTS 16:11–40)

The encounters in Philippi give several signs of supporting a legal agenda. Although an explicit Jewish context (which supports Luke's theme that Paul was not trying to start a new religion) may not be apparent to the modern reader of

Acts, the reference to the Sabbath and particularly to the "place of prayer" by the river would have triggered a Jewish association to the first-century reader.[35] The description of Lydia as "a worshiper of God" marks her as a Gentile God-fearer. If she were Jewish or worshiped Roman gods, Luke would have said so.

Luke's selection of Lydia's story certainly has human interest but he could have chosen any conversion stories referenced in Acts 16:5 or he could have omitted any conversion account. Why does Lydia get the ink? Being female and Gentile, her story advances Luke's "universality" defense of Paul: Judaism has been expanded by God through Jesus to be universal, to embrace everyone. Consequently, Paul is not breaking Roman law as he preaches about Jesus. Luke's remarks that Philippi is a "Roman colony" and that Lydia is a "dealer in purple cloth" (which was prized by Roman aristocracy) connect Paul with any aristocratic Roman reader who might wonder, "What does this Jewish sect of resurrections and miracles have to do with me?"

The prison account of Paul and Silas in the Philippian jail is another indication of Luke's forensic purpose. As we have said of Peter, we would also say of Paul, "He had a rap sheet an arm long." The innocence which Americans are asked to presume for accused people generally does not accord as strongly in the public mind when we hear the accused has an extensive criminal record. Would the Roman mind have worked differently? One may be sure that Paul's accusers trumpeted his arrests as confirmation of the charges against him, such as being: "a troublemaker stirring up riots among Jews all over the world. . . . a ringleader of the Nazarene sect and [who would] desecrate the temple."[36]

Accordingly, it behooved Luke to explain any arrest of Paul by Roman authorities. In Philippi, Paul and Silas were accused of being Jews (!), throwing the city into uproar, and advocating customs unlawful for Romans to accept or practice.[37] The accusation of being Jewish is intended to inflame the Philippian magistrates through appeal to racism, anti-Semitism, or fear of foreigners. Luke repeats them to show that his clients are being accused by people seeking to foment such feelings. He also wants to show that many of Paul's accusers did not see him as a non-Jew; thus any charge being made in Rome about A.D. 62 that Paul was preaching an illegal religion would be seen as inconsistent if not insincere. Paul was proud of his Jewishness and never sought to distance himself from it[38] but rather strenuously resisted those who argued that belief in Jesus was not Jewish. It appears to me that Luke's mention that "the crowd joined in the attack against Paul and Silas"[39] functions to alert a judicial readership that mob or political considerations rather than truth brought about the imprisonment.[40] Let us now venture down another byway of *Acts*.

SLAVERY AND EQUALITY

Slavery permeated the Roman Empire and supported a lavish lifestyle for the aristocracy in Rome. Slave revolts erupted periodically and were brutally suppressed. In 73 to 71 B.C., a slave revolt led by Spartacus resulted in an army of 70,000 runaway slaves defeating the Roman army in several battles before being vanquished. As with the Egyptians before them and the antebellum Americans of the South who would follow them, the Romans rested their social order on this evil institution. Any social movement or religious faith which threatened the foundations of slavery would be seen by the aristocracy as a threat to their economy and lives. It certainly would be scrutinized. If found to be dangerous, such a movement or faith would be repressed forcefully, brutally. The Jerusalem Jewish establishment posed no threat to Roman order for they, too, lived lives made comfortable by slaves. Jerusalem, too, had its special platform for selling humans.[41]

Paul's words that in Messiah there is neither "slave nor free"[42] although radical to Roman society were normative to the Way. We know from other New Testament sources that the teachings of the Messianics and Jesus, while certainly not advocating violent elimination of slavery, did contain principles which were ultimately destructive of that institution.[43] The egalitarianism such as that taught in the letter of Jacob was clearly inconsistent to a rigid class society, not just to its slavery foundation but to the entire social system which supported the aristocracy:

> My brothers, as believers in our glorious Lord Jesus the Messiah, don't show favoritism. Suppose a man comes into your meeting wearing a gold ring and fine clothes, and a poor man, in shabby clothes also comes in. If you show special attention to the man wearing fine clothes and say "Here's a good seat for you," but say to the poor man, "you stand there" or "Sit by my feet," have you not discriminated among yourselves and become judges with evil thoughts?[44]

The aristocracy controlled the legal system. In view of the hot button issues that slavery and equality constituted for the Roman judiciary and hierarchy, the opponents of Paul may have exploited the teachings of the Nazarenes to support the claims that they were a threat to the social order. Does *Acts* give evidence of such charges having been made? Probably.

First, the pervasive attention to the status of Gentiles can be seen as an answer to opponents' charges that the church's disruption of the social/religious status quo (allowing Gentiles to become full members of the faith without circumcision and observance of the Torah) could endanger other areas of Roman society. Second, the account of the deliverance of the slave girl[45] is consistent with refutation by Luke of charges that Paul was teaching or instigating insurrection or at least insubordination by slaves. Paul frees the girl from a demon but her masters react to the deliverance with as much vehemence as if he had helped her escape (which in a way he had). Nothing I have found in Roman law suggests that the Romans would see exorcism as illegal. Hence, it is plausible that Luke included the details concerning the Philippian slave girl to make clear that Paul was not teaching slaves to rebel. Of course, Luke also needed to address the subsequent imprisonment of Paul and Silas.

Paul's acquittal in Philippi comes first from God via earthquake[46] and then the charges are dismissed by the magistrates.[47] Nevertheless, Paul insists on a public acknowledgment of his innocence and lack of proper trial.[48] Luke clearly implies that God sent the earthquake which freed Paul and Silas but he does not say so explicitly. Why not? Probably because he was not writing to believers. Rather, Luke records the deliverance to inform Theophilus of Paul's acquittal by Roman magistrates (and/or that the punishment given, one day in jail and flogging, was not according to Roman law).

In either event, no proper finding of guilt was ever made. Thus, a theological digression about God sending the earthquake would detract from his legal agenda. Also, Luke knows that the exorcism and the earthquake, to which he attests, are remarkable. They would not be forgotten in Philippi. The Roman magistrates, the jailer, the jailer's family, and probably many others could either corroborate this account and help Paul be released from his imprisonment in Rome or they could contradict his account and so assure Paul's execution, and, possibly, Luke's. Conclusion: Luke, the lawyer, is either selecting *verifiable* events which support his legal case or is risking his own execution.

Further, Luke shows that Paul and Silas do not retaliate against the accusers, jailer, or magistrates. They insist upon an acknowledgment of their lawful rights and leave peacefully. Certainly, their behavior would be seen by Roman officials as fully supportive of Roman order. Finally, the question arises why Paul and Silas apparently waited until after their release to assert their Roman citizenship[49] instead of asserting it upon their arrest and thus avoiding the severe flogging[50] and painful imprisonment.

While commentators have proposed many explanations for the apparent delay, one put forth by Brian Rapske seems the most reasoned.[51] If the evangelists did not have citizenship documents on their person, they could have spent debilitating months in jail while their claim was verified. Even if they did have documents (which seems unlikely due to no mention of them by Luke here or in Acts 21:39), the credentials would have been suspect due to their Jewishness.

Thus Paul and Silas chose to wait on their assertion and suffer a "severe flogging," hoping to be freed soon rather than to risk indeterminate months of incarceration awaiting a procedural ruling on their citizenship. To Theophilus, if he is a Roman "fact gatherer," the issue of citizenship would have been moot (not requiring investigation or adjudication) because he would have had ample time to establish the truth of it during Paul's two-year Roman imprisonment (if it had not already been done during his Caesarean imprisonment). This mootness may explain why Luke does not bother to tell Theophilus why Paul and Silas did not assert their citizenship until after their release.

THESSALONICA (ACTS 17:1–9)

A lawyer with a strong position grounded in fact and law will repeatedly stress the supporting facts. Following that principle of good advocacy, Luke continues to emphasize the Jewishness of Paul's mission, always to the synagogue first:

A. "as was his [Paul's] **custom**";[52]

B. "on three **Sabbath** days";[53]

C. reasoning from the [Hebrew or Septuagint] **Scriptures**,[54] explaining [that Jesus is the **Messiah.**][55]

English translations of *Acts* which substitute "Christ" for "Messiah" substantially obscure and disserve the import of Luke's legal argument because to most modern readers "Christ" lacks a Jewish connotation while "Messiah" retains, in the twenty-first century, the connotation that "*Christos*" (the Greek word used in *Luke-Acts*) would have had in the first century. The word *Christos* was perceived exclusively in its Jewish context because a "Christian" identity separate from Judaism had not emerged.

The message of resurrection is not presented as novel but, rather, is tied to Hebrew scripture.[56] The reaction is noteworthy in that *some* Jews believed, whereas a *large number* of God-fearing Greeks and *not a few* prominent women accepted the message. Why does Luke select these details? Probably he is helping his readers see how the Gentile component of the church has come about gradually, incrementally, but only through Jesus and the continued Jewishness of the message.

MOTIVATION OF THE OPPOSITION

Also, Luke is explaining the cause for the ensuing riot[57] which he attributes to "jealousy" among Jews who do not accept Paul's message. If Luke is writing *Acts* to defend Paul, as a good advocate he must not only plead his mentor's innocence but also *articulate plausible improper motives for Paul's opponents* to have brought charges against him. He would assert that those opponents were the true cause of civil unrest.

Jealousy is a theme Luke has developed which ties Paul's opponents together. First, he reports the high priest and his associates are jealous.[58] Then, through Stephen's speech,[59] he cites biblical precedent when Stephen recounts the jealousy of the patriarchs concerning the particular signs of God's favor on Joseph. Then, in Pisidian Antioch[60] jealousy arises when Paul's opponents "see crowds" gathering to hear Paul preach. Apparently, the jealousy in Thessalonica is of the same type because it arises immediately after the "large number" of God-fearing Greeks believe.

Luke is not only attributing an improper motive to Paul's opponents, he is also arguing that the controversy springs more from emotion than theological difference. Although Paul and other apostles argue scriptural proof of the messiahship of Jesus, Luke does not recount any biblical objections or rebuttal by the opposition in Thessalonica. If Luke were writing to believers, he would have good reason to include the theological objections to Paul's preaching and the responses to those theological objections. Explanations of false doctrines and the refutation of them fill the New Testament.[61] However, Luke is writing to a non-Christian Roman official who is being instructed, if he does not already know, that riots and attempted murders do not arise from theological disagreements but from the emotions which accompany those disagreements.

Prior to the arrival of Paul, the Jewish establishment in Thessalonica essentially had a monopoly on the God of Israel. However, if Paul preached truth, that the God of the Hebrew tribe, Israel's God, was the one true God, then he was God not just of Jews but also of Gentiles. If God had revealed through the teaching and resurrection of Jesus, the Messiah, that Gentiles could be included into the people of God by faith in him rather than by circumcision and the observance of extensive ritual, then that monopoly was about to be shattered.

Emotionally, that monopoly brought prestige. The Greco-Roman pantheon offered a myriad of fickle deities, stories, and rituals, while the monotheism of the Jews taught of one true, holy, and eternal God, creator and sustainer of the universe. As sole arbiters of that God to Gentiles and particularly to God-fearers, the Jews had respect and privilege. And, of course, the Jewish establishment held that same position relative to the majority of Jews who were not synagogue or political leaders.

Undoubtedly, many of those leaders had worked hard building their community, attempting to follow the law of Moses and his interpreters, and influencing their Gentile neighbors to believe the Hebrew tribal God was the only God. Now, in only *three* weeks "these men who have caused trouble all over the world"[62] had won a substantial portion of the God-fearing Greeks and some Jews over to a different Jewish worldview, one that is clearly more inclusive and purportedly more scriptural. Levinskaya analyzes the friction:

> The responsiveness of God-fearers to the Christian message posed a serious problem for Jews. Their status quo and a certain social stability which was secured by their links with the God-fearers, many of whom belonged to the upper class of the society, were put at risk. As a response to the Christian mission Jews intensified relations with their sympathizers.[63]

How would you, as a local Jewish synagogue leader, feel? Defensive? Angry? Jealous? Luke's argument is credible to a jurist because it follows human nature. The details about the mob at the home of Jason and the appearance before city officials[64] all invite Theophilus to investigate and verify Luke's account.

In addition to jealousy and fear of loss of status as motivations to oppose Paul, Luke has already stated that some leaders feared being blamed for the death of Jesus.[65] Later he explains that some Jews mistakenly believed Paul was undermining observance of the law among diasporan Jews.[66] John, with a note of irony since Jerusalem had been destroyed by the time he wrote, suggests that the leaders who handed Jesus over to Pilate thought that Jesus would eventually somehow cause Roman reprisal against Israel.[67] The competition over financial support from diasporan Jews, the fear of losing exemption from Roman military service, and the loss of the right to define to Rome "who is a Jew," because of Gentile conversions, are other probable reasons that Paul and the Messianics were persecuted.

THE CHARGES IN THESSALONICA

As one would expect in a document being written for legal purposes, Luke details the serious charges against Paul from this location:

1. **Conspiracy** to revolt against Rome ("caused trouble all over the world").
2. **Harboring** conspirators ("Jason has welcomed them into his house").
3. **"Defying** Caesar's decrees."
4. **Saying** Jesus is king over Caesar.

The only conceivable basis for charges one, two, and three based upon *Luke-Acts* and other historical sources is in conjunction with charge four and Paul's preaching of Jesus as Messiah. The particular assertion that Jesus or his followers sought the forcible replacement of Caesar by Jesus must have been prominent in the charges pending against Paul in A.D. 62 because it is so systematically refuted by the teachings of Jesus which Luke selects for his gospel:

1. "The devil said to Him, 'All this authority [over all the kingdoms of the world] I will give to You ... if you will worship before me ...' And Jesus answered and said to him, '... [It] is written, 'You shall worship the Lord your God, and Him only you shall serve.'"[68]
2. "Blessed are you who are poor, for yours is the kingdom of God."[69]
3. "Love your enemies, do good to those who hate you."[70]
4. "... the Kingdom of God is within you." [71]
5. "... give to Caesar what is Caesar's and to God what is God's."[72]
6. "And one of them struck the servant of the high priest cutting of his right ear. But Jesus answered 'No more of this! ... Am I leading a rebellion ... ?"[73]

These teachings are also reinforced by the actions and teachings of the apostles in *Acts*.

The charges against Paul and Silas in Thessalonica are not adjudicated and perhaps never formally brought. In any event, they slip out of town after nightfall.[74] Meanwhile, "Jason and others" are required to "post bond."[75] The "others" may have included Gaius, Aristarchus, and Secundus as we will see in Acts 19.[76]

Berea (Acts 17:10–15)

Berea is one of only two towns on Paul's second missionary journey where he did not encounter serious resistance from the local Jewish establishment. Any defense attorney would certainly reference this stop because the widespread opposition that Paul encountered can be read two ways:

1. The argument of the accusers: "This man Paul is a troublemaker. Wherever he went he produced rioting. Perhaps if only a few people in a few cities were aroused, one could argue that they, rather than Paul, were the problem, but the reaction of people *everywhere* to Paul's preaching indicates the problem is with him, not them."

2. The argument of Luke: "Paul is spreading the truth." Everywhere he went people believed the message that Jesus is the promised Messiah. In some places only a few believed; in other places, many. In Berea, in fact, many Jews and Greeks believed because, rather than being influenced by their emotions, they considered the evidence: The [Jewish] Scriptures. The only accusers in Berea were agitators from Thessalonica."

Athens (Acts 17:16–34)

Luke begins this passage by recounting that Paul went first to the Jews and God-fearing Greeks. (Unless verse 17 is part of an agenda to underscore the Jewishness of the Way, it appears to serve no purpose.[77]) Next he goes into great legal/theological detail in order to relate Paul's teaching to the monotheism of Abraham. One can be sure that Luke, the evangelist, and Paul, the evangelist/prisoner, would take such an opportunity to plant the seeds of belief in the hearts of polytheistic or philosophic Roman officials who might read the brief. After all, *the primary goal of freeing Paul from prison was to enable him to continue evangelizing,* so if evangelization of leading Roman officials could be accomplished in the process of freeing Paul, how much the better!

Certainly, a lawyer's duty is to represent his client. In that light, Luke's collateral agenda of evangelization would be extraneous, distractive, and even detrimental for a client whose sole goal was freedom, but in Paul, Luke had a client who was in full accord with his goals.[78] Prison was to be endured, not avoided, if it could bring some of God's chosen people (Jews and Gentiles alike) to himself.[79] Nevertheless, the first forensic objective of showing that Paul was teaching authentic Judaism made universal through Jesus, the Messiah, is well served by the account of the Athenian sojourn.

A second and probably more surpassing forensic objective of the Athenian account is to draw upon the legal authority and prestige of the *Areopagus* as a precedent to influence Roman officials to acquit Paul in Rome. Greece was acknowledged by educated Romans to be the social and intellectual superior of Rome. The account of Paul before the *Areopagus* may confuse the modern reader, in that the "debate" with epicurean and stoic philosophers and their comments about a "new teaching" could be seen as a departure from Judaism. Theophilus, however, would not have been confused. T. D. Barnes explains: "The *Areopagus*, before which Paul appeared (17:19, 22) *was also the chief court of imperial Athens.*"[80] (emphasis added) Paul was on trial! Thus, Luke's mention that some accepted Paul's message and became believers, and the fact that the *Areopagus* does not convict Paul of any crime and no violence ensued, appear to be details included to influence Roman officials favorably to Paul's defense, and towards believing in Messiah.

Scrutinizing the interrogation of Paul in Acts 17:18b-34, a Roman official would have seen it to as a trial. Verse 18b contains the charge, *religio illicita*, "advocating foreign gods". Verse 19 suggests that Paul was *arrested* (although he may well have welcomed the arrest and opportunity to explain the gospel). T. D. Barnes says verse 19 is best translated as an "unfriendly taking hold of."[81] Verse 19 also states that Paul was taken before a *tribunal*, the *Areopagus*, and *interrogated*. Paul gives a defense which not only connects the judges with his evangelistic message (the "unknown God" in verse 23), but also brilliantly *defends the legal charge* by asserting that the God he worshiped and was proclaiming was already inscribed on an Athenian altar! Verse 27, "As some of your own poets have said," can also be seen as a legal argument for the proposition that Paul was not teaching a new religion, evidenced by his appeal to authorities that his audience would have recognized.

A final evidence of the forensic thrust of the Athenian encounter is verse 31 which is not just evangelistic: "He has appointed a day on which He will judge the world in righteousness by the Man whom He has ordained. He has given assurance of this to all by raising Him from the dead." God is a "judge" who will decide "justly" through Jesus and has "proved" this by raising Jesus. Although he is on trial, Paul has told the Areopagus that *they* will face judgment. Although Paul's Athenian trial ends inconclusively, certainly Theophilus is being told that the most sophisticated body of philosopher/judges in the known world did not find Paul to be violating the law.

CORINTH (ACTS 18:1–21)

Luke resumes a more explicitly Jewish itinerary as Paul arrives in Corinth. Immediately he introduces two more Jewish evangelists, Aquila and Priscilla, husband and wife. In addition to asserting it, Luke establishes their Jewishness to Roman officials by a technique the modern reader will recognize. To Hitler, a Jew who believed in Jesus was still a Jew to be killed. To Emperor Claudius,[82] a Jew who believed in Jesus was still a Jew to be expelled. It can also be inferred that Aquila and Priscilla did not distance themselves from their Jewishness by asserting they were "no longer Jews" by virtue of following Jesus.

After introducing these evangelists, Luke manages to squeeze three themes words, Sabbath, synagogue, and Jews into one sentence (18:4), and then he reiterates that theme in verse 5 by stating that Paul "devoted himself _exclusively_ to preaching, testifying to the Jews that Jesus was the Messiah." As usual, opposition arose, but this time Paul, in a gesture of protest, declares, "Your blood be upon your own heads; I am clean. _From now on I will go to the Gentiles._"[83] (emphasis added) To the non-lawyer, it might seem strange that Luke would include this quotation in his argument. It could be used to support an argument that Paul has left Judaism and joined or started a new religion. Why did Luke include it when he could have omitted it? The overall context suggests three reasons, any one or combination of which would help Paul's legal case:

1. Paul's accusers may have already quoted this or similar remarks by him to show that Paul had left Judaism. Because the words were true and verifiable, they needed to be addressed and explained in context, lest they be construed as an admission of the false charge of creating a new religion.

2. Luke anticipated the possibility that this or a similar statement by Paul could later surface as a refutation of this defense brief. Since this brief may have been Luke's best opportunity to gain the attention of Roman officials, it would seem best to face the statement and put "I will go to the Gentiles" in context of evangelism to the Jews. The two following sentences show that Paul went _next door_ to the synagogue to meet at the house of a God-worshiping Roman, Titius Justus, and took the leader of the synagogue with him.

3. The theme of universality is furthered by Paul's declaration, "I will go to the Gentiles," and that theme is consistent with Luke's defense: Judaism, knowledge of God, and salvation through his Messiah was destined by God to become universally available.

LUCIUS JUNIUS GALLIO

After Paul's declaration, Luke introduces Gallio, proconsul of Achaia, into the narrative. Lucius Junius Gallio would have been _very well known_ to other Roman officials. He was the son of Seneca the Elder and brother of Seneca the Younger, the philosopher. Gallio was also uncle of the poet Lucan, who was the son of his brother, Mela.[84] Gallio's brother, Seneca the Philosopher, praised him as "No mortal is so agreeable to any one person as this man is to everyone."[85] Thus Gallio was well known _and well liked_. Bruce Winter observes: "Gallio was a noted jurist in his day with very important imperial connections. He was named by Claudius [the emperor preceding Nero] in [an] inscription at Delphi as 'my friend and proconsul'".[86]

Seneca the Philosopher was, not coincidentally, one of Nero's two primary advisers as _Acts_ was being written and until he retired in A.D. 62. Gallio probably became proconsul on July 1, A.D. 51 and did not serve long.[87] Nevertheless, the great prestige which would have flowed from his family credentials, his high office, *and particularly his connection, through Seneca, to Nero* made the citation of the decision he reaches in chapter 18 a powerful legal precedent. Further, Gallio was still alive as *Acts* was written[88] and his brother, Seneca, was still in power.

Consequently, Luke is writing an account which he knows can be verified and apparently hopes will be checked. The first part of the attack made on Paul before Gallio in Corinth sounds a lot more familiar to modern Americans than the rioting and beatings recounted earlier in *Acts* as responses to Paul's preaching: instead of rioting, the opponents in Corinth filed a lawsuit! We are told of plaintiffs (certain Jews), a defendant (Paul), a court, a judge (Gallio), charges ("This man . . . is persuading the people to worship God in ways contrary to the [Roman][89] law), and a decision without a trial: case thrown out of court for lack of jurisdiction.

First observe the charge: "persuading the people to worship *God* [not *the Gods*] in ways contrary to the law." Paul was not being accused of wrong teaching concerning the Roman pantheon of deities; rather, the charge under Roman law appears to be *religio illicita*. Also, the law against illegal assembly, *collegium illicitum*, was probably invoked. Remember that *Jewish assemblies* were exempt from that law. Luke's mention of believers meeting next door to the synagogue, at the house of a God-fearer, and with the synagogue ruler, makes sense in that light.[90] Gallio's decision supports these interpretations:

> "If you Jews were making a complaint about some misdemeanor or serious crime, it would be reasonable for me to listen to you. But since it involves questions about words and names and your own law—settle the matter yourselves, I will not be a judge of such things. So he had them ejected from the court."[91]

For Luke, Gallio's decision functions as legal precedent. As an American lawyer before the U. S. Supreme Court might argue: "A learned federal judge in Boston has already heard a similar complaint and thrown it out of court. His reasoning merits your respect!" As *Acts* progresses from chapter 18, Luke increasingly shifts his brief from a statement of facts and background to an argument of law relying on legal precedent. The logic of modern legal writing is exactly the same: First, give necessary background, next, recite facts relevant to the particular controversy, then, use reason and precedents (law) to argue. Because Luke's assertions are so verifiable concerning Gallio's decision, they ring true.

An interesting sidebar to Luke's argument is his implication Gallio was derelict in permitting a subsequent breach of the peace by allowing the synagogue ruler, who was probably a believer in Jesus (see 1 Corinthians 1; he may well have been the same Crispus mentioned in Acts 18:8) to have been beaten by the anti-Messianics.[92] Why would he undermine the credibility of a judge who has ruled in favor of his "client"? The answer is probably that Gallio's nonresponse to the beating was *consistent* with his ruling. Because the Jews were afforded a measure of self-governance under Roman authority, both those who beat Sosthenes in front of Gallio, and Gallio himself, were, by their respective actions and inaction, implicityly acknowledging that the dispute was purely an internal Jewish matter.

Evangelists Priscilla, Aquila, and Apollos (Acts 18:19–27)

Paul's next stop is Ephesus.[93] Luke may have been relieved to report that no disputing much less persecutions or riots occurred, but only reasoning in the synagogue with the Jews and an open invitation to return, with not a Gentile mentioned. Certainly, this Ephesian interlude underscores that not everywhere did Paul's preaching arouse civil unrest. Moreover, by recounting that Paul traveled with team evangelists Priscilla and Aquila and that he left them in Ephesus, Luke asserts that Paul's ministry was not "hit, riot, and run."

Paul then returns to Antioch in Syria.[94] The second missionary journey ends and the third is beginning. Jews all over the empire have accepted Jesus as Messiah as have many Gentiles. Antioch was a leading city of the empire, cosmopolitan and influential. The introduction of Apollos as a "Jew," a "native of Alexandria" (a commercial and intellectual center of the empire), a "learned man" with a "thorough knowledge of the Scripture," together with the previous introduction of Priscilla and Aquila, furthers several legal objectives:

1. Showing that the spread of the gospel was a **Jewish endeavor**.

2. Showing that Paul was not a singular "troublemaker, but one of many evangelists crisscrossing the empire **spreading faith, not rebellion**.

3. Reemphasizing at this faith, based upon verifiable historical occurrences (particularly the Resurrection which climaxes *Luke* and introduces *Acts*) was not just received by uneducated fishermen and impressionable Gentiles, but **convinced a broad cross-section** of Jews, who were well positioned to question and investigate it.

4. (Possibly) **introducing Apollos** as a witness for Paul's trial in Rome.

---

1 See Acts 18:24–25.
2 Acts 15:36—16:41.
3 Acts 15:36.
4 Acts 15:37.
5 Acts 9:27.
6 Acts 11:22.
7 Acts 11:27.
8 Acts 14:14.
9 Acts 15:13.
10 E.g., Acts 14:11, 19.
11 Acts 16:1.

12 Ibid.

13 Ibid.

14 Ibid.

15 Acts 16:2.

16 Acts 16:3.

17 Ibid.

18 Rom. 16:21.

19 1 Cor. 4:17.

20 2 Cor. 1:1.

21 Phil. 1:1.

22 Col. 1:1.

23 1 Thess. 1:1.

24 2 Thess. 1:1.

25 Heb. 13:23. This passage raises the possibility that Timothy may also be facing charges as *Acts* is written.

26 Acts 21:21; see Acts 6:14.

27 Acts 16:5.

28 Acts 16:7.

29 Acts 16:10.

30 *Prima facie* evidence is evidence which, on its own, proves a point unless rebutted by stronger evidence furnished by the other side; e.g., "His Wisconsin birth certificate was *prima facie* evidence of his U. S. citizenship."

31 Despite decades of scholarly speculation to the contrary, the traditional conclusion that the "we" includes Luke is still the most plausible explanation because every alternative theory has been shown to be flawed. See Stanley E. Porter, "The 'We' Passages" in *Acts in Graeco-Roman Setting*, 545–74.

32 See Acts 24:19.

33 Luke 1:1–4.

34 Norman Geisler and Thomas Howe, *When Critics Ask* (Colorado Springs: Victor, 1992), 385. Also see Lee Strobel, *The Case for Christ* (Grand Rapids: Zondervan, 1998), 98.

35 Acts 16:13.

36 Acts 24:5.

37 Acts 16:21.

38 Rom. 11:1.

39 Acts 16:22.

40 One noted scholar of *Acts*, Brian Rapske, reaches an opposite conclusion: That the crowd is portrayed as more orderly than the owners who "seized Paul and Silas and dragged them." He argues that the crowd functioned in a quasi-judicial capacity: "*Roman jurisprudence showed an awareness of the assembly*, as evidenced by the impact of the presence and action of the people in cases where one's Roman citizenship might be appealed." (emphasis added) Although Rapske may be right, both his interpretation and mine show that another of Luke's details, "the crowd joining in," is seen to have been included more for the benefit of a legal minded reader than for a Christian reader. Rapske, *Paul in Roman Custody*, 121–3.

41 David Fiensy, "The Composition of the Jerusalem Church" in *Acts in Palestinian Setting*, 224.

42 Col. 3:11; Gal. 3:28; see Philem. 16.

43 E.g., Luke 6:31, Philem. 15–16.

44 Jacob 2:1–4.

45 Acts 16:16–21.

46 Acts 16:26.

47 Acts 16:35.

48 Acts 16:38.

49 Ibid.

50 Acts 16:23.

51 Rapske, *Paul in Roman Custody*, 129–34.

52 Acts 17:2.

53 Ibid.
54 Acts 17:2. The New Covenant Greek scriptures did not exist. The few that may have been written would not then have been recognized as "scriptures" and thus would carry no authority.
55 Acts 17:3.
56 Luke is not interested in quoting Scripture at this point, although Paul was probably teaching from Isaiah 53. On the subject of the Jewishness of resurrection, Luke has already quoted Psalm 16:8–11 in Peter's first speech (Acts 2:25–28) and so is skipping supporting biblical passages in Acts 17 to avoid detracting from his main point: Judaism taught that a Messiah would come and be resurrected.
57 Acts 17:5–6.
58 Acts 5:17.
59 Acts 7:9.
60 Acts 13:45.
61 E.g., 2 John 7–11, Jude 3–21.
62 Acts 17:6.
63 Irina Levinskaya, "God-Fearers: The Literary Evidence" in *Acts in Diaspora Setting*, 117.
64 Acts 17:5–6.
65 Acts 5:28.
66 Acts 21:21; see Acts 6:13–14.
67 John 11:49, 18:14.
68 Luke 4:5–8.
69 Luke 6:20 (i.e., not the kingdom of Caesar).
70 Luke 6:27.
71 Luke 17:21.
72 Luke 20:25.
73 Luke 22:50–52.
74 Acts 17:10.
75 Acts 17:9.
76 Acts 19:29, Acts 20:4.
77 Acts 17:17.
78 Tim. 1:8.
79 2 Tim. 2: 9–10.
80 T. D. Barnes "An Apostle on Trial," *Journal of Theological Studies* 22 (1969): 412. See also Gill, "Achaia," *Acts in Graeco-Roman Setting*, 447.
81 Ibid., 414.
82 Acts 18:2.
83 Acts 18:6.
84 Bruce, *New Testament History*, 316.
85 Seneca, Nat. Qurest. 4a, praef. 11, quoted in Bruce, ibid., 316.
86 Bruce Winter, "Gallio's ruling on the legal status of early Christianity" (Acts 18:14–15) *Tyndale Bulletin* 50.2 (1999): 213.
87 Ibid., 316.
88 Ibid., 316.
89 The accusers would not have brought a case of Jewish law violation before Gallio but rather attempted to acquire jurisdiction by framing the charges under Roman law. David Gill and Bruce Winter, "Acts and Roman Religion," *Acts in Graeco-Roman Setting*, 100, agree that "the ultimate intention of Jewish leaders in Jerusalem and the Diaspora" was to have Messianic Judaism declared non-Jewish and thus illegal, a "*religio illicita.*"
90 Acts 18:7–8; Gill and Winter, ibid., 217.
91 Acts 18:14–16.
92 Acts 18:17.
93 Acts 18:18–21.
94 Acts 18:22–24.

CHAPTER 19

ACTS 18:23—20:12

THE THIRD JOURNEY:
"NEITHER THIEVES . . . NOR BLASPHEMERS."
(ACTS 19:37)

THE BAPTISM OF THE HOLY SPIRIT (ACTS 19:1–7)

The account of Paul meeting the disciples of John the Baptizer furthers none of the previously proposed legal agenda of Luke:

1. It does not particularly function to show that Paul was preaching a Jewish faith because the only allusion to the Jewishness of the Ephesian disciples is indirect: they follow John (whom the reader already knows to be a Jewish rabbi/prophet).

2. The Holy Spirit focus is not contextualized in Hebrew scriptures. Although the passages concerning the Holy Spirit found earlier in *Acts*, particularly chapters 1 and 2, are explicitly anchored by Luke in the Hebrew scriptures, here the relation to Judaism may be too minimal for a Roman investigator to appreciate.

3. No charge is made against Paul at this juncture; thus, no defense is needed.

Why then does Luke include this passage? Is a new legal argument being raised? It seems most probable to me that Acts19:1–7 is included to tell about John the Baptizer. The disciples of John, predominantly Jewish so far as we know, had spread throughout the empire and were likely to be known to any Roman official reading the brief. The faith that Paul was preaching needed to be explained in light of John's following.

The question in the mind of Theophilus may have been, "Do Paul and these messianists follow John also? Are the Nazarenes in league with John's disciples as a threat to Rome?" Alan Segal concludes, "Whether or not [the followers of Jesus and the followers of John] were overtly political movements, the Romans interpreted them as a political threat, as is evidenced by the martyrdom of the leaders of each movement."[1] By showing the tie-in between the followers of Jesus and those of John, Luke answers these questions.

This passage also gives a possible explanation for Luke's inclusion of the details about John (his miraculous birth and recognition of Jesus while still in the womb) found in Luke 1:3–25, 1:39–45, and 1:57–80 which are not found in the synoptic Gospels of Mark and Matthew. Also in other passages where *Mark, Matthew* and *Luke* all recount the same aspects of John's ministry, Luke adds details such as "and all mankind will see God's salvation" (e.g., the Isaiah prophecy at Luke 3:6). Such an addition furthers Luke's agenda for *Acts* in three ways. First, it reinforces his argument that God always intended Judaism to be open to all humanity through the Messiah. Hence, Paul was not preaching a "new religion." Second, it reinforces a point made implicitly in the narrative at Acts 19:3–7 that the followers of John were not a sect competing with the Christians but were serious Jews whose doctrine pointed them to Jesus but was incomplete. Third, it allows him to show that John's followers were also spiritual seekers, not revolutionaries. Remember that John's execution by Rome would have necessitated these explanations.

EVENTS AT EPHESUS (ACTS 19:8–41)

Luke's digression, if the seven preceding verses qualify as such, is short. By verse 8, Paul has returned to the venue where his "lawyer" wants him: the local synagogue, where his teaching must have been well received to have extended for three months. Despite the seemingly inevitable opposition which arises,[2] it is not violent but only obstinate and slanderous. That description of Paul's opponents in Ephesus explains why Paul, the citizen respectful of civil order whom Luke seeks to portray, does not resist but apparently moves peacefully to "the lecture hall of Tyrannus" to continue his evangelism. This lecture hall was known to Theophilus. Paul Trebilco describes it as "clearly the chief glory of the city . . . about four times the size of the Parthenon in Athens . . . As a result of its grandeur and widespread fame, the temple was a great attraction to ancient travelers."[3] Events at Ephesus would have been particularly easy to verify. Besides being the third largest city in the empire after Rome and Alexandria, Trebilco notes:

> . . . a college of *tabellarii* (messengers or couriers) was based in the city. Roman military control and the efficiency of their administration depended on rapid communications and so the Romans devised an elaborate series of communication networks. Ephesus, as a base for the college of *tabellarii*, was the centre of the Romans' communications

network for Asia and courier routes would have radiated from Ephesus to all the administrative centres of the province.[4]

The notable facts about this mission were its duration (two years), its reach ("all the Jews and Greeks in the province"), its public visibility, and the extraordinary miracles. These facts are edited to make a lawyer's point: verifiability. Any Roman official questioning the peacefulness or attendant miracles of Paul's two-year ministry in Ephesus need only have sent letters of inquiry to the local magistrates because Luke has asserted:

1. Paul was **known** to everyone.

2. He met **very openly** in a well known **public** arena.

3. The meetings went on for **two years**.

4. His teaching did **not arouse violence**.

Legal writing, even briefs as adventurous as *Acts*, can dry out. Luke has Peter and John in the temple on several occasions, and Paul in about a dozen synagogues with more synagogue and temple experiences to come. When does emphasis morph into monotony? A brief writer is motivated by two countervailing fears:

1. Putting the reader to sleep by excessive repetition.

2. Omitting any relevant fact or precedent or failing to adequately reinforce an argument.

These concerns characterize Luke's writing also but he was free of the one fetter restraining the modern attorney and writer under contract to Thomas Nelson: the page limit. Luke had the luxury of spicing up his brief with humor, he wanted it read. It is not surprising, however, that *Acts* is the longest book in the New Testament. Perhaps because it is of the genre "legal brief," all facts which might influence a judge were included; being of the subspecies "legal brief without page limit," interesting and amusing stores keep the reader's attention. Certainly, the story of the seven exorcists fleeing naked provokes a smile in any culture![5] The story is well placed also because it leads into the massive burning of sorcerer's scrolls and the spread of the word of the Lord. Both the verifiability and universality themes are furthered,[6] but most importantly, the riot[7] which explodes in Ephesus is put in context. However, before Luke explains the riot, he contrasts a peaceful, voluntary, "scroll burning."[8] Paul is at the end of his mission in Ephesus when the riot occurs or, more probably, the riot helps him decide to leave.

ROME AND RIOTERS

Of all the charges against Paul, inciting riots, more even than teaching of an "illegal" religion, would have caught Rome's attention. Rome valued order and commerce. Trebilco notes that in A.D. 59 only about three years before *Acts* was written, the Roman city of Pompeii had a riot after a gladiator show. As a result, many of the leaders of the riot were exiled and the city was barred from such shows for ten years.[9] A threat to civil order was never ignored.

From the extent to which Luke asserts Paul's nonviolence, one may reasonably conclude that Paul's accusers were not about to let Roman officialdom forget a major civil disturbance occurring in the wake of his teaching. Thus, Luke's careful detailing of Paul's lack of involvement suggests the purpose for which he wrote *Acts*. First he names the instigator of the riot at Ephesus: Demetrius.[10] Then he establishes the financial motivation of Demetrius and the rioters: loss of business. Even in the way he presents the accusations of Demetrius (people are deciding not to buy silver shrines of Artemis)[11] Luke asserts that Paul's involvement was indirect. Paul is not forcing, nor is he accused of forcing, anyone to "boycott" but his teaching is clearly persuading many that Artemis is not God.

After the riot begins and two of Paul companions are seized, Paul wants to address the crowd—the evangelist awakens to opportunity![12] Yet Luke, the defense attorney, emphasizes that other disciples kept him from the fray. Aristarchus is probably introduced by Luke because he is eventually imprisoned with Paul.[13] The reader will later learn that he accompanies Paul and Luke on the boat trip from Caesarea to Rome.[14] These known facts about Aristarchus suggest that the charges from Thessalonica (about A.D. 49) or from Ephesus (about A.D. 55) may have caught up with him, and most importantly with Paul, in Caesarea in A.D. 59 or in Rome as *Acts* is being written.

Luke then mentions that provincial officials, "asiarchs,"[15] were friends of Paul and begged him not to enter the theater.[16] Why this detail? If Luke is writing to believers, it does little to further a catechistic agenda. However, if Luke is stressing the political aspects of a legal argument, the mention of Paul having friends in high places probably shows Paul had the approval of the local authorities who would be as concerned as Rome was with civil order.

As explained earlier, law as "abstract justice" does not appear to be a Roman concept. Rather, the legal system kept social order. Strip away naive rhetoric from other legal systems and notice: the law functions to resolve disputes and put criminals in jail and, regrettably, the rich and powerful often get more "justice" than the poor and weak. Consequently, in Acts 19:31 and elsewhere, Luke may be asserting the political connections of Paul to help win his acquittal and/or as a counterweight to opponents who may be using political connections to influence Paul's conviction.

ALEXANDER

Ironically, Alexander, a Jew,[17] and certainly not a follower of Jesus because he is not called a disciple and because Luke says, "The Jews pushed Alexander to the front," gets treated roughly by the crowd.[18] Why does Luke introduce Alexander when he has no other mention in Acts? If Luke were writing to believers, would they care about Acts 19:33–34 much less need to know his name? As a Jew, Alexander was not appreciated by the idol worshipers or the guild of idol makers. The protesters saw no difference between Paul, the Jew, or Alexander, the Jew. All Jews were seen as against idol worship and, therefore, the mob shouted him down. The accusation that Paul was preaching an illegal religion is consequently addressed because the rioters saw him and his message as being as Jewish as the other Jews. Luke also is noting that the uproar is over the anti-idolatry of Judaism in general not just the anti-idolatry of Jewish Christianity. Most importantly, Alexander was probably a witness against Paul in his trial at Rome (see chapter on trial witnesses). Hence, Luke needed to identify him and show he was more involved than Paul and was equally rejected by the crowd.

The naming of Demetrius and Alexander and the reference to the unnamed city clerk (Paul may have forgotten or not known his name) also further the theme of verifiability. The clerk's most important functions in the narrative, however, are to remind Theophilus that:

A. *Law is paramount* in Roman society.

B. As official record keeper[19] of Ephesus, Rome can ask him or check *contemporaneous records* to see if Paul was involved.

C. If Paul had broken any law, he could have been arrested or taken to court (but he was not because he followed the law).

Thus Paul is "acquitted" by the city clerk through lack of prosecution. Although this "acquittal" is not a legal precedent in the modern sense, it certainly functions in *Acts* as an attempt to persuade the reader of the innocence of Luke's client.

MACEDONIA, GREECE, AND EUTYCHUS
(ACTS 20:1–12)

Luke makes sure to recount Paul's immediate departure after the riot in Ephesus. Where his presence could cause trouble, Luke, the legal defender, often shows that Paul walks away (or allows the disciples to take him away) from the fight.[20] Even though he has the right to remain, Luke's client avoids violence. Paul's peaceable travel through Macedonia and Greece is disturbed only by a plot against him by certain Jews. Paul avoids that confrontation too and ends up at Troas[21] where one of the most remarkable miracles of his ministry occurs. Yet, the resurrection of Eutychus is related almost routinely.

From the use of "we" in verse 7, we deduce that Luke, the physician, is still with Paul. As a physician, this miracle presumably was of particular interest. However, instead of exalting Paul, Luke appears to be poking fun at his going "on and on" and putting at least one listener into a deep sleep. The actual miracle is told in one verse and then Paul has some food and resumes teaching! Is this legal writing? Is a conceivable point being made to a skeptical judicial audience?

Actually, Luke may be doing several things in this passage. Simultaneously, he is showing that God has invested Paul with the authority to raise the dead by paralleling the resurrection in Paul's ministry with the only account of a resurrection performed by another apostle, that of Peter.[22] And, with a touch of humor, he is showing that Paul is a regular type of fellow—boring a young man to death then raising him up! Luke certainly makes an effort throughout *Acts* to create a sympathy for Paul in the heart and mind of the reader. Does he do this because his readership is Roman officials who may not be predisposed to like Paul because he is a Jew, or because his reader is a Christian who needs to be convinced Paul is likeable?

Also, Luke again aggressively asserts verifiability. A miracle of this magnitude makes Paul no ordinary Roman prisoner. Luke's assertion is sure to arouse major skepticism among a judicial readership but rather than avoid creating such a reaction by simply omitting the story, Luke specifies the town, name of the young man, and occasion.

The "lawyer as witness" is unusual, of course, but it only underscores Luke's confidence. If Roman officials investigated this story further (as could be anticipated with a claimed miracle of this magnitude) and found it concocted, Luke would, at best, find himself in prison with Paul and quite likely facing execution. If the account was investigated and corroborated, then Luke could expect that the credibility of his account of the life of Jesus would be enhanced.

The humanization of Paul on which Luke focuses in the preceding verses, continues apace as Paul journeys back near Ephesus.[23]

---

1   Segal, *Paul the Convert*, 110.

2   Acts 19:9.

3   Trebilco, "Asia" in *Acts in Graeco-Roman Setting*, 323.

4   Ibid., 309.

5   Acts 19:13–16.

6   Acts 19:10, 17–20.

7   Acts 19:23–41.

8   Trebilco, "Asia," 315, observes that this particular incident would stand out due to its noncoercive nature in contrast to "virtually all of the accounts [of book seizures/burnings] in the Graeco-Roman period." Presumably, a Roman official concerned with civil order would take note of the greatly different behaviors produced by adherence to Messianic Judaism and Artemis worship.

9   Trebilco, "Asia," 345.

10   Acts 19:24.

11   The Artemis cult would have been known to some Roman officials from forty years earlier. In A.D. 23 they voted to deny Ephesus the honor of having the second temple in the province of Asia dedicated to worship of the emperor because the "state worship" was considered to already center on the cult of Diana [Artemis]. Trebilco "Asia," 327. Twenty years later [A.D. 44]

the temple of Artemis was censured by the Romans and put under regulations due to apparently pervasive corrupt practices. Ibid., 343–4.

12 Acts 19:30.
13 Col. 4:10.
14 Acts 27:2.
15 See generally R. A. Kearsley, "The Asiarchs," in *Acts in Graeco-Roman Setting,* 363–76.
16 Acts 19:31.
17 Acts 19:33.
18 Acts 19:34.
19 Trebilco, "Asia," 351.
20 See Acts 19:9; 17:14; 16:40; 15:2; 14:20.
21 Acts 20:6.
22 Acts 9:40.
23 Acts 20:13–38.

CHAPTER 20

ACTS 20:13—21:14

"*WITH ALL HUMILITY OF MIND*"
(ACTS 20:19)

Judges and government officials, most lawyers have learned, are not just moved by logic, facts, documents, and legal arguments. Certainly politics in the trial of a prisoner as prominent as Paul could affect the outcome. Were his accusers powerful or insignificant, friends or enemies of the Roman state or of Emperor Nero? Would an acquittal of Paul weaken Roman control in the provinces or undermine the domination of the Roman state religion, previously absolute, apart from Judaism?

These, and similar considerations, transcended the guilt or innocence of a single individual. Both Paul and Luke had enough wisdom and insight into human nature to understand that the Roman legal system could fail to do justice. Even in our own American society, the most highly legalized in the history of the world, those who operate within it understand that the law is not untouched by emotions, predilections, and politics. Human systems (legal or political) ultimately are linked to humans for their success or failure, humans who, unlike Spock, love and hate, laugh and cry.

Political undercurrents abound in *Acts*, but to understand Paul's speech beginning at Acts 20:18, one must go beyond factual presentation, legal arguments, or political positioning to hear a lawyer helping a reader identify his own human experience with the friendships, laughs, failures, and tears of his client.

To introduce the speech, in verse 16, Luke takes another opportunity to emphasize the Jewishness of Paul's ministry: his urgency to reach Jerusalem (the capital of Israel) by the day of Pentecost (the Jewish holiday, also called *Shabuot*, and understood by the *Talmidei Yeshua* to symbolize the outpouring of the Holy Spirit and the beginning of the harvest of Gentiles, "nations," unto the God of Israel). It is from Acts 20:18 to 21:6, however, that the sub-theme of Paul's intimacy with and love for his disciples is elaborated. Virtually every verse can be paraphrased or summarized with emotion:

20:18	how I lived with you.
19	humility and tears amidst persecution.
20	putting the interests of the disciples first.
22	compelled by the Spirit to an uncertain future.
23	facing prison and hardship.
24	a life laid down for others.
25	I will never see you again.
28	watch over yourselves, my children, and my grandchildren.
29	protect them from savage wolves.
30	even our friends will betray us.
31	tears day and night.
32	I leave you in God's hands.
33–4	You know love, not money, was what drove me; you see my hands with which I supported myself.[1]
35	I helped the weak and so must you.
36	kneeling together in prayer.
37	weeping, embracing, and kissing.
38	grief and farewell.
21:1	tearing away.
4	more urging not to go.
5–6	time to go; separation from families; prayer and good-byes.

This passage is Luke's plea to the heart, the implicit argument of which can be restated as: "You who sit in judgment, as you have human tenderness and compassion, see this man as a man like you. He is not a lawbreaker much less a rebel, but a Jew moved by the love of God shown by Jesus crucified to tell that this love is available to Jews and Gentiles alike through faith in Him. I do not argue for mercy because he is not guilty. Rather, I appeal to the love of truth within you to focus on the facts; do not be swayed by false accusations, prejudgments you have made against Jews or Christians, or even by supposed political expediencies of Rome." Also, Luke utilizes a dramatic technique frequently favored in romantic films of the '30s. Two lovers stand by a train. One is departing. The conductor signals. Do not our hearts agonize over separation? Roman officials from an earlier era of transportation would well have appreciated "the tide which stays for no man"[2] and felt that surging emotion.

Lest his point be missed, Luke continues his depiction of Paul as a loving and beloved teacher. Paul doesn't stay with "disciples" but with "brothers."[3] When he arrives at the house of Philip in Caesarea (on the way to Jerusalem), he receives a powerful warning from the prophet Agabus who predicts Paul's imprisonment when he goes to Jerusalem.[4] Luke uses this meeting to further his agenda:

A. The people "plead" with Paul not to go; Paul responds, "What do you mean by weeping and breaking my heart? For I am ready not only to be bound, but also to die at Jerusalem for the name of the Lord Jesus."[5] Paul is a man consumed with speaking Truth even at the cost of his own life. His message and these events are true; the charges against him are false.

B. The declaration of Paul in verse 13 also epitomizes what Acts and the New Testament Epistles show to be the attitude of Paul as he prepared to face trial. Luke is asking Theophilus to hear: "For I am ready not only to be bound, but also to die [in Rome] for the name of the Lord Jesus."

C. He reminds that the struggle remains one among Jews: "the Jews of Jerusalem ... will hand him over to the Gentiles."[6] It is not Paul but his accusers who bring a religious dispute before Nero.

D. Boldly, he reminds any Roman official who would read over Theophilus's shoulder that Paul is under authority. Paul's declaration, "I am ready ... to die ... for the name of the Lord Jesus," tells the reader that Nero may judge the prisoner but the prisoner has and will conduct himself in accordance with God's higher purposes. The implicit plea and warning to the reader is that he likewise would do well to encounter and follow this God.[7]

E. Luke is asserting that Paul before Nero will be like Jesus before the Sanhedrin, Pilate, and Herod Antipas in Luke 22:66—23:9 in that truth will not be subordinated to expediency.

Having revealed Paul's heart, Luke now invites his reader to accompany the apostle to Jerusalem and a series of dramatic confrontations.

---

1   See the defense concerning handling of finances.
2   Diary of Plymouth Colony Governor William Bradford.
3   Acts 21:7.
4   Acts 21:8–14.
5   Acts 21:13.
6   Acts 21:11.
7   As has been noted, the earthquake which opened the Philippian jail, the Resurrection of Jesus itself, and the continual reference of Luke to verifiable events all reinforce the plea and warning.

147

CHAPTER 21

ACTS 21:15—22:22

"*LISTEN NOW TO MY DEFENSE*"
(ACTS 22:1)

PAUL'S ARRIVAL (ACTS 21:15–26)

Paul's arrival at Jerusalem to stay with Mnason and his meeting with Jacob and all the elders is the next step in a narrative which has become *very detailed regarding location*. From Acts 20:3 to the end of *Acts* everyplace Paul went is named. The time span of about five years includes two jail stays of about two years each.[1] As suggested, evangelists elsewhere in the empire also may have been evoking tumultuous responses, and the chances of them being laid on Paul were apparently not remote. For example, the remark of the Roman commander who arrests Paul, "Do you speak Greek? ... Aren't you the Egyptian who started a revolt and led four thousand terrorists out in the desert some time ago?"[2] suggests that Paul may have faced some wild and absurd accusations from other quarters. Since Luke could neither know every accusation circulating against Paul nor anticipate every accusation which could be presented at trial, it made sense both to *defuse* them generally with humor and to *preclude* them through the details of Paul's itinerary.

The meeting with Jacob and the elders has essential forensic applications. First, the elders declare how thousands of "zealous for the law" Jews have believed. Luke wants Theophilus to know that the faith in Jesus remains Jewish completely. Also, the mention of the meeting itself reiterates that an alternative authority structure exists within Judaism to declare the meaning of faith in the God of Abraham. The priests as possessors of the temple and the Sanhedrin by virtue of tradition had presumptive authority to declare whether Paul or the *Talmidei Yeshua* were Jews.

Against this backdrop, Luke must argue skillfully that his "government in exile" is legitimate: this government is in Jerusalem, it is organized, it leads many zealous-for-the-law Jews, it was established by God[3] as Luke has already shown, and most importantly for this passage, the Jerusalem elders exercise authority over the Gentiles. In fact, the authority exercised (abstain from food sacrificed to idols and the meat of strangled animals and from sexual immortality) is exactly the type of authority that supports Luke's legal and evangelistic arguments:

A. The **salvation through Jesus** which God has revealed **centers on faith in him** rather than *Torah* observance. A sophisticated Roman official aware of the pervasive legal system of contemporaneous Jewish practice must have been astonished that these "Way" followers could call themselves Jews and impose so few rules on their Gentile brothers.

B. The directives of the Jerusalem Council[4] to Gentile Christians were based on instructions given in Leviticus 17 and 18 for aliens living among the Israelites.[5] In Acts 15:19–21, Jacob summarized the Leviticus provisions. If Luke were writing to a Gentile Christian or a seeker, he would have had a *huge* incentive in Acts 15 or Acts 21 to explain the theological justification for those instructions. That he fails to do so evidences that his **reader is not concerned with such theology**.

Paul was being accused of leading Jews, who live among the Gentiles, "away from Moses."[6] The charge which the elders said was being made in Jerusalem is one of the charges Paul, the prisoner, faced as Luke wrote *Acts*. Of course, the charge being leveled in Jerusalem was not intended primarily as forensic when made; rather, it was intended to discourage Jerusalem Jews from considering the possibility that Jesus was the Messiah. Likewise, the response of Paul in taking purification rites was not originally intended to provide legal cover but was to show the unbelieving Jewish community that these "Nazarenes" remained Jews in heart and custom and faithful to the teachings of Hebrew scripture even as they rejected pharisaic and priestly authority. The legal reason Luke includes this charge here is to take one more occasion to cite evidence disproving it.

PAUL'S ARREST (ACTS 21:27–36)

Apparently, the plan of the elders had the desired effect initially because Paul and the four men with him were unhindered in the temple for several days. Because the assault on Paul did not come from observant Jerusalem Jews, Luke has allowed for the inference that nonviolent dialogue occurred. Taking purification rites, however, had an inherent risk. To the extent Paul publicized his Jewishness, he also publicized his presence. It is Jews from the provinces of Asia Minor who see Paul in the temple and incite the riot. The persecution Paul had received in the provinces and the previous assassination attempt in Jerusalem[7] made his act of going to the temple life-threatening. In fact, the prophecy from Agabus of his capture and handing over to the Romans[8] may have even been a comfort—at least he wouldn't be killed! Luke, the lawyer, now countercharges Paul's opponents:[9]

A. They **stirred up** the crowd, with shouting.

B. They **seize** Paul.

C. They **falsely accuse** Paul of teaching against the Jewish people and Jewish temple.

D. They **mistakenly accuse** him of bringing non-Jews (Greeks) into the temple.

E. Without trial or any legal process, they **attempt to kill him.**

F. Luke is implying that the **riot and attempted murder were premeditated,** in that the perpetrators had seen Paul in the city earlier in the week and thus had opportunity to ask for his arrest if he had broken any civil law.

This passage is a powder keg for a legal defender. From his own experience, Paul knew his mere presence could arouse violent opposition. Roman officials knew Jerusalem teetered continually on the edge of explosion. [10] Reading *Acts*, one of the first questions from an investigator would be, "Luke, Paul knew his presence created turmoil and he knew Jerusalem was particularly volatile. Why didn't he just stay away?" Rather than face such a question, an attorney would edit this passage from his brief—why attack the opposition when the attack could backfire? The only explanation for its inclusion consistent with the premise of this book is that Paul, in Rome, was being charged with inciting this riot in Jerusalem. Therefore, Luke has to answer these charges squarely and he does so in Acts 21:27 through 22:22.

PAUL'S SPEECH TO THE CROWD— (ACTS 21:37—22:22)

Ancient authors often quoted speeches of others in their works. The objective was not to capture a speech in its entirety or verbatim, but to be faithful in conveying the true sense of the speaker's message. [11] In contrast to the dialogue before the Sanhedrin in Acts 23:1–9, it is unlikely Paul's speech to the crowd in Jerusalem was recorded contemporaneously even in abstract. Nevertheless, Luke has reconstructed and edited Paul's speech, perhaps from Paul's own recollection, to serve broader purposes. Its overall message is Paul's conversion retold to Luke's readers (primarily for evangelistic purposes), with the exclamation point in Acts 22:21 (primarily for forensic purposes) that faith in Jesus did not upset the Jewish crowd so much as did inclusion of Gentiles into God's plan! While surely one can enjoy from afar the broad effect of Luke's and Paul's literary architecture, true appreciation of the construction of his speech comes from a metaphorical building tour.

1. **Respect** is the entranceway.

2. **Humor** is the decoration.

3. **Jewishness** is the framework.

4. **Witnesses and evidence** are the roof and walls.

5. **Jesus** is the foundation.

<u>Respect</u>: Paul first shows deference by asking the commander for permission to speak to him.[12] Then he asks permission to address the crowd.[13] When he speaks, it is with great courtesy, "Brothers and Fathers,"[14] and in their native Aramaic language rather than the foreign Greek that many of them knew. So as we enter the speech, we note that Luke wants his audience to see the difference between an evangelist and a provocateur.

<u>Humor</u>: Paul is mistaken by the commander for an Egyptian rebel leader! Given Paul's emphatic nonviolence in the face of numerous assaults and given his learnedness, the reader would immediately see the irony of the commander's assumption. If Paul was slightly built and/or his eyesight severely myopic as many scholars have concluded, and if these conditions were known to Theophilus, especially if he had seen him, then the humor of the misidentification would have been especially apparent.

<u>Jewishness</u>: The reader hears that Paul is Jewish![15] Haven't we heard that before? Next, the reader is told that Paul is Jewish![16] Could Luke be trying to make a point? In the unlikely event any reader could miss his emphasis, Luke then quotes Paul in giving his Jewish credentials:

A. As a **student** of Gamaliel.

B. As a **persecutor** of the Way.

C. As **authorized** by the high priest and council.

Subsequent to his encounter on the road to Damascus, he is instructed more fully by Ananias who is described as a "devout observer of the law" and "highly respected by all the Jews living there."[17] Paul returns to Jerusalem and is praying in the temple and arguing with God when the Lord cuts him off with the words which, when repeated in Paul's speech, will put the crowd back into a frenzy.

<u>Witnesses</u>: The bricks, mortar, and roofing of the oratory are witnesses and evidence. A legally discerning reader would recognize these assertions:

A. Paul, himself, **a former persecutor,** now a **witness**.

B. The high priest and the **council as witnesses**; paraphrase: "You can ask them yourselves."[18]

C. Letters, **written evidence,** authorizing the persecution.

D. **Paul,** himself, **as witness** to his encounter on the Damascus Road.

E. Companions as **witnesses saw the light**.[19]

F. **Ananias, a witness.**

    G. The **Jews in Jerusalem as witnesses**, who knew of Paul's persecuting the Messianics.[20]

    H. **Stephen, as witness** (martyr).

<u>Jesus</u>: To finish the metaphor, Jesus is the foundation of the speech. He is the focal point and primary speaker in the narrative. Five times he is quoted in Luke's synopsis of Paul's defense. His words to Paul convey to the Roman reader (as opposed to the Jerusalem listener):

    A. That his persecutor, Paul, and by implication, the persecutors of Paul, **do not understand their own motivations**: "Saul! Saul! Why do you persecute me?"[21]

    B. That he, **Jesus, is the Messiah**. "Who are you, Lord?" I asked. "I am Jesus of Nazareth whom you are persecuting," he replied.[22] The Messianic identification for the reader is reinforced by the words of Ananias calling him "the Righteous One."[23]

    C. That Paul is on a **preordained mission** from God, not on his own campaign: "go into Damascus. There you will be told all that you have been assigned to do."[24]

    D. Paul's testimony to the identity of Jesus **would be rejected**, perhaps violently. "Quick!" he said to me. "Leave Jerusalem immediately, because they will not accept your testimony about me."[25]

    E. The message **will reach the Gentiles** through Paul: "Go, I will send you far away to the Gentiles."[26]

Each of the components of the speech, respect, humor, Jewishness, witnesses, and Jesus and each of statements of Jesus, advance previously identified legal themes. Many also support the evangelism objective which I feel Luke had when he wrote this legal defense. However, those who hold to the viewpoint that *Acts* was written to a Gentile Roman *believer or believers* in Jesus must explain why Luke included certain features in Paul's speech and throughout *Acts*. Particularly: Why such a heavy emphasis and reemphasis on the Jewishness of the faith to Gentiles who already understood that the Messiah of Israel was their Lord?

As I read the New Testament Epistles whether written to predominantly Gentile congregations, to mixed congregations such as in *Romans,* or to Jews in such letters as *Hebrews* and *Jacob,* I see no signs that Gentiles were rejecting Israel's God, the Jewishness of their faith, or the Messiahship of Jesus. Scholars note several controversies and discern many fault lines in the early church, but rejection by Gentiles of the essential Jewishness they embraced to become believers is not one.[27]

The second feature of Paul's speech (also found throughout *Acts*) is the pervasive emphasis on judicial witnesses who could attest the veracity of Luke's assertions. If

Luke is writing for believers, they already are convinced of the truthfulness of Paul's message. It would be strange indeed for them to have committed their lives to the truth of his message but still require detailed and extensive proof of his innocence of breaking Roman law. Yet, in the next encounter with the commander of the Roman garrison, Paul explicitly asserts his innocence under Roman law.

1   Acts 24:27; Acts 28:30.
2   Acts 21:38.
3   Acts 1:15–26; 6:1–7.
4   Acts 21:25.
5   Lev. 17:8, 10, 12, 13, 15; 18:26.
6   Acts 21:21.
7   Acts 9:29.
8   Acts 21:10.
9   Acts 21:27–31.
10 From the analytic perspective of this book, it is inconceivable that *Acts* was written after the revolt of A.D. 66. No legal advocate could fail to contrast the peace teachings of Jesus (see Luke 6:27–30; 20:26; 22:49–51) with that assault on the enforced Roman order.
11 Conrad Gempf, "Public Speaking and Published Accounts," in *Acts in Literary Setting*, 259.
12 Acts 21:37.
13 Acts 21:40.
14 Acts 22:1.
15 Acts 21:39.
16 Acts 22:3.
17 Acts 22:12.
18 Acts 22:5.
19 Acts 22:9.
20 Acts 22:19.
21 Acts 22:7.
22 Acts 22:8.
23 Acts 22:14.
24 Acts 22:10.
25 Acts 22:18.
26 Acts 22:21.
27 The historical rejection of the essential Jewishness of faith in Jesus occurred over time; for an overview of the development of anti-Judaic theology see Elijahnet.org and Dan Gruber's *The Church and the Jews* (Hanover, N.H.: Elijah Publishing, 1997). Paul considers heart circumcision rather than physical circumcision to be essential Judaism for the Gentile.

CHAPTER 22

ACTS 22:23—23:35

PAUL, BEFORE THE COMMANDER, THE
SANHEDRIN AND JESUS:
"*CONCERNING THE RESURRECTION*" (ACTS 23:6)

After the crowd starts shouting at Paul's account of his commission by Jesus to reach the Gentiles, Luke shifts gear. *Because Luke's readers are Gentiles, the anger of the Jewish crowd against a man to whom God had spoken favorably concerning Gentiles is bound to elicit empathy.* Many would even perceive the crowd's reaction as anti-Gentile. But more than just Gentiles in general, Luke's readership, as I've proposed, is the Roman official investigating charges against Paul and other officials to whom he would show *Acts*.

Therefore, Luke segues into Paul's Roman citizenship. He eschews criticism of the centurion and commander, Claudius Lysias, who are about to flog Paul because when they learn of his citizenship they immediately desist. Rapske convincingly observes, "Paul's insinuation of, rather than insistence upon, his rights encourages two conclusions: First, Paul will not so stridently insist upon his Roman rights as to undercut his religious commitment to Judaism before Roman eyes. . . . Second, while his self-disclosure [of citizenship] indicates that he has some confidence that his Roman citizenship may make a difference in his treatment, its manner suggests that Paul is still prepared to suffer or even die without complaint (see Acts 21:13), if it is disregarded."[1]

To Rapske's analysis I would add that whereas, in Philippi, it would have been a lengthy matter to establish his citizenship (and therefore give him reason to endure flogging) in Jerusalem, his citizenship, if questioned, could have been quickly established through witnesses.[2] If Rapske's conclusion is correct, this passage shows Paul honoring God first but also respecting Roman law in its proper place as subordinate to God. This is exactly the tenor one would expect to find in a legal brief on behalf of an evangelist whose primary concern is to spread the message of salvation. This paragraph contrasts the law-respecting nature of the Romans (and by extension of Paul himself as a Roman citizen) with the disdainful attitude of his opponents.

Luke makes a lawyer's classic argument: "Your honors, Paul's accusers, when it suits their purposes, want to use the law to silence him, but when it doesn't, they ignore it. The law is to protect the law-abiding. Don't let them misuse it." This principle is widely established in one-branch of Anglo-American jurisprudence. The Equity or Chancery Courts which issue extraordinary remedies such as injunctions will often not grant an injunction even against a malfeasant defendant unless the plaintiff is also blameless, unless he has "clean hands." Luke is arguing that Paul's accusers should be prevented from pursuing the charges against him due to their own disdain of Roman law. "Their hands are dirty!" This argument is repeated and magnified as Luke recounts a hostile hearing before the Sanhedrin, a concerted murder plot, and irregular legal proceedings before two Roman governors.

THE SANHEDRIN

Connecting the riot and the assassination attempt is a mini-trial of Paul before the Sanhedrin in the presence of Lysias, the Roman commander of Jerusalem. Paul's opening statement is direct: "Men and brethren, I have lived in all good conscience before God until this day."[3] The persecution from various Jewish opponents has not drawn Paul into condemning the Jewish people at large or separating himself from them. He calls them "Brothers" and dares, with his characteristic chutzpah, to win a few over.

In contrast to Paul's assertion of good conscience, Luke recounts the high priest Ananias ordering that Paul be slapped. *Luke wants Roman officials to feel the slap.* The action of Ananias insults Roman authority because their commander has convened the parties in a quasi-judicial capacity "to find out exactly why Paul was being accused," yet his investigatory authority is immediately disrespected! Paul himself reacts by calling the high priest a "whitewashed wall" but immediately apologizes when he is informed that the man he was addressing, the man who ordered him to be slapped, was the high priest, the holder of an office due respect according to Hebrew scripture.[4]

This encounter almost certainly would be recounted at Paul's trial in Rome: it was the last direct meeting between him and the Jewish leaders officially recognized by Rome, it followed immediately after the alleged temple desecration by Paul, and a Roman official was present who could corroborate or dispute the differing versions of the litigants. Could Paul's opponents be arguing to Rome that Paul was slapped *after* he insulted the high priest? Certainly Paul's opponents would seek to characterize any disrespect for the high priest as disrespect for *authority constituted by Rome*. Luke's explanation of these details has the hallmark of a litigant refuting or anticipating an opponent's charge. Although we may never know with certainty why Luke incorporated particular details such as these, the legal defense explanation consistently appears plausible.

Knowing that the Sanhedrin contained Sadducees and Pharisees, Paul then decides to exploit theological rifts on the issues of resurrection and angels. Soon the Sanhedrin is at odds with itself. In this passage, Luke is not concerned with the furtherance of resurrection or angelic theology. His prior accounts in *Acts* leave no doubt that both resurrection and angels are part of God's program. Rather, Luke's first point is showing that the foundational event of Christian faith, the Resurrection of Jesus, as well as the angelic appearances such as recounted earlier[5] and the one which would follow in *Acts*, were totally consistent with Jewish theology, as understood at the highest level of official Judaism (i.e., that Messianic Judaism was not an illegal new religion). Second, Luke is arguing to his Roman audience that the theological issues need to be separated from the determination of Paul's guilt because even his opponents would not agree among themselves on major points. Luke's third point is that even among the most educated and presumably mature Jewish leadership the passions on these issues led to violence. It is the Roman commander, detached from the emotions of the dispute who saves Paul again!

Along with the legal points, Luke has an additional incentive to recount this confrontation. Because the Sanhedrin had at least two scribes to record the proceedings at every session,[6] Theophilus will immediately recognize that a written record to verify Luke's account does exist. If he chose to investigate this episode, as any professional pretrial investigator for the Roman emperor would,[7] then this is the best set of facts from which to present an argument: facts memorialized by a contemporaneous written record created by the opposition! More importantly, if the record *contradicts* Luke's account, for example by stating that Paul was violent, then such a document could be used by Paul's opponents very effectively at trial. It would especially behoove Luke to refute a potentially false record.

After making his legal arguments through verse 9, Luke then tells Theophilus that the opposition, even the presumably Roman-law-respecting Sanhedrin, becomes violent. Commander Lysias must again rescue Paul from a "mob." He returns him to protective custody where he will meet with Jesus.

BEFORE JESUS

The appearance of Jesus to Paul in the night following the confrontation with the Sanhedrin may be singular in one sense. Because the entire lives of Luke, Paul, and the believers rested upon whether Jesus rose from the grave, another post-Resurrection appearance could not be fairly omitted even from a selective chronology of the early church. Luke may consider an appearance of Jesus to Paul just too important an event to omit from the "brief" even though it does not advance and may obscure his agenda. On the other hand, we have no way of knowing whether Jesus appeared on other occasions to Paul or other disciples, with such appearances omitted from *Acts*. Also we do not know if Jesus spoke other words to Paul on the particular night he appeared to Paul because Luke does not tell us. Nevertheless, we need not speculate about omitted appearances or words because the two-sentence encouragement from Jesus which is recorded is highly relevant to a Roman tribunal: "Take courage! As you have testified about me in Jerusalem, so must you also testify in Rome."

How would Luke's secondary audience, Roman officials, besides Theophilus, being asked to investigate the charges or otherwise participate in the trial, react to this account? With incredulity, fear, anger, awe? Of course, much depends on the individual. Yet they would share one viewpoint. Would not magistrates, senators, military men, lawyers, administrators, Burrus, Seneca, or Nero himself all ask, "Who is this is no-name Greek 'lawyer' from some flyspeck provincial town with his know-it-all Jewish client? How dare he say, 'This trial is now before you because the resurrected Jesus, who is God, appeared to my client one night and said it would be!'"? The further implication in verse 13 can be paraphrased as, "You are the judges but God controls proceedings from the beginning!" Such an implication is far from the deferential, if not humble, posture expected of attorneys for men on trial for their lives. Would not many Roman officials take offense, thinking: "These Jews can have their own God and believe their delusions, but when they assert that their God has control over, or even a say in our proceedings, they go too far! We make our own decisions. Jewish legions do not occupy Rome! It is Roman legions and Roman gods that rule the world!"

Is Luke committing legal malpractice by including this passage in his brief? Yes and no. If Luke does not believe his account of Jesus appearing and speaking to Paul, he is rashly risking his life by lying to save his "client"/mentor/friend. However, if Luke believes Jesus did appear, then he had good reason to be bold, even with those who held the power of life and death over Paul. *Acts* leaves no doubt that Luke and Paul completely believed Jesus was alive and directing their paths. As I argue throughout, Luke's and Paul's goal as evangelists was to evangelize. Paul's freedom probably would further that end but the means must not be allowed to obscure the goal. If Jesus did stand near Paul, Luke has a compelling reason, even contrary to his own logic, to risk offending the readers: the Lord has spoken! Because they believe Jesus really is in control, Luke decides to take his chances.

Lest the reader think I am reading too much into this passage, skip ahead to Acts 26, particularly verses 28 and 29. My understanding is that when he writes a defense brief, Luke, the disciple, had the same attitude as his rabbi, Paul. Luke shows that Paul is more concerned with convincing Gentile judges, who hold the power of life and death over him, to believe in Jesus than with his own freedom, or with telling angry Jewish crowds about Messiah than his own physical safety. In the process, Luke is revealing to us, the modern readers, his own advocacy strategy: state the facts fully, argue the law vigorously, proclaim the truth about Jesus, and leave the results both of the evangelism and the trial to Him because the Holy Spirit will reveal the truth to those determined to know it.

The drama of the appearance of Jesus immediately segues into the drama of another plot to murder Paul.

Conspiracy to Kill Paul: "Questions of Their Own Law" (Acts 23:29)

The account of the conspiracy of forty or more men to murder Paul is great both as legal argument and theater. We all know that in modern trial practice, lawyers use theatrics when appropriate to convey their point. Brief writing also affords such opportunities, albeit less frequently. The drama of Acts 23 is whether the conspirators will succeed in killing Paul through ambush before the Roman army can move him to safety, the heroism of Paul's nephew, and the humor of forty men vowing not to eat or drink until they kill Paul. The reader suspects they must be hungry! In the midst of this suspenseful account, however, Luke weaves no less than six of his legal themes:

A. <u>Internal Jewish Dispute.</u> The intended victim and the conspirators are all Jews, Paul's nephew is a Jew, and the plot immediately follows the theological dispute in the Sanhedrin and appearance of the Jewish Messiah to Paul. The inclusion of Gentiles into the Israel of God now appears to cause more tumult than the question of the messiahship of Jesus.

B. <u>Enmity to Rome.</u> The enemies of Paul are enemies of Rome: The conspirators clearly intended to shed Roman blood, if necessary to kill Paul. Their attack was coordinated with the highest levels of leadership: the "chief priest and elders."[8] If Paul had been brought to the Sanhedrin or ambushed *en route*, Roman guards would have been present and at risk of death. *Luke is, in effect, accusing the leadership not only of conspiracy to commit murder, but also of conspiracy to commit treason against Rome.* That the commander understood the threat is clear from his dispatch of two hundred soldiers to escort Paul.

C. <u>Hypocrisy.</u> At the same time, the enemies of Paul are hypocritical in using the legal system to prosecute him. The next day meeting in the Sanhedrin[9] was to be a pretext. By implication the charges pending in Rome against Paul, inciting riot or creating an illegal religion, are uses of Roman criminal law as a pretext for their theological agenda and self-interest.

158

D. **Innocence**. Regarding accusations of fomenting rebellion, Paul, in Roman custody, possibly in chains, and outnumbered forty to one, obviously cannot be the instigator of this threat to the peace!

E. **Verifiability**. These actions took place about four years before *Acts* was written. The time, place, and participants are identified. Luke quotes a key confirmatory document: a letter from Claudius Lysias, the commander of the Roman garrison in Jerusalem, to the Roman governor.[10] As a good "lawyer," Luke makes this letter what modern lawyers would call Exhibit B to his brief.[11] (The Jerusalem Council letter concerning Gentiles is Ex. A) As memories fade and recollections of events vary, nothing helps a case as much as a contemporaneous written record by a third party or government agency.[12] A letter such as that of Lysias would be expected to exist. After all, one does not rise to the level of commander of the Roman garrison in Jerusalem without being wise enough to establish some record for dispatching two hundred soldiers to the Roman governor in the middle of the night! That the letter is preserved is extremely instructive. Luke's version of the letter could be verified in Caesarea, Jerusalem, or possibly even in Rome where copies of many official reports were sent. If Luke forged or changed this letter, he and Paul would have faced execution.

F. **Legal Precedent**. The court of Caesar functioned as the highest tribunal. As with any tribunal which heard disputes from many different parts of the empire, the Roman officials would ask, "What did our lower courts say?"

Because the Roman military governance in Judea differs so considerably from the American system, no modern equivalent for the letter from Lysias exists. Its influence on and credibility to Theophilus and other judicial officials would exceed that of a police report but be less than that of a complete judicial determination. Echoing the prior decision of proconsul Gallio,[13] this report from Lysias states that Rome has *no jurisdiction* because the dispute was a matter of Jewish law (theology) and that Paul has done nothing meriting imprisonment. In fact, Paul's "defense" that the real lawbreakers are his accusers is found to be true.

The letter has a humorous sidelight which is internal and further evidence of its authenticity: Lysias gives himself credit for rescuing Paul "the Roman citizen" from the mob.[14] However, Luke far more plausibly recounts that Paul's Roman citizenship was not discovered until he was about to be flogged. Did the Roman commander learn of Paul's citizenship in the midst of a riot? Lysias is even implying he would not have rescued a man from a mob if he were not a Roman citizen, hardly commendable behavior from the man charged with keeping order! No, Lysias did not learn of Paul's citizenship while the crowd was "shouting, throwing off their cloaks and flinging dust in the air."[15] Rather, Lysias is lying to protect himself; he almost flogged a Roman citizen without trial and he feared personal repercussions.

On the question of whether the mob and the conspirators were attempting to kill Paul, Lysias and the rest of Luke's narrative agree totally.[16] The authentication internal to *Acts* of Luke's copy of the letter lies in the discrepancy concerning when Lysias learned of Paul's citizenship. If Luke were to have forged or distorted the letter, he would have strengthened his argument by having Lysias agree with his account in Acts 22:25 (Paul's question of the legality of the flogging) rather than letting the commander (one of his key "witnesses") look so foolish! Luke makes sure to note that the letter is delivered with Paul directly to the governor, Felix, who imprisons him in Herod's palace.[17] Luke provides this detail so Theophilus will know that the subsequent trial before Felix (and two-year imprisonment without verdict) was conducted by him with full knowledge of evidence fully exculpating Paul.

With the citation of Lysias' letter, the transition of *Acts* from a necessary factual background of the history of Christianity (Acts 1–12, 15) to an account of the travels and intermittent imprisonments of Paul (Acts 13–14, 16–23) and finally to the official legal proceedings against Paul (Acts 24–28) is now complete. Henceforth, no question can be raised about whether any action by Paul violates Roman law because he is always in Roman custody. Thus, Luke relaxes his recitation of facts and focuses the rest of *Acts* on Roman law and procedure and incidents which further his legal or evangelistic agenda.

---

1 Rapske, *Paul in Roman Custody*, 143.

2 See Acts 23:16.

3 Acts 23:1.

4 Acts 23:3; see 22:29 where the Roman soldiers immediately withdraw when they realize they have made a mistake.

5 E.g., Acts 12:7.

6 Rapske, *Paul in Roman Custody*, 105, footnote 197.

7 Would you enjoy being Nero's chief investigator and at Paul's trial sitting through contradictory testimony concerning this encounter? The deranged emperor, irritated by the different versions, turns to you and asks that the Sanhedrin's scribal records be read. If you have failed to request those records, how do you feel? More importantly, given the time and resources to do so, would you not have anticipated the importance of these records and obtained them?

8 Acts 23:14.

9 Acts 23:20.

10 Acts 23:26–30.

11 According to Bruce Winter, "Official Proceedings," 309, "Such a document would have been available to the Defendant."

12 Except perhaps a record created by the other side; see commentary on Acts 22:22–29.

13 Acts 18:14–15.

14 Acts 23:27.

15 Acts 22:23.

16 Compare Acts 21:31–33 with 23:27 and 23:21(b) with 23:30(a).

17 Acts 23:33–34.

CHAPTER 23

ACTS 24

PAUL BEFORE FELIX: "ALL THINGS . . . WRITTEN IN THE LAW AND PROPHETS" (ACTS 24:14)

Felix has read the letter exonerating Paul but apparently decides the situation is so important that he will have his own trial. Luke, the lawyer, is in full legal stride. When arguing an "appellate" case,[1] as Luke is when writing *Luke-Acts* to Theophilus, a lawyer draws facts and arguments also from trial transcripts of the lower court. Acts 24:2–22 and several following passages are exactly that. These "transcripts" inform the original readers of *Acts* of the exact procedures followed, evidence presented, and arguments made in the lower court.

Of course, Luke's excerpts are not complete transcripts. Much as a contemporary American lawyer would in his appellate brief, Luke has carefully selected portions of the proceedings which support his argument. His legal editing can be seen in each sentence. Paul is certainly the primary source of these accounts, although Luke and other believers may also have been present. *Official Roman records of this trial would also exist and be available to Roman investigators* and to Paul as a criminal defendant. The accusers in this case are the high priest Ananias and some elders[2] represented by a Greek or possibly Roman lawyer, Tertullus.[3]

Why is the identity of the accusers so important? And why is it so important to them to prosecute Paul? The identity matters because Luke is hammering home the point that the dispute is intra-Jewish and theological, thus beyond Roman jurisdiction. If the accusers were civil authorities or private parties claiming injury by Paul, the issues would be different. However, by introducing the accusers as plaintiffs in an official religious capacity, Luke reminds the reviewing court what the case is about before Tertullus opens his mouth. When he does speak, his introduction sounds lawyerly.[4] It is polite, deferential, flattering, and accompanied by a hallmark of authenticity: a litigator's promise of "brevity"![5]

The "three counts" of the complaint, of course, are framed to avoid theological appearance:

I. Inciting Jews to riot throughout the world.

II. Being a "ringleader of the Nazarene sect."

III. Desecrating the temple.

<u>Count I. Incitement To Riot</u> is the lead charge and, therefore, probably considered by Tertullus and his clients as most likely to succeed. Certainly, the introductory compliment to Felix, "We have enjoyed a long period of peace under you," is a not-so-subtle reminder that civil order is *job one* for a Roman governor. Luke concurs with that job description yet reminds Theophilus by citing the words of the opposition and through sarcasm of the questionable sincerity of the high priest and his entourage due to the previously noted participation of the leadership in the assassination plot against Paul.[6]

However, this charge carries much apparent credibility. Many cities where Paul preached eventually had a riot or serious civil disturbance. The gravity of that charge is evident throughout *Acts*. Luke has painstakingly detailed each civil disturbance to show how and why it arose. By the time he gets to the formal charges made through lawyer Tertullus, Luke does not detail the rebuttal given by Paul because he presumes his reader will realize they are groundless and hypocritical based upon all of the previous factual evidence compiled in the brief.

Felix had very good reason to treat the charges against Paul with extreme care. David Gill, a leading expert on *Acts*, notes that it was probably during the following two years while Paul was imprisoned at Caesarea that riots broke out between the Jewish and Greek residents over the issue of whether Caesarea was to be considered a Jewish city. *Josephus records that Felix had brought troops into the marketplace and ordered the Jews to disperse. Upon their failure to do so, many were killed and their property plundered.*[7] Consider the effect of Luke's narrative on his reader: Theophilus is reviewing a trial before a judge who Theophilus certainly knows has botched the most primary of official responsibilities. Theophilus would have instantly recognized the irony of the Tertullian flattery.

<u>Count II. The Charge Of Being A "Ringleader"</u> is similar to the rioting charge. Here is additional evidence the "Nazarenes" were associated with more civil disturbances that just those following Paul's missionary trips.

From Tertullus's charge, Luke seizes a forensic concession. A wise lawyer knows the best way to prove a case is to use admissions of the opponent who then cannot deny his own words when they are turned against him. Tertullus calls the Nazarenes a "sect." This means that these particular accusers, *which includes the high priest*, do not contend that the Jewish Christians have founded an illegal religion, but they explicitly concede they are a branch of Judaism.[8] This position contrasts to the more reckless accusers such as the Thessalonians who said, "They are defying Caesar's decrees, saying that there is another king, one called Jesus."[9] It is highly instructive that no charge is made concerning the Resurrection of Jesus. If proof of his non-resurrection did exist, such as a body or witnesses in Jerusalem who had seen it removed from the grave, here is where Paul's accusers would have raised it: "This Nazarene sect says its leader, Jesus, rose from the dead after being crucified—but you Romans, through your former Governor Pontius Pilate, disproved their lie long ago. These Christians are deceivers and madmen!"

<u>Count III. The charge of temple desecration</u> was the hottest. Luke does not quote Tertullus's description of the desecration because the charge obviously echoes Acts 21:28, "bringing Greeks into the temple area." To the extent the alleged temple desecration was a theological issue, it was unlikely to arouse the sympathy of a Roman court ("these Jews are always arguing about their god"), but to the extent the charge has civil order implications it is potent. Paraphrase: "Paul invaded the holiest place of our religion by bringing in a non-Jew. His action hurt, insulted, and infuriated every true Jew in Jerusalem. This was trespass and assault. A response was required just as surely as if he had swung his fist." While such accusations might attract the governor's interest, the problem is they were untrue (as Luke has already detailed), most certainly because of the absence of the Greek (Trophimus, Acts 21:28) or Greeks who Paul supposedly brought into the temple area and who would have been seized by the angry crowd.

Most bold in Tertullus's plea is the assertion that Paul will convict himself upon examination.[10] Why would a lawyer take such a risk? Several possible answers:

A. Tertullus has no evidence of his own so he hopes that grudging admissions by Paul will give some life to his baseless case. (I discount this explanation because his accusers apparently had some testimony to present.)[11]

B. Tertullus thought his charges were true. Paul was known as a truthful fanatic. Tertullus hoped Paul's own fanaticism would be his undoing.

C. Tertullus and his clients were stalling. They would assert that the truth of their allegations was well known in Jerusalem. If Paul denied their allegations, then they could ask the court for time to locate witnesses to contradict him.

D. Perhaps Tertullus viewed this encounter more as an opportunity for the ancient equivalent of a pretrial "discovery deposition": Paul would be examined, his alibi pinned down, and in due time, exposed as a lie at a later trial.

E. The strategy of Tertullus was actually to persuade Felix to surrender jurisdiction to the Sanhedrin.[12]

Whatever the reason for Tertullus's assertion, it failed. Paul's defense is a sharp counterattack: *"The issue is not me, it is resurrection!"* Just as Tertullus had, Paul opens with remarks which may be construed as respect or flattery. Then he launches into one of Luke's favorite themes: verifiability! Paraphrased loosely, verses 24:11–16 read: "I arrived a week and a half ago—check it out! How could I have done half the things they accuse me of! Where's the proof? Sure, I believe the Jewish scriptures and belong to a group of faithful Jews who believe Jesus rose from the dead. Is that a crime?"

Luke then invokes yet another legal principle: the right to confront witnesses against oneself.[13] Those charging Paul were from the Sanhedrin, they were not witnesses to the "temple desecration." Given the weakness of the complainants' Count III, Luke quotes Paul as focusing his argument against this count because:

A. Defense lawyers usually attack the weakest charges first. A victory against any charge both weakens the credibility of and gives a psychological discouragement to the complainant.

B. The alleged temple desecration is the most recent and closest geographically: it is the most verifiable. Paul clearly wanted the truth to come out quickly so he went on a two-part counteroffensive. His first counterargument is essentially:

1. I categorically deny any desecration.[14]

2. The charges in Count I and II are vague and concern events more distant in time and location than Count III.

3. Please investigate Count III which is at your doorstep and you will see how untrue it is.

4. You will conclude that any plaintiffs who bring such serious charges as Count III without an appropriate fact investigation (or even to have lied to the court) are also probably lying or speaking in willful ignorance concerning the substance of Counts I and II.[15]

5. Thus, you should throw this case out now or after you have investigated the riot at the temple.

The second prong of Paul's counteroffensive is jurisdictional and evangelistic: "[I have committed no crime] unless it was this one thing I shouted as I stood in their presence: 'It is concerning the resurrection of the dead that I am on trial before you today.'" As we have seen before, Luke's forensic point is that intra-Jewish theological disputes are beyond the competence of the Roman courts. He is also pointedly reminding Theophilus (as Paul was reminding Felix and his accusers) that Paul's accusers had no evidence to present at that point and that Felix ignored Roman law by allowing Paul to be partially tried without witnesses to any wrongdoing by him. Felix's response is equivocal: he "adjourned the proceedings."[16] It would not have been fair to the prosecutors to force a trial if Ananias and the complainants had witnesses who could be presented *within the next several weeks.*

For Paul's apparent benefit, Felix says he wants the commander, Lysias, to be present. Certainly, the testimony of Lysias as a presumably neutral Roman official who was to some extent an eyewitness and who investigated the facts should be most persuasive in any court.

If Felix has not realized the point as Paul speaks, the Roman officials reading Luke's brief probably have: the high priest and Jewish establishment had a major "conflict of interest" in claiming to speak for all of the Jewish people. Luke has already shown that an alternative and/or independent system of authority within Judaism and at Jerusalem had been established. If Paul, or other followers of the Way, succeed in persuading more Jews to believe in Jesus, the "establishment" would lose power, prestige, and money. Especially on the issue of the resurrection of Jesus, the ruling Jewish officials had an incentive to disregard, if not conceal, the evidence.

Luke makes two more points for Rome to consider.[17] First, that Felix was "well acquainted with the Way." Luke wants Theophilus to acquire such familiarity. That is why Luke takes such pains in *Luke-Acts* to recount the history of what we now call "the early Christian church." Theophilus needed background to investigate Paul's case properly. In contrast, Felix already had the background, even promising to decide the case when "Lysias comes," which leads to Luke's second point. By the time *Acts* was written, Paul had spent two years in Caesarea and two in Rome in prison or under house arrest. Any fair person can see that keeping a person in jail without trial for a long time is, itself, an injustice. Even if the accused is guilty, the period of imprisonment could exceed the appropriate sentence for the crime, but if the accused is not guilty, an innocent person has been punished. Consequently, Luke is complaining that Felix is more concerned about politics than truth, more about retention in office than justice.

He says Felix had everything at his disposal to decide the case, promised to decide, but instead kept Paul under arrest.

This pattern of judicial influence is not remote from the twenty-first century. Any American litigator weighs the merits of filing in state versus federal court in a politically sensitive case. Invariably, one consideration is that the federal judge is appointed for life and does not need to worry about political repercussions. A state judge, however, is usually elected or appointed for a set time. If the judge wants to stay on the bench, she could think twice or see just the evidence that suits her self-interest.

Felix was not only subject to such pressure, but also corrupt! If he convicted an innocent Roman citizen who had a dedicated following and probably the ability to press the issue of his innocence to Rome, he might lose his job when the facts came out. On the other hand, if Felix set Paul free, Paul's accusers could bring pressure to bear on Rome to have him removed. Being "well acquainted with the Way," Felix probably knew the box the chief priests had put Pilate in when Jesus was on trial for his life.[18]

To avoid both risks he puts off a decision but decides to interview Paul privately. Felix soon regrets his decision. As Paul discourses on "righteousness" and the "judgment [of God] to come," Felix begins to fear God and His judgment on unrighteousness. Thus, Luke is telling Theophilus that Felix, himself, was in a box between the Jewish leaders and possibly Rome on one side and God, Paul's followers and possibly Rome on the other side. One possible escape from the box was a bribe; if Paul gave Felix some money for his efforts, the bribe giver would be unlikely to squeal, Felix could not be nailed for convicting an innocent man, and Felix could rationalize away his fear concerning God's righteousness and judgment.

Eventually, since Paul would not bribe him, Felix leaves him under arrest for two years and, at least, Felix salvages some favor from the accusers.[19] Luke's accusation of Felix as being corrupt is risky. If Felix still holds an influential position in the Roman Empire as *Acts* is written, Luke may make a serious enemy. However, Felix's corruption probably was known to Roman officials either while he served in Caesarea or had been exposed by A.D. 62.[20] As noted previously, his failure to keep the peace certainly was known. In either event, the long incarceration of Paul without a decision was unjust in itself. Luke wants Theophilus to see that Felix broke Roman law and to prepare him to see that legal violations would continue under Festus.

---

1 In many senses, Paul's trial before Nero would not be an appeal, but a trial *de novo* (witnesses and evidence presented afresh). However, the distinction between trial and appeal would not have been as marked under the Roman system. Particularly in a trial before an egomaniac such as Nero it seems logical that he would pick and choose, based on his interest, how much of the trial he wanted to hear and to what extent he would choose to rely on decisions of his staff (such as Theophilus) and on provincial officials.

2 Acts 24:1.

3 See Rapske, *Paul in Roman Custody,* 159.

4 See Bruce Winter, "The Importance of the Captatio Benevolentiae in the Speeches of Tertullus and Paul in Acts 24:1–21," *Journal of Theological Studies* 42 (1991): 505–31.

5 Acts 24:4.

6 Acts 23:14.

7 David Gill, "Acts and Roman Policy in Judea" in *Acts in Palestinean Setting*, 24. I have paraphrased the account of Josephus from *The Jewish Wars* 2.24.

8 Steve Mason adds further import to Tertullus' words. He contends that the Greek word translated "sect" more properly means "school" in this context. That is, a school "alongside the other Jewish schools." If Mason is right, then Paul's opponents on this occasion are not arguing that Christianity is not Jewish. Steve Mason, "Chief Priests, Sadducees, Pharisees and Sanhedrin" in *Acts in Palestinian Setting*, 154.

9 Acts 17:6.

10 Acts 24:8.

11 See Acts 24:9.

12 Such a maneuver is most logical legally because it gives the opponents two opportunities to convict Paul: first before their own court, but if they cannot try him there, then before Felix. This interpretation is strongly bolstered by the variation textual reading found in the AV and NKJV (in quotes): We seized him "and wanted to judge him according to our law. But the commander Lysias came by and with great violence took him out of our hands, commanding his accusers to come to you." and by the explicit "pre-trial motion" made by the chief priests.

13 Acts 24:17–19.

14 Acts 21, 26–29.

15 The presence of Tertullus works greatly to Luke's advantage here. Judges usually give a lot more leeway to a *pro se* plaintiff because non-lawyers are most often less precise in their presentation of charges and evidence and because they are less familiar with procedural requirements, such as making sure a reasonable basis for a charge exists before bringing it before the court. Because the complainants have their own Roman lawyer, they have no such excuse. The statement of Tertullus in verse 8, "By examining him yourself, you will be able to learn the truth about all these charges we are bringing against him," is an example of the care a lawyer should take when presenting charges because it tells the court, up front, that no evidence will be presented except to use the defendant as a witness against himself. Thus, the judge is not subsequently angered when no witnesses are called. The variant reading of part of verses 6–8 is, "and even tried to desecrate the temple; so we seized him *and ordered his accusers to come before you.* By examining him yourself ..." (emphasis added) The variant implies that Tertullus can get some witnesses to back up the charges, but needs some time to do so. (If he had witnesses who were present, Tertullus's request that Felix ask Paul to prove the case against himself or Paul's demand to be confronted with his accusers make no sense.) Tertullus may not have had the time (he had at most five days and probably only a day or two) to interview witnesses. Thus, he was in the situation of any lawyer just brought into a case: He must rely on the version of the facts given by his client. It is, however, clear that he did not want to stick his neck out too far. After all, he did not know that this case would cause his name to be remembered throughout history, he only knew that he had some mega-important clients and he was going before the Roman governor. Tertullus had better speak carefully or his reputation and ability to earn a living could suffer!

16 Acts 24:22.

17 Ibid.

18 See Luke 23:2.

19 Acts 24:27.

20 Bruce, *New Testament History,* 344–6.

CHAPTER 24

ACTS 25:1–22

PAUL BEFORE FESTUS:
"*NO WRONG . . . AGAINST CAESAR*"
(ACTS 25:8)

Despite his equivocation, Felix loses his position and is replaced by Festus who, upon arriving in Judea, visits Jerusalem. Luke's initial description of Festus portrays him as diligent (immediately introducing himself to the leaders of the subject people) and fair-minded (refusing to do them the favor of changing *venue*[1]). When Luke writes of a proposed change of location he sounds like he is speaking of a recognized legal maneuver to Roman officials who understood the validity of such a move. However, when he states[2] that the purpose of the maneuver is to ambush and murder Paul, he is reminding them that the accusers of Paul fundamentally have no respect for the law or authority of Rome and only regard it as expedient to their self-interest.

After introducing Festus as fair, Luke shifts to a description in which Festus appears to be pro-[Sadducean] establishment.[3] Festus invites them to travel "with me"[4] and he spends eight to ten days "with them."[5] In modern legal terms, Luke is indicting the judge as "having numerous *ex parte* (with one side only) communications" and of giving "an appearance of partiality," both of which are serious detriments to the administration of justice. Even though Roman jurisprudence was not as developed in these areas as modern law, Luke is nevertheless appealing to principle: if a judge is "friends" with one party, how can he be trusted to be neutral?

The trial before Festus proceeds like the one before Felix in that "many serious charges" fly but no proof is established. However, the trial differs in that the accusers have no lawyer. This would be correct procedure under Roman law. The accusations are more difficult to sort out, being labeled "many serious charges" as opposed to the relative specificity of Tertullus before Felix.[6] However, the procedure is less judicial, with Luke describing the accusers as having "stood around" Paul. This behavior was a clear violation of Roman procedure which allowed only one accuser.[7] Also there appears to have been no *inscriptio* (written charges), another patent violation of Roman procedure.[8]

Paul is at a serious disadvantage in this trial because the prosecution and the judge have, so to speak, just arrived on the same bus[9] and the judge has informed him that trial is to begin at once. Paul is outnumbered, not allowed the opportunity to obtain a lawyer (another violation of Roman procedure), and not given the opportunity to line up, much less call, witnesses on his own behalf. He is able to confront his accusers but Luke does not tell us whether he is allowed to cross-examine them. The trial would be considered a sham even by primitive, not to mention Roman, legal standards. Deducing from the defense he presents, the charges against Paul appear to be the same that have been leveled against him throughout his missionary journeys and are probably the ones which follow him to Rome. Paul answers: "I have done nothing against:

A. the law of the Jews;

B. the temple; or

C. Caesar."

By this summation, Luke is again arguing: the case is principally about religious rather than civil issues and, to the extent it is civil, it is groundless. At this point Festus appears to have yielded to the impulse to gain favor in the eyes of his subjects and he, himself, suggests the "change of *venue*." Why he asks Paul about his willingness to go to Jerusalem rather than just ordering the trial to reconvene there is unclear. Five explanations come to mind:

1. Festus, despite his pro-prosecution proclivities, wants to be, or at least wants to appear to be, fair on this point.

2. Festus feels he is "calling a bluff" by Paul and/or his accusers about finding the evidence in Jerusalem.

3. Festus, as a matter of Roman law, is deferring to the rights of Paul as a citizen.

4. Festus suspects that Paul knows he will be murdered on the way or once he gets there. Although Festus would not want a citizen murdered while in his custody, he is, in fact, bluffing, knowing that Paul will smell a trap (a plot to assassinate or a conspiracy to convict) and will appeal to Caesar.

5. Festus is giving Paul a choice to submit to a Jewish tribunal because the Romans had given the Jews the right to try Jewish legal cases before Jewish courts.[10]

From what we can glean from the text, explanations three and four appear most likely. Paul does immediately appeal to Caesar.[11] He certainly realized that after two years in custody he was being stampeded to trial. Further, Paul certainly knew of Lysias's letter to Felix exonerating him and he knew that Festus had to have read that letter (if Paul himself had not already brought it to the attention of Festus during the "pretrial proceedings"). Finally, Paul perceives the move to Jerusalem as removal from the protection of Roman law: "No one has the right to hand me over to them."[12] This response even implies that Festus is suggesting that the Sanhedrin try Paul (option five above). Logically, if Paul is arguing that the charges against him are matters of Jewish theology, then Jewish theologians are the appropriate judge. The problem with such reasoning is that the apostles had rejected the official hierarchy as having authority (at least theological authority) over them as early as Acts 4, and both Paul and Festus know the trial would be a sham because he would be tried by his accusers.

Whatever Festus's motive in giving Paul a say in whether the trial should be in Jerusalem, Luke has not put Theophilus in suspense. Jesus had already appeared to Paul two years earlier[13] and told him he would "testify about me" in Rome. Thus, Luke is also showing that Paul, as a follower of Jesus, obeyed when he saw the opportunity to go to Rome. Festus apparently confirms the legality of Paul's appeal by conferring with his subordinates. He also had no option but to grant the appeal or set Paul free. If Festus had failed to honor Paul's appeal and had punished Paul in any way, Festus himself would have faced forced exile.[14] However, Festus probably gladly granted the appeal. In just his first month in office, Festus has rid himself of a problem prisoner!

Shift from a legal to a business framework: a new chief executive has just been brought in to turn around a money-losing business. Usually his first step is to tell the accountants to recognize the losses his predecessor had been hiding or postponing. If the losses are to come out eventually, the new CEO wants them disclosed immediately so he will not be blamed for the errors of previous management. If Paul's case had gone to Rome under Felix, Felix may not have looked good. Officials there may have questioned his integrity or competency as facts were presented. Felix hoped the case would disappear so he sat on it. Festus recognized a hot potato was in his lap the first day he spent in Jerusalem. He got rid of it before he became identified with it!

HEROD AGRIPPA II

Having relieved himself of responsibility (and jurisdiction), Festus now talks about the case with King Agrippa and Bernice who arrive a few days later. Agrippa (Herod Agrippa II) was the son of the Herod (Agrippa I) mentioned in Acts 12 and was a puppet king for Rome over the largely Gentile territories in the areas north and northeast of Israel. Festus knows that even as a puppet king, Agrippa can write directly to Emperor Nero to expose any improper behavior, so he shows his judicial face. His explanation of his behavior is somewhat self-serving in that he describes himself as judicially precise:

A. not the "Roman custom" to hand over a man before trial.

B. right to face accusers respected.

C. opportunity to defend.

D. no delay in justice.[15]

The next part of Festus's explanation[16] rings more true, particularly that the case was "about a dead man named Jesus who Paul claimed was alive." To a new governor who was not familiar with the Way and apparently not knowledgeable about Judaism, the claim of a resurrection probably would seem strange if not absurd. Festus had rightly discerned the central issue but then protested being "at a loss as to how to investigate," as if witnesses, documents, and physical evidence could only be sought in Jerusalem if Paul had been willing to go there for trial! Luke the lawyer/editor has several reasons for including the Agrippa consultation[17] in his brief:

A. He wants Theophilus et al. to see that the governor "ducked the case."

B. He hopes to keep the focus on the Resurrection and related religious disputes rather than the civil charges.

C. He needs to introduce Agrippa as a Roman official and honest man who exonerates Paul in a virtual trial.

Exactly how Luke learned of the Festus/Agrippa conversation is unstated. Perhaps it was recounted the next day when Festus and Agrippa spoke to Paul. Whatever the source, if *Acts* is indeed a legal brief, then the account is quite likely to be accurate, if for no other reason than Luke would know that either Festus, Agrippa, or both could be summoned by Theophilus, Nero, or other Roman officials to testify or give deposition statements concerning the accuracy of Luke's representations. As a result of the trial before Festus and the behind-the-scenes maneuvering with Agrippa, Luke has also succeeded in showing his Roman readership that Paul's case is both highly political and highly important. Agrippa seems genuinely interested in hearing Paul, so Festus immediately grants his wish.

---

1   *Venue* is collectively a series of legal principles and statutes which determine the place where a trial will be held as opposed to where it could be held. It is also similar to the legal concept *forum nonconveniens* (inconvenient court location). Paul's accusers probably felt that even if they couldn't kill Paul (Act 25:3) they had a better chance of convicting him on their home court of Jerusalem.

2   Acts 25:3.

3   Acts 25:6–7.

4   Acts 25:5.

5   Acts 25:6 .

6   Acts 24:5.

7 Robinson, *Criminal Law*, 5.

8   Ibid., 5.

9 Acts 25:6.

10 Andrew Clarke, "Rome and Italy" in *Acts in Graeco-Roman Setting*, 467–8.

11 Acts 25:10.

12 Acts 25:11.

13 Acts 23:11.

14 Rapske, "The Role of the Magistrate in Sending People into Custody," *Paul in Roman Custody*, 52.

15 Acts 25:16–17.

16 Acts 25:18–21.

17 Acts 25:13–22.

CHAPTER 25

ACTS 25:23—26:32

PAUL BEFORE AGRIPPA:
"*NOTHING BEYOND THE PROPHETS AND MOSES*"
(ACTS 26:22)

Luke recounts that this "trial" was well attended by "high ranking officers and leading men of [Caesarea]."[1] His purpose in this observation is verifiability. Luke constantly selects *very public* trials, speeches, healings, or preaching to further his narrative. Because Agrippa will soon "acquit" Paul, Luke wants the Roman officials reviewing his background history and legal defense to know that these proceedings are verifiable from many sources in addition to emphasizing that Paul's guilt or innocence was a matter of major public concern in Caesarea. Luke wants his brief widely and carefully read. If Paul's case is about just another minor sect and a rabble-rousing leader from a distant province, it might be reviewed cursorily by only a few officials. If, however, it speaks of far-reaching public concerns, decisions rendered by several high-ranking Roman judges, and claims to address the eternal existence of each human, then it merits mega-attention and reading by Nero and officials throughout the empire.

The first thing Luke wants his reader to note about this trial is the self-serving introduction of Festus. Festus says he had already found Paul "not guilty" at least of capital charges.[2] Because this declaration contradicts Luke's account of the trial, that Festus made no decision but merely offered a change of *venue*[3] (trial location), Luke is telling Rome that their man Festus is just as two-faced as his predecessor Felix. Secondly, Festus admits[4] he has no specific charges against Paul, a man who has been held in Roman custody for two years! Verse 26 is another key to understanding the audience of *Acts* because *Festus says that he will be writing up charges to send to Nero himself.* Festus had reason to expect such a letter to be read:

1. He was the governor of the province and thus required to communicate directly with the emperor on important matters.

2. This would be his first or one of his first official reports since taking office, thus it would probably be read with more care.

3. The charges would pertain to a Roman citizen brought to Rome for trial, not to a person of lesser legal status.

4. The charges had a powerful constituency pushing them.[5]

5. The charges alleged provoking of civil unrest in many areas of the empire. This was not a "local" matter.

6. As has been shown, the decision of the case would have profound implications on Roman politics, military affairs, and its treasury.

7. The claims of these Jewish agitators concerning the resurrection of their leader, miracles, and eschatology were extraordinary. If the summary from Festus of charges brought by others (of which we have no copy) was headed directly to the emperor, then the response, Luke's brief, could be expected to end up there also.

The readers, as we can deduce from the foregoing seven considerations, would not only include Nero, then only age twenty-two, but his advisers Seneca and Burrus. Whether *Acts* was ever read by Nero, we do not know. However, an advocate as thorough as Luke collaborating with a defendant as opportunistic as Paul would certainly write his brief with the hope and intention it be read not just by the advisers but by Caesar himself. We lawyers often agonize over whether our cleverly insightful arguments or brilliant witticisms will be enjoyed by the judge or wasted on an unappreciative law clerk. We have no control over, and usually no knowledge of, to whom the judge delegates the reading of our briefs, but I have yet to meet an attorney or read a treatise on legal writing that advocates writing to the clerk's level. All arguments are focused for the ultimate decision maker.

Acts 25:26 tells us Festus intended to submit a written report to Nero. Remember that under Roman law the prosecuting party had to submit an *inscriptio*, written charges. These facts and the significance and complexity of the case make it almost certain that the Roman court would allow the defense to submit a written response. A narrative such as *Acts* precisely fits the profile of such a document.

Finally, we note that this "trial" has no prosecutor or complaining witness, only Paul to defend himself. Festus purports to hope that an examination of Paul will provide sufficient evidence to bring charges against him.[6] In this regard, he is echoing Tertullus and, from a forensic viewpoint, overreaching as much. If the petitions of "the whole Jewish community [a patent exaggeration] . . . in Jerusalem and here in Caesarea"[7] did not suffice to provide specific or sufficient charges to send to Nero, it is not reasonable to expect a defendant to do so.

Luke is leading the reader to a conclusion: this case arose from anger about admission of Gentiles into the Jewish faith and was brought only from political motives. Festus was a hypocrite not to have said so. He continued a legal charade when he could have admitted the truth: "I am holding Paul because powerful forces within the Jewish establishment want him eliminated as a threat to their influence and position. As a political matter, you, most excellent Nero, should decide whether executing Paul to please his opponents justifies the cost in diminished credibility of our legal system."

Paul's Testimony (Acts 26)

In chapter 26, Luke, for the third time, recounts Paul's conversion. The analytical reader, ancient and modern, may ask, "Why is Luke repeating this account? I've already read about the Damascus Road encounter and reread it when Paul stood before the crowd at the temple?" Several possible reasons are consistent with what we have already learned of Luke's agenda:

A. To act as a vehicle to introduce **new legal arguments**.

B. To reemphasize important **legal themes**;.

C. **To evangelize** through repetition of a powerful encounter with Jesus.

D. To court **political influence**.

Let us consider Luke's strategy:

A. **New Legal Arguments:**

1. Theophilus knows that Agrippa,[8] like Felix[9] but unlike Festus,[10] is "well acquainted" with Judaism and the sect called Christians or Nazarenes. Consequently, his "acquittal" of Paul should be accorded substantial weight by any subsequent investigator or court.

2. Luke has led the reader through trials and quasi-judicial proceedings. A trial seeks truth in the resolution of a particular conflict. Just as in legal proceedings, persons concerned with finding historical truth and even scientific truth must ultimately rely in part on the judgments and findings of others. In the legal/historical branch of truth inquiry, such procedure includes evaluating testimony of witnesses and the relevance and reliability of witnesses. Of course, in all cases of reliance, the relier must judge the degree of reliability by the source: is the witness credible; does the witness have a reputation for truthfulness? Luke is arguing that Agrippa evaluated the key event in Paul's testimony, indeed of his life: the encounter with the resurrected Jesus on the road to Damascus. Paul's claim is so outrageous or hope-inspiring, depending upon one's viewpoint, that it could lead to:

    (a) charges of insanity;[11]
    (b) conclusion charges against Paul must be true;
    (c) faith in the Resurrection;[12] or
    (d) acquittal (even if faith does not result);[13]

Luke is presenting his argument to a nonbelieving Roman Gentile audience where the possibility of a reaction similar to that of Festus[14] is substantial. A man such as Agrippa, familiar with Jewish teachings and particularly with the Hebrew scriptures, would be in a far better position to judge whether Paul's claims about Jesus had a solid rational basis or were delusional than would a Roman tribunal with a pagan or Greek philosophical worldview: "I am saying nothing beyond what the prophets and Moses said would happen—that the Messiah would suffer and, as the first to rise from the dead, would proclaim light to his own people and to the Gentiles."[15]

Thus, Luke uses Agrippa's reaction to Paul's testimony to enhance Paul's credibility.

B. **Legal themes reiterated**: When an event in Paul's life allows Luke to reinforce legal arguments, he includes it in *Acts* because every major event which is recounted supports one or more themes. In this conversion account Luke touches on:

1. **Verifiability**—"they . . . can testify . . . that according to the strictest sect of our religion, I lived as a Pharisee."[16]

2. **Intra-Jewish**—nature of the dispute.[17]

3. **Universality**[18]—Paul sent to Jews and Gentiles.

4. **Jurisdiction**—The court is reminded that the "legal" issue, as presented in the trial before the Sanhedrin, is really about the resurrection of the dead[19] and therefore not a legal issue at all. Paul's assertion is that all the charges (e.g., sedition, rioting, creating a new religion, desecrating the temple) can be traced to his proclamation of Jesus' resurrection or to the anger of his opponents caused by inclusion of Gentiles.

C. **Evangelism**: Luke's brief was part of Paul's opportunity to share the gospel in the highest councils of Rome. Paul had received a progression of at least four prophecies which charted his way to Caesar: (1) At the time of his conversion, Paul learned that Gentiles would be prominent in his ministry.[20] (2) Agabus had foretold Paul's arrest and handing over to the Gentiles (Romans).[21] (3) Jesus had stood before Paul at night and encouraged him. "As you have testified about me in Jerusalem, so you must also testify in Rome."[22] (4) Finally, after the inquiry before Agrippa (but before Luke writes this brief) an angel of God will tell Paul, "You must stand trial before Caesar [Nero]."[23]

So, even as *Acts* is written, Luke and Paul have become the most committed, brilliant, and elaborate liars imaginable (for the most unfathomable reasons), or they have become totally convinced they are to go before Caesar through a plan that God had already established. Such assurance would fuel an effort to evangelize the highest of the Roman rulers. ***Paul boldly turned his interrogation before***

Agrippa into an inquiry into the reality of Agrippa's faith. Likewise, Luke has turned the brief in defense of his mentor Paul into a challenge to Theophilus and those who would read over his shoulder that they, themselves, confront, and answer the question: "Who is the man Jesus who could move Paul and these other Jews and Gentiles to risk death and incur persecution?"

This interpretation of *Acts* is strongly confirmed in Paul's letter to the Colossian church, written while he was awaiting trial before Nero: "And pray for us, too, that God may open a door for our message, so that we may proclaim the mystery of Christ [Messiah], for which I am in chains. Pray that I may proclaim it clearly, as I should." (NIV)[24] What better "open door" for the proclamation of the "mystery of Messiah" than a pretrial brief to explain the story of Jesus and the message Paul was preaching? How better "to make the most of every opportunity" than to suffuse the brief with the gospel?

Paul and Luke firmly believed that Paul's fate was not in Nero's hands but God's. Nevertheless, they clearly felt it was God's will to present their case as thoroughly and forcefully as possible so that truth would be established. Because they had apparently reached a point in their spiritual development where truth was more important than approval, freedom, or even life, Luke had permission from his client to use his testimony to win hearts to Messiah even if it did not advance Paul's legal interests. However, the internal evidence of the conversion passage[25] shows that Luke used it to convey both legal argument and evangelistic messages.

D. **Political Influence:** Luke had a final political/legal/evangelistic reason to feature Paul's encounter with Agrippa and Agrippa's response: Agrippa and Nero were close. After Nero took office he increased Agrippa's kingdom by giving him more cities and territories. In gratitude, Agrippa changed the name of his capital from Caesarea–Philippi to Neronias. Obviously, Agrippa's declaration of Paul's innocence was hoped to carry weight with Nero's court. Thus Luke concludes the Caesarean imprisonment of Paul with the literary technique of an innocent man peacefully sailing toward a gathering storm of destruction.

1	Acts 25:23.	14	Acts 26:24.
2	Acts 25:25.	15	Acts 26:22b-23.
3	Acts 25:9–10.	16	Acts 26:4–5.
4	Acts 25:26.	17	Acts 26:22b-23.
5	See Acts 24:27.	18	Acts 26:17–18.
6	Acts 25:26.	19	Acts 26:6, 8.
7	Acts 25:24.	20	Acts 26:17–18.
8	Acts 26:3.	21	Acts 21:10.
9	Acts 24:22.	22	Acts 23:11.
10	Acts 25:19–20.	23	Acts 27:24.
11	Acts 26:24.	24	Col. 4:3–4.
12	Acts 26:28.	25	Acts 26:4–20.
13	Acts 26:31–32.		

CHAPTER 26

ACTS 27:1—28:16

PAUL BEFORE THE STORM:
"*THOU MUST BE BROUGHT BEFORE CAESAR*"
(ACTS 27:24)

The journey to Rome is an adventure. Yet, what do storms, shipwrecks, and healings have to do with a legal brief? A good eyewitness account[1] like this begs to be told and Luke enjoys telling it! Luke is also constrained by the chronological organization of *Acts* to include the remarkable journey from Caesarea to Rome. Nevertheless, drama and chronology alone are insufficient reasons to devote so much space in such an important legal defense to a storm and shipwreck. Unless plausible legal and/or evangelistic purposes can be discerned in this account, it is fair to conclude that our proposed explanation for the composition and readership of Acts is wrong, or at least incomplete or oversimplified. Accordingly, let us examine again Luke's narrative.

27:1—Paul is put in the custody of "a centurion named Julius of the Imperial Regiment." These details shout: "*Verify, verify, verify.* Our story will be confirmed by your own high-ranking loyal soldier!" The details concerning Julius would be of little interest to a Christian audience and no parallel to such details exist where centurions are mentioned in the New Testament outside of *Acts*. Textual evidence again points to a non-Christian audience.

27:3—Julius allows Paul to go ashore to get supplies from friends. The message: this is no criminal. Given ample opportunity to flee, he remains in custody. He respects the law.[2] *He is innocent.*

27:9—"It was after the Fast" (*Yom Kippur*). This detail says, "Paul, I (Luke), and Aristarchus were running on a Jewish calendar (not by the dates of another religion or even of the Roman Empire)."

27:10–11—Paul's prophecy of a disastrous voyage says, "This man hears from God. Think twice about convicting him. Be warned by what almost happened to those who ignored him."

27:13–20—The storm at sea begins fulfillment of the first prophecy and prepares Theophilus for the second. The presence of God amidst the storm and Luke's desire to show his reader that Paul is sent by God are a powerful wind driving this portion of the narrative.

27:23–26, 37—The second prophecy of Paul is amazingly accurate in detail:

(a) Shipwreck.

(b) Aground on some island.

(c) Not one in 276 men will die.

The specificity with which Luke records this prophecy challenges Theophilus to *verify*, to confirm Paul's assertion of divine connection; check the facts with Centurion Julius.

27:29—Injects humor. If even the Salts were praying, the danger was extreme!

27:31b—Paul speaks again, "unless these men stay with the ship, you cannot be saved." Unlike the beginning of the voyage,[3] this time the centurion listens. First, Luke is asking, "How does one lowly prisoner, outranked by a pilot, ship owner, and a centurion[4] end up running a huge ship carrying 276 men and bringing them all to safety unless his claimed connection to the true God is real?" Then Luke is *warning* the reader, "Julius heeded Paul's words and was saved. *Will you heed them?*"

27:33–6—By now the crew and passengers have such faith in Paul that they eat and prepare to run aground by jettisoning their cargo.[5] This detail reiterates, "If 276 men came to trust this man with their lives, you should believe him when he tells you he is innocent and when he says Jesus is the way to salvation."

27:41—Paul's prophecy[6] is quickly fulfilled.

27:42–3—The soldiers plan to kill the prisoners to prevent their escape. Though they have just had their own lives saved through a prophecy from God, they still feared a Roman law which provided severe punishments, even death, for allowing a prisoner in Roman custody to escape.[7] However, Julius retains such faith in Paul at this point that he vetoes such a "sensible" precaution and takes charge of evacuating the disintegrating vessel. Luke explains that Julius forbids the executions of the other prisoners because he wants to spare Paul. The centurion is yet another witness who believes that Paul is an innocent man sent by God.

28:1–6—Paul, despite his acquired status as a leader within the group, is still portrayed as having the heart attitude of a servant as he gathers firewood to warm the other survivors.[8] Then the viper strikes. We know from other sources that Paul's theology fully comprehended unseen spiritual forces of Satan operating to control or influence perceived reality: "Put on the whole armor of God, that you may be able to stand against the wiles of the devil. For we do not wrestle against flesh and blood, but against principalities, against powers, against the rulers of the darkness of this age, against spiritual hosts of wickedness in the heavenly places."[9]

Luke saw reality through the same worldview.[10] With the viper's attack, Theophilus, as well as the islanders of Malta, must wonder, "What is happening?" The chronicle of events implies a concerted Satanically led assassination plot against Paul not to be equaled in our literary heritage until the Schwartzenegger *Terminator* sagas. Were Luke, or Paul through Luke, writing to Christians, these events would surely have evoked an explanation from the writer, as teacher, of the functioning of the unseen enemy. However, such an explanation would be inappropriate if the reader is a Roman official because a such theological teaching would unnecessarily digress from the legal agenda.

28:7–8—Luke then locates himself and Paul at the estate of Publius, "the chief official of the island," where Paul heals the father of Publius from "fever and dysentery." During this three-month stay on Malta, it is evident that Paul had many remarkable experiences:

1. The rest of the sick on the island came and were cured.[11]

2. They honored us in many ways.[12]

3. They furnished us with the supplies we needed.[13]

Why does Luke omit details of all the experiences except the hospitality of Publius and healing of his father? The deduced answer consistent with the rest of *Acts* is that an encounter with a high-ranking Roman official would most resonate with his audience of other officials and would provide the highest degree of verifiability. In summary, the storm, the shipwreck, and the Malta accounts and their verifiability and chronological proximity to the reading of *Acts* by Theophilus (two years) function primarily to enhance the testimony of Paul, the witness, soon to be confirmed by two Roman gods and ultimately delivered to Nero.[14]

TRUTH AND PERJURY (ACTS 28:11)

In this transition paragraph summarizing a journey of about two weeks from Malta to Rome, Luke gives the reader fascinating details. They sailed on an Alexandrian (Egyptian) ship "with the twin gods Castor and Pollux." If *Acts* is written to acquaint the Roman hierarchy with the Jewishness of faith in Jesus and to defend Paul against his accusers, what conceivable purpose does Luke have in including this detail? Of course, the same question must be asked if one assumes *Acts* was written to Christians. If anything, the Castor and Pollux details and the uneventful sail from Malta to Rhegium to Puteoli, when juxtaposed with the preceding catastrophic storm and shipwreck, imply that the protection of the pagan gods was superior to that of the God of Israel!

Brian Rapske notes that D. Ladoucer suggests that the function of the particular gods, "*the guardians of truth and the punishers of perjurers*" (emphasis added), may be set forth as "one more argument in a sequence calculated to persuade the reader of Paul's innocence."[15] This is not a detail (twin Roman gods) which Luke would include to persuade Messianics of the truth of Paul's defense. Rather, it is a "coincidence" which would be immediately appreciated by a pagan Roman jurist without explanation by Luke. In addition to the forensic reinforcement from the Castor/Pollux detail, Luke may be evangelizing again. Just as Paul used the "unknown God" in Athens to point Greek intellectuals to Jesus,[16] Luke appears to be using Castor and Pollux to point polytheistic Romans to Paul as the messenger of God's truth.

Our author then mentions that some (Christian) brothers heard of their arrival and provided hospitality and encouragement on the way from Puteoli to Rome. This passage furthers Luke's legal agenda by showing that the gospel has already spread to Rome in a benign way: these are "brothers" who show love and serve others; they are not "aliens". Also Luke does not mention whether these "brothers" are Gentiles, Jews, or both. Their background matters not, they are simply brothers. Luke is saying this sect is no threat to Rome.

When Paul arrives at Rome[17] he lives by himself with one guard. The Christians are not about to help Paul escape and he has passed up every opportunity to do so. Why? Luke wants Theophilus to know his "client" does not behave like a criminal because he is not one. Luke then writes, "Paul was allowed to live by himself, with a soldier to guard him."[18] Modern lawyers use such facts to their client's benefit: "Your honor, even though my client was accused of treason and armed violence, the judge who conducted the preliminary hearing set a reconnaissance bond" (bond without cash deposit). Some magistrate had determined the conditions of Paul's imprisonment in Rome. Rapske notes that Paul was granted "a very light form of military custody."[19] A reader conversant with the Roman legal system would immediately recognize that those conditions were an indication that the Roman official who had heard the charges (probably with input from Julius) had determined that the charges were not strongly supported by evidence at that point.

Theophilus would also understand that Paul's custody would allow him the freedom to address the Jewish leaders in Rome.

---

1 Acts 27:1.
2 See Rom. 13:1–7.
3 Acts 27:11.
4 Ibid.

5   An interesting detail confirming the accuracy of this account is: "Quite apart from the spoiling of cargo, grain which gets wet can swell so dramatically doubling in size, that a full load can split the plates of even a modern ship," Rapske, "Acts, Travel and Shipwreck," 35, quoting G. E. Rickman, "The Grain Trade under the Roman Empire" in *The Seaborne Commerce of Ancient Rome Studies in Archaeology and History,* J. H. D'Arms and E. C. Kopff, eds., (Memoirs of the Amer. Acad. in Rome 36; Rome: American 1980), 265.

6   Acts 27:26.

7   Robinson, *Criminal Law,* 103.

8   Acts 28:3.

9   E.g., Eph. 6:11–12.

10 See Luke 4:1–2.

11 Acts 28:9.

12 Acts 28:10a.

13 Acts 28:10b.

14 Col. 4:3–4.

15 D. Ladoucer, "Hellennnistic Preconceptions of Shipwreck and Pollution as Context for Acts 27–28," HTR 73 (1980), 446, quoted in Rapske, "Travel and Shipwreck," 44.

16 Acts 17:23.

17 Acts 28:16.

18 Ibid.

19 Rapske, "Paul in Roman Custody," 182.

CHAPTER 27

ACTS 28:17–31

PAUL BEFORE THE JEWS OF ROME:
"*JESUS, FROM TORAH*"
(ACTS 28:23)

The first thing Luke records Paul doing in Rome is convening leaders and telling them of his loyalty to the Jewish people and of the "hope of Israel." Luke's forensic message[1] is that Paul has done everything and continues to do everything in the open; nothing is hidden, no threat to Rome exists. Luke now begins the summary of his defense, selecting those portions of Paul's speech which further that summary as Paul recounts his arrest to the Roman Jewish leaders:

A. Nothing has been done out of anti-Jewish motive; or

B. Contrary to the customs of their mutual Jewish ancestors;

C. After being turned over to the Roman judicial system I was exonerated; but

D. "the Jewish authorities"[2] objected;

E. I was compelled to appeal to Caesar;

F. I have no charge against my own people; and

G. My trial and the opposition against me boil down to one issue: "The hope of Israel," the messiahship of Jesus.

Some have argued that Luke uses the phrase "the Jews"[3] in a perjorative sense because he, as a Greek, is harboring antagonism toward them for a variety of possible reasons. A less contentious explanation, which I believe, is that Luke has gone to extraordinary lengths to show that the dispute of Paul and the Jewish Christians with the non-Christian Jews is an internal Jewish matter. The modern reader might see the controversies as a theological dispute in the context of Christians versus Jews or in the light of centuries of persecution of Jews by people in the name of Christ. But they would be reading into the dispute historical events that had not occurred.

The Jewish sects of the first century, Sadducees, Essenes, Zealots, Nazarenes, and Pharisees, had many passionate disputes among themselves. The battle between the Jewish believers in Jesus and non-Messianic Jews is probably the most vehement because it brought the Jewish faith to the Gentiles on a worldwide scale and upended submission to parts of the existing Jewish authority structure. Still, it was an internal Jewish controversy. All of the leaders among the "Christians" that we know of at this time are Jews, all of the evangelists are Jews, and most of the theological controversies, Messiahship of Jesus, resurrection of the dead, whether God ever speaks aloud, and angels, are Jewish ones.

In verse 17, for example, Paul is talking to Jewish leaders to convince them he is not anti-Jewish. Thus it strains logic to conclude that his use of the phrase "the Jews" in verse 19 in that same speech would have any intended (or perceived) anti-Jewish connotation with the original audience.

WHY DOES LUKE'S ATTITUDE TOWARD JEWS MATTER?

This discussion concerning the purported anti-Judaic tilt in Luke's writing is important to his reader. Luke's legal agenda is to show that the *Talmidei Yeshua* remain true to the Jewish faith and are not starting a new religion. If he is portraying Paul and the other Messianics as separating themselves from their "brothers and fathers,"[4] then he is destroying one of his key legal arguments.

Luke continues his summary of the meeting by noting that the Roman Jewish leaders had received no letters concerning Paul, and even "brothers" who had traveled from Jerusalem had no bad reports about Paul. Luke is asserting that if Paul's opponents had solid evidence against Paul they would have sent it to Rome immediately or that it would have already been well-known to the Jewish leadership there. However, the internal evidence of the text we have examined thus far, particularly the implied refutations, strongly suggest that *by the time Luke writes Acts, two years later, letters have been sent and charges gathered from Jerusalem* and various cities where Paul's message aroused opposition.

Although the Roman Jewish leaders have heard nothing bad about Paul specifically, they have heard a lot of talk against "this sect."[5] Luke is now summarizing again:

A. Paul is not a one-man show; Messianics and evangelists are popping up in many places.

B. The *Roman* Jewish leadership at this time considers the Way a *sect* of Judaism rather than a different religion.

Paul's continued attempts to evangelize this Jewish community are from "the Law of Moses and from the Prophets," not from any later writings or revelations Paul had received. Thus, Luke, through the last paragraphs of *Acts*, wants the reader to remember the Jewishness of the debate. Some believe. Some do not.[6] Through Luke, Paul then makes his final challenge:[7]

"The Holy Spirit spoke the truth to your forefathers when he said through Isaiah the prophet:

> And He said, "Go, and tell this people: 'Keep on hearing, but do not understand; Keep on seeing, but do not perceive.' Make the heart of this people dull, And their ears heavy, And shut their eyes; Lest they see with their eyes, And hear with their ears, And understand with their heart, And return and be healed."[8]

Therefore, I want you to know that God's salvation has been sent to the Gentiles and they will listen."

Why does Paul quote such a confrontational passage and why does Luke end his brief with it?

<u>Paul's reason</u>: Paul loved his Jewish brethren so passionately that he wanted to do whatever he could to save as many of them as possible. When "some were convinced" and "others would not believe,"[9] he was not satisfied. He knew many had closed their hearts to his message so his last appeal was to their minds and their very Jewishness—the history of Israel. Accordingly, to their minds he presented the words God Himself spoke when Isaiah received his call as a prophet: "The people of Israel will hear but not understand, will see but not perceive." Paul hoped some of his hearers would realize those words of God were not symbolic but actually applied to them, then and there. If they realized what was happening, perhaps they would decide to open their hearts.

Paul had said all he could, the words of God Himself were his finale. Yet Paul knew, as did the Roman Jewish leaders, that the commission of God to Isaiah ended with his message eventually being received; God had promised Isaiah that someday after a long dispersion[10] the people of Israel would understand (Isaiah's message) with their hearts and turn and be healed. Meanwhile, if Paul could provoke a few more of his people to jealously and thus to salvation by allowing them to see that God's love was now going forth to the Gentiles also,[11] he would do so.

The second thrust of Paul's final appeal was to Jewish history. Most great Jewish leaders or prophets in the Hebrew Bible, Joseph, Moses, David, Isaiah, Jeremiah, were first rejected by the people, often dramatically, but eventually embraced. Paul was hoping that some of his listeners would realize that God's words to Isaiah had been fulfilled again and again and that with Jesus the Messiah, the greatest of Israel's leaders and prophets, the rejection would be the greatest, most vehement, and longest.

<u>Luke's Reason</u>: Luke had a different perspective in writing than Paul did in speaking; their audiences were different, although their agendas overlapped. For example, a Roman member of Nero's *consilium* may not have heard of Isaiah

much less understood the immediate context[12] (a day would come long beyond the natural life of Isaiah when his words would soften rather than harden hearts) or the larger biblical context (the longstanding custom of Israel to reject God's prophets). Likewise, the question foremost in the minds of Paul's Jewish listeners, "Is Jesus really the 'Hope of Israel'?" would be formulated differently by Luke's Roman Gentile reader: "If the God of the Jews is the one true God and Paul is speaking the truth about Jesus being the Messiah, why is Paul's message so forcefully rejected by so many Jewish leaders?" Luke is answering the latter question. He has previously argued that an internal struggle in Judaism was raging over authority: biblical vs. traditional; apostolic vs. Sanhedrinic/priestly. Now in his summation he brings both sub-themes back to the fore.

On the question of biblical authority he quotes Isaiah, making sure to identify him as "the prophet" for those Roman readers who might not know. Not only does he quote the biblical prophet, but for good measure he quotes the prophet's direct quotation of God! On the issue of apostolic authority Luke has Paul speaking for himself: "The Holy Spirit spoke the truth to your forefathers when he said through Isaiah the prophet: . . ." [13] Although Luke is using Paul as an authoritative source who derived this authority from God, he is also saying that Paul has authority because his teaching agrees with the Hebrew scriptures. Luke concludes his summary with a prophecy from Paul that echoes Jesus's introduction of Acts in 1:8: "you shall be witnesses to Me in Jerusalem . . . and to the end of the earth." Paul ends by saying: "the salvation of God has been sent to the Gentiles, and they will hear it!"[14] Luke has reprised his theme, Christianity is Judaism made universal through Jesus, for the final time and has explained to Theophilus that the rejection of Paul's message by many Jewish leaders was all a part of what God foreknew.

The final two verses of *Acts* give us the last pieces of our jigsaw puzzle. Two years pass without an incident considered worthy by Luke for inclusion in his defense! These two years are closest in time to the writing of *Acts* and, therefore, the most easily remembered. If Paul "preached" boldly, certainly many notable conversions and miracles occurred, or this was the most aberrant period of Paul's ministry. Why then are no events recorded? Two good and complementary explanations come to mind:

A. Once Paul was under imperial guard in Rome itself, no charges could accrue against him. Luke had no charges to refute. Since *Acts* was written as a defense brief, its work ends at Acts 28:29.

B. In addition to preaching, teaching,[15] and writing to believers (see chapter on Paul's prison letters), Paul's incarceration was dedicated to helping Luke write *Luke* and *Acts*. The Gospel was the easier task. Based on *Mark* and other available sources, Paul, Luke, and perhaps others might have completed in a few months the copying and the addition of the parts uniquely helpful to the legal agenda to create *Luke. Acts*, however, was a far more difficult assignment. Almost all of the material was original. Luke probably got source material from Peter and Paul but he had to edit and rewrite it. Luke himself states that his work is the product of careful investigation and fact gathering.[16] His writing evidences thoughtful crafting of facts, legal arguments, themes, progressions, drama, humor, precedents, and evangelism. Even if the gathering of evidence and marshaling of witnesses began when Paul and Luke arrived in Rome, the writing could easily have taken a year or more.[17] Thus, I conclude that verses 30 and 31 of Acts 28 were written just at the end of the two years referenced in verse 30. The text gives good reason to support that conclusion.

We must now ask whether the careful observations made on our journey through *Acts* afford us any other *systematic* ways to test the thesis that *Acts* is formally a legal defense of the charges pending against Paul. They reveal several.

---

1 Acts 28:17–20.
2 The Greek word *Ioudaioi*, which originally meant "Judeans" and means "Jews" is often mistranslated as "Jews" when, in context, it means "Jewish leaders" as is the usage in passages such as Acts 28:19 and John 7:13. See also *The Expositor's Greek Testament*, vol. 1, A. W. Robertson Nicoll, ed. (Grand Rapids: Eerdmans, 1983), 709, 763.
3 E.g., Acts 28:19.
4 See Acts 22:1.
5 Acts 28:22.
6 Acts 28:24.
7 Acts 28:26–27.
8 Isa. 6:9–10.
9 Acts 28:24.
10 Isa. 6:11–12.
11 Acts 28:28; see Rom. 11:13.
12 Isa. 6:9–13.
13 Acts 28:25b.
14 Acts 28:28.
15 Acts 28:31.
16 Luke 1:3; see 1 John 1:1.
17 See Rapske, "Paul in Roman Custody," 319, on trial delays necessitated by evidence gathering; 329 on pretrial case preparation; and 333 discussing 2 Tim. 4:13.

CHAPTER 28

TRIAL WITNESSES AND DOCUMENTARY EXHIBITS

Trials require witnesses. The witness theme permeating *Acts* is expressed both in the legal and evangelistic sense, which is reflected in the thesis of this book. Putting the evangelistic purposes aside, if *Acts* was written in contemplation of Paul's trial then perhaps the text would introduce witnesses to be presented. Of course, a witness can be identified, and his credentials and background established, when his testimony is presented. Nevertheless, if Theophilus is a Roman official gathering evidence, if he is Paul's lawyer, or is going to be a decision maker, it makes sense to give him the background on the witnesses to be called before trial.

In modern practice, witnesses are identified and witness lists exchanged *long* before the actual trial. This practice helps both sides prepare their case. I am not suggesting that Roman law had a formal procedural rule requiring witness identification, merely that the logic underlying the modern practice also would apply to a major Roman trial. In modern civil practice each side deposes the potential witnesses of the opposition. However, it is logical that potential witnesses would be introduced in the narrative, since private litigants certainly lacked the resources and authority to take such steps and since, in trials before the emperor, a specific official was assigned to pretrial investigation. If Theophilus is that official and *Acts* is written for that purpose, the presence or absence of such witnesses in the text is a test we can use to measure the validity of the legal brief hypothesis.

Who might those witnesses be? Please revisit the charges we know or deduce to have been brought against Paul (see Chapter 1 chart). Then, thinking as defense lawyers, let us ask, "Whom should we call?" In answering that question, we would consider:

A. How **directly** the testimony of the witness bears upon the charges in question:

　　1. With respect to the charges relating to riot incitement, an **eyewitness** to most or all of the events will be superior to an eyewitness of only some events, and an eyewitness will be superior to a hearsay witness.

　　2. With respect to the "illegal religion" accusations, a Jewish Christian would be superior to a Gentile Christian, and a **Judean Jewish Christian** would be superior to a diasporan Jewish Christian.

B. How **credible** the witness is as measured by the likelihood that a Roman court would find him or her to be honest, knowledgeable, mature, and of good memory.

C. The degree of the witness's **self-interest;** a non-Christian Roman would generally be perceived to have less bias than a Nazarene.

D. The **ability to communicate** to and favorably influence the judge through the same language (Greek or Latin) or similar background (Roman aristocracy). However, this factor would not be helpful in presenting a witness on the authentic Jewishness of Hebrew Christianity. In that event, a native Aramaic speaker with a heavy accent in his Greek would be most convincing.

If those particular witnesses are profiled in *Acts*, then we can count those profiles as evidence that Luke wrote *Acts* with trial preparation in mind. If the profiles are irrelevant to any legal issues, then we can count them as evidence that Luke's agenda was non-forensic. Peter, Philip, Gallio, Sergius Paulus, Silas, Mark, Timothy, Priscilla, Aquilla, Apollos, Barnabas, Jacob the Just, Claudius Lysias, Felix, Agrippa, Festus, and others could all give relevant testimony and they generally meet many or most of the qualifications for a witness as set forth above. Luke takes care to identify even minor characters who could be favorable witnesses such as Sopater, Aristarchus, Secundus, Gaius and Trophimus.[1] Although some characters such as Publius[2] may only figure in the evangelistic agenda, Luke does not introduce characters who are irrelevant to either a legal or evangelistic agenda.

It does not, however, mean that all or most were called to testify. By setting forth this information to the Roman official charged with investigating trials before the emperor, that official could have questioned or had many of those individuals deposed by other Roman officials in their home cities. Or, at a minimum, he could have confirmed or disproved the facts which Luke alleges through written records or third party testimony.

JACOB AND PETER

Jacob the Just (a/k/a James) and Peter would be at the top of my witness list. Consider the credentials of Jacob:

1. Brother (or close relative) of Jesus.

2. Originally not a follower of Jesus.

3. Leader of the Jerusalem church.

4. Presided at meeting allowing Gentiles into the church without circumcision based upon scriptural authority.

5. Strong emphasis on *Torah* observance for the church.

6. Apparently good reputation with non-Christian Jews in Jerusalem.

Consider the credentials of Peter:

1. Original disciple of Jesus.

2. Leader of the disciples.

3. Preacher on day of Pentecost.

4. Evangelist to the Jews.

5. Evangelist to Centurion Cornelius and family, first group conversion of Gentiles.

Both of these men would be great witnesses on the question of the Jewishness of faith in Jesus. Both are frequently mentioned in *Acts*. With Jacob particularly, Luke appears to make a special effort to establish his authority and involvement in the issues concerning Gentile circumcision[3] and *Torah* observance by diasporan Jewish Christians.[4] Jacob was killed in Jerusalem sometime in A.D. 62 by order of the high priest. We do not know the reason for the execution, but we can presume he never got to testify in Rome. However, the execution of Jacob is certainly consistent with a theory that the execution order was given to prevent him from testifying. Luke probably would not have known of Jacob's death at the time he wrote Acts. Therefore, I conclude that the introduction and details about the individuals named above as potential trial witnesses from *Acts* is, at least, consistent with the hypothesis that *Acts* is a legal brief.

ANANIAS

We also have the question of who will testify *against* Paul at his trial. Because Paul could not control who would be called to testify against him, it is far less likely he would identify prosecution witnesses in a trial brief. Nevertheless, if an adverse witness was a key participant in an event forming the basis of a charge, it makes sense Luke that would mention him. The high priest Ananias is one possible candidate as an accuser or adverse witness. He is mentioned by name in Acts 23:2 and 24:1 and alluded to in Acts 25:2. His position as high priest would give much weight to his testimony. In the trial before Felix, he is willing to travel to Caesarea to prosecute Paul or testify against him. On the issue of the Jewish authenticity of faith in Jesus he would certainly be an authority and his testimony could cut both ways:

A. "These men have left Judaism—they do not circumcise their converts"; and/or

B. "I concede that they follow many of the teachings of the Pharisees (resurrection, angels, God speaking audibly) and use the Hebrew scriptures as their authority."

As an eyewitness to civil insurrection charges, he has little to add except as to Paul's conduct before the Sanhedrin in Acts 23:1–10. Because he is not mentioned in Paul's prison letters, the possibility of his being a witness in Rome must remain an open issue. Nevertheless, because of the vehemence with which Paul was persecuted on so many occasions, some delegation of Jerusalem elders (see Acts 24:1) certainly would have gone to Rome to press the charges against Paul.

ALEXANDER

An even more intriguing witness possibility is Alexander who is mentioned as a Jew, not a follower of Jesus, and who addressed the rioting Ephesian metalworkers in Acts 19:33 (See pp. 141–2). We have already mentioned that there is no apparent reason for Luke to identify this individual if he is writing to believers. However, Alexander certainly was an eyewitness to the riot and thus competent to testify if Paul was charged with inciting it. Besides deducing that Luke must have had a reason for mentioning his involvement and naming him, we can also deduce that the Jews must have had a reason for pushing him to the front.[5] They must have concluded that something about Alexander would allow him to influence the rioting craftsmen, but we are not told what that something is.

Had we no more information about Alexander, we would not have enough evidence to mention him as a possible witness. However, in probably the last of his prison letters, Paul mentions a certain "metalworker" who "did me a great deal of harm."[6] What harm could be done to Paul while in Roman custody? Certainly not physical harm. Given that Paul was awaiting trial, the most obvious type of harm is legal. His opposition to Paul's message (2 Tim. 4:15) is not a harm against Paul *personally*. The mention of this metalworker occurs in an important context. In verse 16 of 2 Timothy 4, Paul says that he has already had one trial appearance. Thus the most obvious inference is that the metalworker gave damaging testimony against Paul because he opposed Paul's message. If this metalworker is the man referenced in Acts 19:33, it would explain why the Jews pushed him before the rioting craftsmen:

1. **He shared the same or related trade as the crowd** and would be known to many of them and more likely to receive a sympathetic hearing from them.

2. **He had knowledge of and could oppose Paul's teachings** which were ultimately the cause of the uproar.

Based upon these circumstances and parallels between Acts 19 and 2 Timothy 4, it is plausible that both refer to the same man. Because both are named Alexander, I conclude they are almost certainly the same.

One further bit of evidence supports this conclusion. In 2 Timothy 4:12, Paul says, "I sent Tychicus to Ephesus." Tychicus was Paul's courier delivering the prison letters to the neighboring towns of Ephesus and Colossae to encourage the believers there.[7] It makes sense that during the interlude between Paul's "first defense" and the trial he is awaiting as 2 Timothy is written, that he would seek additional evidence since the first defense was apparently not a concluded trial. Tychichus was probably present during the Ephesian riot,[8] therefore he would be an obvious choice to obtain written statements from the city clerk, Roman officials,[9] or other witnesses there concerning Paul's involvement. The mention of Alexander the metalworker doing harm to Paul is one sentence removed from Paul's statement that he sent Tychichus to Ephesus. 2 Timothy 4:12 and 14 dovetail with the information Luke supplies about Alexander of Ephesus in *Acts*.[10] Because the foregoing evidence fit our thesis so well, Acts 19:33 further supports the thesis that Luke has written *Acts* as pretrial background and legal defense. A consideration of "potential trial exhibits" perhaps provides even stronger evidence for the thesis.

POSSIBLE TRIAL EXHIBITS

In presenting a trial, written documents are extremely important, especially if they were created contemporaneously with the events they record. For example, a MasterCard record of a purchase signed by an individual would strongly corroborate a person's testimony that she was in the city and the particular store on the date the purchase was recorded. In fact, if the witness insisted that she was only in that city on the day *previous* to the purchase or that she bought a dress instead of a sweater noted on the charge slip, the judge or jury would usually believe the written record over the witness's sworn testimony. Why?

1. Written records are far less likely to "forget."

2. They are often created by disinterested parties who have no reason to lie (the MasterCard merchant in our hypothetical case, for example, if the issues on trial did not involve the purchase).

Under Roman trial procedures, relevant documents and written pretrial depositions were acceptable evidence. [11] In the first century, of course, written records were less common than today and their photocopy machines were excruciatingly slow. Because of the relative scarcity of documents (compared to the twenty-first century), those that did exist would have been all the more persuasive. Every logical reason exists to conclude that in certain cases involving many accusations, many witnesses, and many locations, such as the trial of Paul, written records would be more important than in other cases. Numerous examples exist of documents figuring prominently in Roman trials.[12] If *Acts* was written with a view toward defending Paul and, by extension, the Way against the charges brought against him in Rome, then one would expect it to:

A. Reference relevant documents.

B. Quote from those documents.

C. Focus on events which can be corroborated by those documents.

D. Address events where written documents furnished by the opposition could be used adversely.

Thus, in yet one more way we can test the thesis that *Acts* is fact background and legal argument in defense of Paul by considering whether such documents or situations where documents exist are referenced. If they are not, or referenced only infrequently, then that will be a piece of evidence against the thesis. On the other hand, if such documents or situations are frequently referenced, we can count those references as evidence supporting the thesis.

Of course, a careful historian, writing in a nonlegal context, also may tend to record events which are documented.[13] Therefore, if *Acts* is a statement of historic facts selected for legal purposes rather than a history written for other purposes, we would expect the "paper trail" particularly to follow the legal issues rather than, say, the biographical or theological issues. Let us first attempt to list the documents that in A.D. 61–62 may have been either in Luke's possession or accessible through the offices of the Roman government. The following chart lists documents which were certain or virtually certain to have existed at some point. After listing the documents, I have assigned a degree of probability of their availability in A.D. 62 giving the greatest weight to:

1. **Explicit reference** in *Acts* or *Luke*.

2. **Nearness in time** from date of composition to the presumed writing date of *Acts*.

I have given some, but lesser weight to:

3. Customary Roman/Jewish **record-keeping practices**.

4. Possible **allusion in *Acts*** to the document.

5. My **sense as a litigator** of *Acts* being written to "lay a foundation" for use of a document at trial.

Thirty-Three Documents Possibly or Probably Available as Exhibits for Paul's Trial in Rome

	Document	Possible	Probable	Very Probable
1.	Many "accounts" of the life of Jesus (Luke 1:1)			X
2.	Gospel of Mark		X	
3.	Septuagint (Greek) translation of Hebrew Scriptures			X (certain)
4.	Sanhedrin trial "transcript" (Acts 4:5–21)	X		
5.	Sanhedrin trial "transcript" (Acts 5:27–40)	X		
6.	Sanhedrin trial "transcript" of Stephen's speech (Acts 6:12—7:60)	X		
7.	Letters of authorization (Acts 9:2; 22:4)	X		
8.	Service record of Centurion Cornelius (Acts 10:1)	X		
9.	Peter's prison record (Acts 12:4)	X		
10.	Proconsular records of Sergius Paulus (Acts 13:7–12)		X	
11.	Letter from Jerusalem elders (Acts 15:24)			X
12.	Philippian jail/ municipal records (Acts 16)		X	
13.	Citizenship records for Paul (Acts 16:37, 22:25)			X
14.	Thessalonian jail/ municipal records (Acts 17:1–13)	X		
15.	*Areopagus* trial transcript (Acts 17:16–32)	X		
16.	Proconsular records of Gallio (Acts 18:2–17)		X	
17.	Commendation of Apollos (Acts 18:27)	X		
18.	Ephesian municipal records (Acts 19:38)	X		

Document	Possible	Probable	Very Probable
19. "Log" of Luke's travel (Various, e.g. Acts 20:13–16)	X		
20. Purification notice (Acts 21:26)	X		
21. Sanhedrin trial "transcript" (Acts 22:30—23:10)		X	
22. Letter from Commander Lysias (Acts 23:25–30)			X
23. Transcript of trial before Felix (Acts 24:1–21)		X	
24. *Narratio*, "N" document— written summary of Tertullus for his oral argument	X		
25. Prison record of Paul in Caesarea (Acts 24:27)			X
26. Transcript of trial before Festus (Acts 25:6–12)			X
27. Letter from Festus to Nero (Acts 25:26)			X
28. Transcript of "trial" before Agrippa (Acts 26:1–32)	X		
29. Centurion's or captain's report of voyage and shipwreck (Acts 27)	X		
30. Records of Publius (Acts 28:7–10)	X		
31. Magistrate's decision fixing conditions of Paul's custody (Acts 28:16, 30)			X
32. *Inscriptio*, charges against Paul (see Acts 28:21 and commentary on that verse)			X
33. Depositions—(written statements) of Roman officials and other witnesses			X (many such documents)

What does this chart tell us? Where does the paper trail lead? Excluding the Scriptures or Scripture sources (Nos. 1, 2, and 3), I have categorized fourteen or more documents as probably or very probably in existence at the time of Paul's trial. Another sixteen possibly exist. Almost all of the documents are explicitly legal or would be relevant to defend the charges against Paul. The one which I consider to have only a tangential relevance to legal issues, the commendation of Apollos, is mentioned by Luke in passing. While some documents clearly have a general historical or theological relevance, many of the documents do not fit into an "*Acts* is a biography of Paul" paradigm (such as the letter from the Jerusalem elders). Likewise, other documents which may be seen as part of Paul's biography do not fit into an "*Acts* is a theological history" paradigm. Is *Acts* primarily an evangelistic treatise? The paper trail doesn't seem to lead that way either. However, virtually all the documents (*thirty-two out of thirty-three!*), whether explicitly or implicitly referenced in *Acts,* could be used to corroborate the facts asserted or the legal arguments which, I believe, Luke is making throughout *Acts.* The paper trail leads to the courtroom.

1 Acts 20:4; 27:2.
2 Acts 28:7.
3 Acts 15.
4 Acts 21:21–24.
5 Acts 19:33.
6 2 Tim. 4:14.
7 Eph. 6:21–22; Col. 4:7–8.
8 Acts 20:8.
9 Acts 19:31.
10 The Alexander mentioned in 1 Tim. 1:20 could be the same individual as mentioned in 2 Timothy and Acts 19, but that question is too attenuated from the purpose of this book to discuss.
11 Robinson, *Criminal Law,* 5.
12 E.g., Rapske, "Paul in Roman Custody," 249, quotes Cicero as asserting that he will prove the guilt of Verres by use of testimony and prison records. Cicero, "Verres" 2.5.142.
13 Although beyond the scope of this book, one could also compare *Acts* to ancient historical monographs known to be written for nonlegal purposes (see chapter on dating and genre) to see how frequently documents or documented events are referenced.

CHAPTER 29

THE MISSING EPISTLES AND PAUL'S PRISON LETTERS

I s something missing? The previous chapter noted how selectively Luke references documents which can support a defense of Paul and Christianity. However, if Luke is writing to Theophilus for other reasons, such as to record history, give instruction in the faith, or argue theology, or if Luke really has no focused purpose and is just stringing events about Paul together for the reader's enjoyment, then why, we must ask, are references to other categories of documents absent from Acts? Where are the references to commercial documents or to historical records which do not connect to a legal/evangelistic agenda? *Most importantly why does Luke not mention any of Paul's letters?*

In addition to the thirteen letters attributed to Paul in the New Testament canon, we also know Paul wrote other letters.[1] These letters apparently were circulating beyond the Gentile congregations Paul had started and were well respected.[2] If Luke was with Paul on his journeys or during his imprisonments in Caesarea or Rome, he certainly would have had occasion to note that Paul spent time writing "to strengthen and edify the churches." If Luke is writing to believers, one presumes he would have at least mentioned *some* of Paul's letters. Why this omission which some commentators have called "notorious"?

One school of thought holds that Luke was unaware of this correspondence. If *Acts* was written between A.D. 85 and 90 as one scholar opines,[3] then the "ignorance explanation" becomes implausible because many of the letters would have circulated.[4] No writer who was so minutely conversant with the events of Paul's life would have been ignorant of their existence or, if aware, would have failed to mention them if he was writing to believers. Paul is the hero of *Acts*. His speeches are recorded frequently. Obviously Luke would mention the letters if his audience is *Talmidei Yeshua*.

On the other hand, if *Acts* was written around A.D. 62, Luke would have had to spend much time with Paul and used him extensively as a source. He would have seen Paul writing the letters (he is mentioned in three of them!).[5] In *Philemon* and *Colossians*, Luke joins in "sending greetings." Accordingly, based on strong evidence, I conclude that Luke knew of much of Paul's correspondence and probably knew of most or all of it. Consequently, the question: Why did Luke write so much about Paul and omit all reference to his many letters?

One reasonable answer is that Paul's letters to believers would be substantially irrelevant, or even counterproductive, to Luke's legal strategy. If *Acts* was composed to defend Paul and Christianity, and to be read by a Roman official gathering facts for Paul's trial, the letters:

(a) would **differ in content and purpose** from that of *Acts*—instruction, edification, and encouragement for believers versus background and legal and evangelistic persuasion for Roman officials.

(b) were **less credible** because they did not come from third parties but contained what are known in modern law as "self-serving declarations by the accused."

(c) **could expose** other believers[6] to persecution.

(d) could have provided **ammunition for Paul's opponents,** such as taking his teaching on divisions in the church and using them out of context to support the argument that the Messianics were socially disruptive.

The omission of any reference in *Acts* to Paul's letters is significant and almost certainly deliberate. That omission must be accounted for in any understanding of the purpose of *Acts*. Admittedly, an argument from silence is difficult to make. However, some silences are louder than others. The omission from *Acts* of any mention of Paul's epistles is a thundering silence, and it lends support to the legal brief hypothesis simply because their omission from a legal brief is plausible while their omission from a letter to a seeker or believer is implausible.

PAUL'S LETTERS FROM PRISON

We know that many of Paul's letters in the New Testament were written while he was in prison. Although *Acts* does not allude to these, the letters frequently allude to the events in or circumstances of *Acts*. Paul had two major imprisonments:

1. Caesarea—two years (A.D. 59–60—Acts 24:27).

2. Rome—two years (A.D. 61–62—Acts 28:30).

In addition, some scholars believe he may have been released after his Roman imprisonment and been incarcerated in Rome again around A.D. 65.

Four of the letters, Ephesians, Philippians, Colossians, and Philemon, appear to have been written during the Roman imprisonment of A.D. 61–62. The fifth letter, 2 Timothy, was written from Rome also, but either during A.D. 61–62 or possibly during a second imprisonment from A.D. 65 to 67.

What, if anything, can we learn from Paul's epistles which bear upon our thesis? Let us examine passages which reference Paul's imprisonment, our author Luke, or both, and use them to test our understanding of to whom and why *Acts* was written:

Ephesians

6:19–20: "and [pray] for me, that utterance may be given to me, that I may open my mouth boldly to make known the mystery of the gospel, for which I am an ambassador in chains; that in it I may speak boldly, as I ought to speak."

As Paul closes this letter, his uppermost personal need is boldness to share the gospel despite his imprisonment. His attitude, as shown in his request for prayer, is fully consistent with the agenda we have seen of his disciple, Luke, in his legal brief. Luke is sharing the gospel in written form, Paul wants to share it verbally. More than just being consistent, the objectives of Paul and Luke complement each other.

Philippians

1:12–14: "But I want you to know, brethren, that the things which happened to me have actually turned out for the furtherance of the gospel, so that it has become evident to the whole palace guard, and to all the rest, that my chains are in Christ; and most of the brethren in the Lord, having become confident by my chains, are much more bold to speak the word without fear."

1:20: "according to my earnest expectation and hope that in nothing I shall be ashamed, but with all boldness, as always, so now also Christ will be magnified in my body, whether by life or by death."

4:22: "All the saints greet you, but especially those who are of Caesar's household."

These and other verses in Philippians show that although Paul hoped to be released from prison and reunited with the other believers, his overarching and exceeding priority was to proclaim the gospel boldly. To whom did he want to preach, when he asks for prayer to speak fearlessly? As a prisoner, he did not have a lot of options. The obvious and only certain audiences we know of are (1) the palace guard, (2) Caesar's (Nero's) household, and (3) those who would preside over, participate in, or attend his trial. The third category includes Nero, his *consilium*, Roman senators, aristocrats, and judicial officials as the majority of that category. Paul places the goal of courageously speaking "the word of God" above his own life. These expressions in Rome are fully consistent with Paul's attitude on his way to Jerusalem in Acts 21:13: "For I am ready not only to be bound, but also to die at Jerusalem for the name of the Lord Jesus."

Therefore, we can conclude the evangelistic agenda of Paul described by Luke in *Acts* and the evangelistic goal and readership for which I believe *Acts* is written are fully consistent with the objectives and priorities expressed by Paul in Philippians. This consistency tells us Paul saw himself and Luke saw Paul with the same eyes in the critical area of life purpose. Because Luke was Paul's disciple and because, by any interpretation of *Acts*, Paul is not only a central character of *Acts*, but a hero, we can fairly surmise that if Luke wrote *Acts* to defend Paul before Nero, he would have every predisposition to use his legal writing as an opportunity to present the gospel.

Colossians

4:3–4: "meanwhile praying also for us, that God would open to us a door for the word, to speak the mystery of Christ, for which I am also in chains, that I may make it manifest, as I ought to speak."

4:14: "Luke the beloved physician and Demas greet you."

Again, Paul asks for prayer specifically to proclaim clearly "the mystery of Messiah." And Luke is with him. The confluence of Paul's attitude and Luke's opportunity make clear the conclusion that Paul encouraged Luke to share his objective of using his imprisonment as an opportunity to spread the gospel. What better "open door" to reach many Roman officials than the very "statement of facts" which the defense would be submitting? What "clearer proclamation" than *Luke-Acts*?

Philemon

23: "Epaphras, my fellow prisoner in Christ Jesus, greets you,

24: as do Mark, Aristarchus, Demas, Luke, my fellow laborers"

From these two verses, we learn much that is relevant to our inquiry. First, this letter is probably written early in Paul's Roman imprisonment. We will see from 2 Timothy 4:9–11 and 4:13 that Mark, Aristarchus, and Demas eventually leave Paul; but, at this point they have not left. Second, Mark is with Luke. If Mark is indeed an author, contributor, or even just a partial transmitter of the Gospel which the early church attributed to him, then he would have been a source for or helped Luke compose the Gospel of Luke. Third, and most importantly, Luke is present with Paul while Paul is in prison. Paul is the obvious source for much of *Acts*, Luke is the obvious writer, their time together in Rome is the obvious time for its composition. Could the obvious explanations for source, author, and dates possibly be the true explanations?

2 Timothy

2:8–9: "Remember that Jesus Christ, of the seed of David, was raised from the dead according to my gospel, for which I suffer trouble as an evildoer, even to the point of chains; but the word of God is not chained."

4:9–11: "Be diligent to come to me quickly; for Demas has forsaken me, having loved this present world, and has departed for Thessalonica—Crescens for Galatia, Titus for Dalmatia. Only Luke is with me. Get Mark and bring him with you, for he is useful to me for ministry."

4:16–17: "At my first defense no one stood with me, but all forsook me . . . But the Lord stood with me and strengthened me, so that the message might be preached fully through me, and that all the Gentiles might hear. Also I was delivered out of the mouth of the lion."

This letter tells us that as Paul approached trial, "everyone" deserted him. However, 4:11 makes it probable that the "everyone" did not include Luke.

Further, the trial did not result in an execution but turned out to be a "first defense." Some speculate that Paul was released and then re-imprisoned around A.D. 65–67 during the time when he wrote 2 Timothy. However, I believe the second defense was probably an adjournment of the first trial rather than a whole new imprisonment and trial because Paul says "first defense" rather than "first trial" and because the tone of 2 Timothy 4 suggests a continuity of imprisonment. In any event, "only Luke" is with Paul as he awaits a second defense. If Luke had researched and written *Luke-Acts* as a defense of Paul and if he had absorbed the attitude of Paul depicted in *Acts* of proclaiming the gospel regardless of personal cost, it makes sense that he would want to be with him and that he could contribute both to the first and second defense by writing *Luke-Acts*.

We also learn that the Lord stood at Paul's side and strengthened him, which is consistent with His exhortation to "Take courage!" in Acts 23:11. "Be of good cheer, Paul; for as you have testified for Me in Jerusalem, so you must also bear witness at Rome."

Finally, Paul tells Timothy that the strengthening of the Lord enabled him to fully proclaim the message so all the Gentiles might hear it. It seems that prayers requested of the Ephesians, Philippians, and Colossians have been answered. The most obvious explanation of this passage is that Paul believes that by his testimony to those attending his "first defense" he has won or will win some to faith. Reaching "all the Gentiles" should be read broadly as in "all France rejoiced at the triumph of their Olympic gold medalist." Paul has spread the word widely, in to many parts of the empire. Now he has reached its highest social and political stratum.

SUMMARY OF PRISON LETTERS

Certainly many critical verses in Paul's prison letters support the legal brief thesis. Nevertheless, the greatest test of the proposition must come from the biblical source closest to *Acts*, the Gospel of Luke.

---

1   See 1 Cor. 5:9.
2   See 2 Pet. 3:15b.
3   Maddox, *Purpose of Luke-Acts,* 180.
4   See Col. 4:16.
5   Col. 4:14; 2 Tim. 4:11; Philem. 24.
6   See Romans 16 and Paul's apparent care not to mention names of believers in Caesar's household, Phil. 4:22.

CHAPTER 30

HOW THE BOOK OF LUKE FITS IN

Before analyzing the details of *Luke*, I must propose that without *Luke*, *Acts* makes no sense. No legal defense of Paul was possible without an understanding of Christianity. No understanding of the Way was possible without understanding the life and teaching of Jesus. Thus the substance of *Luke*, the principal parts, as opposed to the unique details which are the focus of this chapter, are fully consistent with the evangelistic legal brief thesis because *Luke* provides factual background.

To analyze the purposes and audience of *Acts*, we must carefully consider the well established scholarly consensus that *Acts* is not a solitary work but is coupled with the Book of Luke in (1) a chronological continuum, (2) apparent unity of authorship (Luke), and (3) unity of immediate audience (Theophilus). *Luke*, however, differs from *Acts* in that its core is shared with and evidently borrowed from *Mark*, with generous additions from other sources. Scholars have named the primary other source as "Q," defining Q as passages common to *Matthew* and *Luke* but not found in *Mark*. *Matthew*, *Luke*, and *Mark* present Jesus to the reader with similar eyes (the synoptic Gospels recounting the life of Jesus). To determine the exact intended readership of each Gospel, scholars have rightly focused on the *differences* between them. Particularly with *Matthew* and *Luke*, scholars have concluded that the author took *Mark* and Q and then shaped those sources and added other passages to reach a particular audience. Accordingly, in analyzing to whom the Book of Luke, a borrowed account, was written, one must look to the *distinctives* between *Luke*, *Mark*, and *Matthew*. In contrast, in analyzing *Acts*, an original work without parallel, to discern the readership one must look to the entire work and indeed each detail therein.

To further clarify the relationships between Luke (L), Mark (Mk), Matthew (Mt) and Q, allow me to remake the preceding point in formulas. The *unique* portions of *Luke* we shall designate UL, likewise the unique portions of *Matthew* we shall label UMt:

$$L = Mk + Q + UL \qquad\qquad Mt = Mk + Q + UMt$$

$$L - Mk - Q = UL \qquad\qquad Mt - Mk - Q = UMt$$

and

$$L - Mk - UL = Q = Mt - Mk - UMt$$

Although using formulas can help us understand the relationship of various texts, I do not mean to imply that Mark was written before Matthew (some scholars believe Mark derived from Matthew). Likewise, we need not solve the mysteries of Q or add to its mystique. Finally, it is also beyond our scope to examine aspects of *Luke* except as they bear on the reasons *Acts* was written. Rather, my point is simple: UL, portions of Luke unique from the other Gospels, does exist. By focusing on UL we can call one more witness to the stand.

If UL furthers the legal/evangelistic agenda, then because of the close connection between *Luke* and *Acts* we have evidence that the purpose of Acts is as we have supposed. If UL contradicts the thesis, if it is primarily catechistic (akin to 1 Corinthians 12), theological (akin to John 3:1–21), exhortational (2 Timothy 1, 2), prophetic (1 Thess. 4:13–18), or relational (e.g. Romans 16), then "our" witness, UL, is hostile and our thesis may be wrong. With each UL passage, let us ask whether it appears to have been added to make *Luke* more understandable or connect it more closely to a Roman official or to further a previously identified legal agenda which would be carried forward into *Acts*. The interpretations of UL which follow are not intended to be exhaustive, only to show that those passages support or at least are not inconsistent with our thesis:

Luke 1:1–4: See chapter "The Investigator."

Luke 1:5: "In the days of Herod, the king of Judea . . ."

Luke 1:5–80: An explanation (to the Roman) of how to better know that John the Baptist foreshadowed the coming of Jesus, to establish John's Jewishness against the argument that the Messianics had started a new, illegal religion, and to establish the peaceful spiritual mission of John against the presumption (due to his execution) that he was a revolutionary.

Luke 2:1: "In those days ... a decree went out from Caesar Augustus . . ."

Luke 2:21–40: constant emphasis on the dedication of Jesus being in conformity with the Law of Moses. Why is Gentile Luke the only gospel writer who felt it necessary to mention the circumcision of Jesus? Possibly he felt his reader needed an emphasis on the thorough Jewishness of Jesus in the context of charges that Paul and the Messianics were starting a new religion and not circumcising converts.

Luke 2:41–52: Although Luke could have many reasons for including the account of Jesus, at twelve years, learning at the temple, certainly it shows a continuity in his Jewishness by linking his circumcision, education, baptism, and calling. (Luke 4:16–21)

Luke 3:1: "In the fifteenth year of the reign of Tiberius Caesar . . ."

Luke 3:12–13: Tax collectors (Roman agents essential to the security and power of the empire) are baptized and instructed to follow Roman law.

Luke 3:14: Soldiers (the means by which Rome maintained power) are told to be honest and "be content with your [Roman] pay."

Luke 3:19–20: Explanation of why John really was arrested; i.e. he was not instigating civil unrest or rebellion.

Luke 3:23–38: The genealogy of Jesus extended beyond Abraham (see Matthew 1:1) to Adam. Jesus is not just for Jews; through faith in him Judaism is made universal.

Luke 4:5–13: Satan offers Jesus "all the kingdoms of the world." Jesus' reply, "It is written: 'Worship the Lord your God and serve him only,'" is a dramatic renunciation at the beginning of his ministry of any political goals in competition with Rome. Although Matthew 4:8 contains a similar passage, the conclusion in Luke certainly bolsters the background for the legal defense.

Luke 4:23 and 4:28–30: Early indications of the rejection of Jesus by many Jews also lays foundation for the upcoming legal defense.

Luke 4:24–27: The widow of Zarephath and Naaman the Syrian are non-Jews to whom God's prophets from Israel, Elijah and Elisha, bring blessing to the explicit exclusion of "widows in Israel" and "lepers in Israel." Similarly, Jesus and Paul are God's prophets who bring blessings to Gentiles.

Luke 6:12–16: Calling of the apostles lays the foundation for Acts 1:15–23.

Luke 7:2–10: Healing of a centurion's servant and commendation of the centurion's great faith. (This passage recurs in Matt. 8:5–13 but it so obviously puts Jesus in a loving light to a Roman governmental official that it merits notice.) Also, only *Luke* records the special commendation at Luke 7:9: "I say to you, I have not found such great faith, not even in Israel."

Luke 7:18–35: More background on John the Baptizer especially as a prophet who considered that Jesus could be the Messiah.

Luke 7:39: Rejection of Jesus by Pharisees and experts in a law lays a foundation to explain why many Jewish leaders had rejected Jesus.

Luke 8:3: Herod's household manager mentioned (see Acts 13:1).

Luke 9:9: In recounting Herod's execution of John only *Luke* relates that Herod sought to see Jesus.

Luke 11:14–26: "[A] house divided against itself will fall" certainly can be taken by a Roman official as an implicit warning concerning the condition of the Roman government.

Luke 11:29–32: Both recipients of the warning from the prophets of Israel who heed the message are powerful Gentiles: Ninevites, representatives of a great city, and Sheba, a queen of a large "kingdom." Similarly, Jesus and later Paul are prophets of Israel who warn the nations (Rome and the Roman Empire) to repent.

Luke 11:53: Pharisees and teachers of law further oppose Jesus; Luke continues to lay the foundation for legal argument explaining the rejection of Jesus by many Jewish leaders which will be expanded in *Acts*.

Luke 12:11–12: Prophecy concerning the trials that Peter, Paul, and other disciples would be facing as subsequently chronicled in *Acts*. Parallel passages do exist at Matthew 10:17–20 and Mark 13:11–13. Although each passage is essentially identical, the *Matthew* and *Mark* passages are followed by a passage stating that the resulting divisions will result in death. The possibly corresponding *Luke* follow-up passage, 12:49–53, perhaps for the benefits of the Roman audience, is softened by omitting any reference to death. This change could be to assure that Jesus was not misconstrued as advocating violence.

Luke 12:49–53: Jesus' statement about the turmoil which his ministries and followers will face can help the Roman observer to understand and contextualize the upheaval surrounding his disciples. The parallel *Matthew* passage, 10:34b, quotes Jesus as saying, "I did not come to bring peace but a sword." In *Matthew* Jesus is speaking metaphorically; given the charges against Paul, however, Luke avoids the metaphor by eliminating a passage which could easily be misunderstood.

Luke 12:57–59: Luke clarifies the preceding passage by explaining that the "turmoil" and "division" of the prior passage is *not* civil insurrection and Jesus warns the people to be law-abiding and peacable.

Luke 13:1: Referencing a slaughter by the Roman official Pilate, Luke bypasses a made-for-television opportunity to quote Jesus as denouncing the man who will sentence him to crucifixion or denouncing the rule of Rome. Instead, Jesus teaches on universal sinfulness and the need to repent.

Luke 13:31: Herod mentioned again. This Roman official is mentioned six times in *Luke* and only twice each in *Mark* and *Matthew*.

Luke 14:1–6: Healing on Sabbath: Luke is continually laying a foundation to explain why Paul and the followers of Jesus could behave differently from Jews familiar to Theophilus and still claim to be Jewish.

Luke 14:25–33: The cost of discipleship: Luke has picked out a teaching of Jesus which foretells and begins to explain the motivation and behavior of Peter, Stephen, Paul, and other evangelists in *Acts*.

Luke 15:8–10: Parable of the lost coin: This unique passage could be included for many reasons. Certainly it reinforces the preceding parable of the lost sheep and is a call to conversion. Also, it can appeal in Luke's usage to a Roman official just as it was used by Jesus in the original context (Luke 15:1–2) to appeal to "sinners" by telling them the Pharisees did not control access to salvation.

Luke 15:11–32: Parable of the two sons: In this context Luke is not only telling Theophilus he is a child of God but is planting the seed which may convince him of the plausibility of the jealousy motivation attributed in *Acts* to the accusers of Paul.[1] Luke may intend the reader to see Israel as the older son and the Gentiles (Romans/Greeks) as the younger.

Luke 16:1–14: Parable of the shrewd/dishonest manager: This passage and its summation: "You cannot serve both God and money"[2] is a missile aimed at some of Paul's accusers and particularly the charge that Paul was an evangelist for monetary gain.

Luke 16:16–17: Jesus' prophecy concerning the forceful proclamation of the "good news" certainly prepares Theophilus for the events chronicled in *Acts*.

Luke 16:18: Short teaching on divorce: What matters here may be the omissions. *Mark* and *Matthew* have extensive passages on divorce which pertain to interpretations of Jewish law (see Matt. 19:3; Mark 10:2). Luke may have dropped or shortened those passages simply because they were irrelevant to his agenda and audience. The only real puzzle is why it was not eliminated altogether because it is difficult to understand without the context of the Jewish law, as well as how it is intended to relate to the verses preceding and following. The reason for its retention may be that divorce and adultery were extremely important public issues in Roman law[3] and subject to statutory regulation and severe penalties. Luke may simply have wished to contrast the variability of Roman law with the permanence of God's law asserted in the preceding verse 17.

Luke 16:19–31: The rich man and Lazarus: This passage has lessons discernible on several levels for just about any reader and can be read to support most theories concerning readership. Regarding the evangelistic/legal brief understanding, verses 29–31 function to further explain why so many Jewish leaders are rejecting Jesus.

Luke 17:12–19: Ten lepers are healed: The one "foreigner" is commended by Jesus. Thus Theophilus is told salvation is available to non-Jews who acknowledge Israel's God but that many Jews will miss the message.

Luke 17:20–37: Jesus says, "the kingdom of God is within you" (v. 21). It is not a kingdom which supplants the kingdom of Caesar and not an external kingdom. The passages concerning the days of the Son of Man (vv. 22, 26, and 30) apparently relate to the second coming of Jesus. Possibly Jesus' teaching about his return was used by the opposition to frighten Roman leaders that the Second Coming was really a *forthcoming revolt* against Rome. In that context, the kingdom of God teachings of the Gospels and the Messianics would be perceived as advocating the establishment of an earthly kingdom in opposition to Rome. The teaching here, especially when introduced by Luke 17:21,[4] is included to emphasize that the Second Coming is a divine rather than manmade occurrence.

Luke 18:9–14: The Pharisee and tax collector: This passage gives hope to those who are not part of the religious "inner circle," to outsiders, among whom Theophilus must have felt when observing Jewish piety. It is a recurring theme, but one which required repetition to bridge the wide religious/cultural chasm between the perceived exclusivity of pharisaic Judaism and the new covenant Judaism which was offering faith to all. Further, Luke may have selected this parable because tax collectors would be sympathetic characters to a Roman since they formed the backbone of the financial system supporting the empire, its lifestyle, and military. Tax collectors were *hated* by the populace. Consequently, Luke's selection of a parable about a tax collector appears to be highly consistent with an intention to show Rome that Jesus was not capitalizing on popular resentment to forment rebellion.

Luke 19:1–10: Zacchaeus, the tax collector, a Roman collaborator and a "sinner," finds God's grace. This account shows the Nazarenes were no threat to Rome's income because there is no animosity toward Zacchaeus, only mercy and forgiveness.

Luke 20:1–8: The authority of Jesus relative to the chief priests, teachers of the law, and elders is discussed. "Authority" becomes the lead legal issue addressed in Acts 1.

Luke 20:20–25: Paying taxes to Caesar: Although both *Mark* and *Matthew* also have this passage which strongly supports the evangelism/legal brief hypothesis, *Luke* adds the particular details about the explicit political aims of Jesus' opponents in verse 20. These details precisely predict the defense argument of Paul: his opponents are hypocritical, accusing him of breaking Roman law solely to further their own agenda, not because they care about the law (see Acts 17:7).

Luke 21:12: Signs of temple destruction: *Luke, Matthew,* and *Mark* all record the prophecy of Jesus that the temple will be destroyed. However, the predicate—"But before all these things, they will lay their hands on you and persecute you, delivering you up to the synagogues and prisons. You will be brought before kings and rulers for My name's sake."—functions especially well in preparing Theophilus to understand the persecution of the apostles by the Jewish leadership and God's foreknowledge that Paul would stand trial before Nero.

Luke 21:24: Times of the Gentiles: In recounting Jesus' prophecy of temple destruction, only *Luke* records there will be a period of human history known as the "times of the Gentiles". This detail not only is of special interest to a Gentile reader, but reinforces the legal theme that in Jesus, faith and salvation in Abraham's God is made universally available.

Luke 22:51: The arrest of Jesus: Although *Mark* and *Matthew* recount the cutting off of the ear of the servant of the high priest (an act of violence which clearly can counter defense arguments that neither Jesus, Paul, nor their followers were fomenting a rebellion), *only Luke* recounts the rebuke of Jesus, "No more of this," *and* the healing of the ear. Jesus' rhetorical question: "Am I leading a rebellion . . . ?" although also found in *Mark* and *Matthew*, certainly is consistent with the hypothesis that Luke is writing as a legal apologist.

Luke 23:2a: "We found this fellow perverting the nation." This charge is recorded *only* in *Luke*. Its overt political overtones are echoed in the charges against Stephen: "They also set up false witnesses who said, 'This man does not cease to speak blasphemous words against this holy place and the law; for we have heard him say that this Jesus of Nazareth will destroy this place and change the customs which Moses delivered to us.'"[5] And echoed against Paul: "but they have been informed about you that you teach all the Jews who are among the Gentiles to forsake Moses, saying that they ought not to circumcise their children nor to walk according to the customs."[6] All of the emphasis throughout *Luke-Acts* on the authentic Jewishness of faith in Jesus makes sense in light of these changes.

Luke 23:2b: Charge of tax rebellion: "He opposes payment of taxes to Caesar . . ." Only *Luke* records that Jesus is accused of leading a tax rebellion, clearly a serious attack on Rome's power! Luke has already prepared the reader[7] to understand that the rebellion charge is ridiculous. That he carefully refutes the charge first in chapter 20 and then sets it forth in the mouths of Jesus' opponents supports the proposition that *Luke-Acts* was to be read by Roman officials who had this thought in mind: "How does this Jesus, these Messianists, this Paul affect the peace, income, and stability of Rome?" In contrast, *Matthew, Mark,* and *John* all omitted this charge despite obvious opportunities to do so[8] suggesting that their nongovernmental readerships would have found that detail unimportant.

In addition to refuting the charge, Luke belies it by the account of Zaccheus in Luke 19. The naming of Zaccheus and his identity as *chief tax collector* and a *resident of Jericho* are verifiable details perhaps inserted to allow Rome to confirm the falsity of the tax rebellion charge.

Luke 23:2b (continued): "He . . . claims to be Messiah, a king." All the gospel writers record the reaction of Pilate and the answer of Jesus: "Then Pilate asked Him, saying, 'Are you the King of the Jews?' He answered him and said, 'It is as you say.'[9] But *only Luke* records the charge, the double exoneration of Pilate (vv. 4 and 14) and the reported exoneration of Herod (v. 15). Such additional details certainly support the proposition that *Luke-Acts* was tailored as a legal defense.

Luke 23:1–16: Pilate and Herod: *Only Luke* records the interplay of these two Roman officials in the sentencing of Jesus. Why? If he was writing an account of Jesus' life which would be read by Roman officials familiar with the extensive legal record keeping of the empire, they and Luke would realize that official records of an event occurring thirty years earlier could be in existence. Possibly those records could be as self-serving as those of Lysias.[10] Accordingly, in an era where no formal system of briefing existed, Luke needed to anticipate an adverse record popping up and to preemptively assert the facts as understood by Paul and the followers of Jesus.

Luke 23:18–25: Release of Barabbas: All of the gospel writers agree that a criminal named Barabbas was released in place of Jesus. John 18:40 (NIV) indicates he had "taken part in a rebellion." *Matthew* simply calls Barabbas "notorious."[11] *Mark* goes further and says, carefully, that Barabbas "was chained with his fellow rebels; they had committed murder in the rebellion."[12] *Luke* goes much further. If *Mark* is Luke's source, Luke reaches the sound legal conclusion that a participant in a group committing a serious crime likely to involve killing (insurrection) is guilty of murder even if the participant did not touch the victim and had no weapon. Accordingly, *Luke* records[13] that Barabbas had been charged with insurrection *and* murder. These details are particularly cogent to Roman officials concerned with maintaining order in a vast empire which periodically erupts with rebellion. They are apparently set forth in *Luke* to assert that in freeing Barabbas the true interests of Rome were subverted just to placate certain Jewish leaders. The thesis that *Luke* is factual background for a legal brief in defense of Paul well explains Luke's unique description of Barabbas.

Luke 23:26–31: "Daughters of Jerusalem weep not for me." If *Luke* is written after the destruction of Jerusalem in A.D. 70, the writer may include this passage because it can be read to show that Jesus was indeed a prophet. Some scholars have attributed great importance to this particular verse in support of dating *Luke* in the 70s or later.[14] That support is weak for many reasons:

1. Clearly *Acts* was written after *Luke*.[15] If Jerusalem had already been destroyed by the time *Acts* is written, the narrative of *Acts* affords dozens of reasons and opportunities to allude to it.[16]

2. All the arguments in *Acts* about the authority and place of the temple and priests relative to the authority of the apostles and the charges against Paul would have been *totally moot*! Luke would have wasted a lot of ink on a nonissue.

3. Other internal evidence supporting/confirming a dating of *Luke* later than A.D. 70 is scant, sometimes only a handful of verses depending how one defines "support" and "confirm," while the evidence of an evangelistic/legal defense is massive, discernible in virtually every chapter of *Luke* and *Acts*, often in every sentence.

4. The argument that Luke 23:26–31 is a post-A.D. 70 addition because it appears to reference the destruction of Jerusalem suggests anti-supernatural presupposition or even bias. Scholarship, like law, is ultimately about the pursuit of truth. An argument which says a passage must have been written after the fact assumes that God cannot reveal the future and/or that Jesus could not know the mind of God. It is as much lacking in scholarly objectivity as an "analysis" which concludes a particular passage must be true because it is in the Bible.

Christianity, at core, is a faith based on an historical event, the Resurrection.[17] Its claim invites, and really demands, rigorous historical scholarly investigation and cross-examination. Yet the investigator must be careful about his own biases if truth is to be discovered. Lawyers and scholars, despite their self-proclaimed objectivity, are sometimes poor judges of truth because their advocacy leads them to see facts selectively. In the area of biblical studies almost all scholars approach the Bible with presuppositions as to the degree to which, if at all, God has inspired it or miracles can occur. These presuppositions, if not vigilantly policed, will filter out or minimize uncomfortable or contradictory facts, thwarting the search for truth. How does one objectively criticize any book or faith system, which claims divine inspiration and divine intervention? Certainly not by presupposing miracles do not happen, or that they must happen. Two key rules of interpretation are:

A. The same methods and procedures must be used as in other truth seeking activities of the same type: the historicity of the events in *Acts* or *Luke* must be judged in the same way one judges the historicity of Julius Caesar's history, *The Gallic War*. No special privileges for *Luke-Acts*, no special burdens.

B. When a claim is made which defies verifiability because it is beyond the legal, scientific, or historical methods of establishing truth, then one must test the internal consistency of the asserted facts. Of course, the character of the writer or prophet can also be considered.

Having set forth four reasons why Luke 23:26–31 does not prove a post-A.D. 70 dating, we must ask why Luke is the only gospel writer to provide this detail. At least one plausible answer presents itself:

Luke recognizes this passage as a *timely* prophecy. Jesus' words connote that the fulfillment would be about a generation after his crucifixion: "weep for yourselves and your children," the next generation. Thus, in A.D. 62, if he believed the prophecy of Jesus which he recorded (and we have every reason to believe Luke's sincerity), Luke may sense that its fulfillment was imminent. If so, the evangelistic impact of including this passage becomes apparent when his reader later sees the prophecy fulfilled.

My conclusion is that Luke 23:27–31 can be used to show that Luke was written after A.D. 70 but only to those whose worldview precludes the prophetic. Even at that, it is not a strong piece of evidence and several reasonable arguments against its late dating exist. Further, at least one reasonable argument for its early dating exists. Thus the passage is inconclusive as far as dating is concerned.

Luke 24:13–35: Two disciples encounter Jesus on the road to Emmaus. This event is mentioned briefly in Mark 16:12–13, but Luke elaborates significantly because it furthers his legal agenda on several levels:

1. The "witness" theme of Acts 1:8 is foreshadowed.

2. The climactic event of the book is kept in the context of Jewish scripture[18] when the Roman reader could be inclined to conclude that this very event was putting the followers of Jesus outside of Judaism.

3. The battle lines of *Acts* which have already been established in *Luke* are set forth again[19] so that the reader of *Acts* will see the continuity between the persecution of Jesus and that of Peter and Paul.

Luke 24:50–53: The Ascension: This transition passage concludes what Luke 1:31 started. Jesus came from heaven and returned. At the same time it allows Acts 1 to "pick up where we left off."

The differences between *Luke* and *Acts*: Although *Luke-Acts* has been shown in many ways to be one book, with the same author, stated audience, language, and themes, a few differences nevertheless are worth noting. These differences show that *Luke* and *Acts* were intended to be "detachable" parts:

1. *Luke* was written to evangelize, give factual background for *Acts,* and pre-pare the reader for the legal arguments which would be pressed in *Acts.* Only to those who understand the basics of Jesus' life can *Acts* be seen as a stand-alone evangelistic book. The facts it presents are far more imme-diately relevant to the charges against Paul. The legal defense is explicit and powerful.

2. *Luke* was written before *Acts,*[20] not at the same time. Apparently, Luke, the author, did not think his legal apology could make much headway with-out the background of the Gospel.

3. *Acts* was harder to write than *Luke.* As has been seen, the gospel writer had many sources to draw on and incorporate in his first book. If *Mark* originally existed as an oral work, a one-man play if you will, for evan-gelists to recite/perform,[21] then Luke, with Paul's help, needed only to add Q and make the additions and revisions which would help further his legal agenda. I do not mean to say that the writing was easy, it was laborious. Nevertheless, Luke and Paul had the time[22] and probably the necessary support.[23] *Acts,* in contrast, is written from original oral sources. Certainly, Luke includes many passages from Tanakh[24] and some correspondence.[25] Nevertheless, at a minimum, Luke would have had to interview Peter and Paul extensively to obtain such details as Acts 1:20, 4:6, 5:7, 10:30, 12:8, 12:13–15, 14:12–13, 14:26, 17:34, 18:17, 21:40—22:2 (and possibly interview Philip at the time of Acts 21:8 to get some of the details in Acts 8:4–40). Most of these details would have been unimportant to a later audience of Christians. However, they mat-ter forensically and were given by Luke to support his legal arguments. Therefore, it easily took many months and probably closer to a year, to write *Acts* after *Luke* was given to Theophilus. *Luke* does not need *Acts*, but *Acts* needs *Luke* because it makes no sense to someone who knows nothing of Jesus.

These differences matter because the conclusion that *Luke-Acts* is one book for *all* purposes can lead to a wrong understanding of the author's focus. In *Luke*, the focus is on Jesus while the groundwork for the understanding of the legal/political/religious controversy is being laid. In *Acts*, especially with the introduction of Paul at 7:58 and accelerating at his trial before Felix in chap-ter 24, the emphasis changes to legal defense. Scholars have noted much of this pattern for decades. Ironically, they have missed the forensic thrust of the total-ity of *Luke-Acts* probably because of unfamiliarity with the components of legal argument, the specifics of Roman law or possibly by trying to impose a theo-logical paradigm on an essentially nontheological work. In any event, because scholarly enthusiasm for deconstruction has helped us examine, and test *Acts* in its components, now we can reassemble the book with a fuller understanding of how it works. In so doing we must answer squarely, the final obstacle to our thesis: the combined insights of scores of excellent scholars who have reached different conclusions about the purpose of *Acts*.

---

1   Acts 13:45, 7:9.
2   Luke 16:13c.
3   Robinson, *Criminal Law*, 58–64.
4   See also comment on Acts 1:6.
5   Acts 6:13–14.
6   Acts 21:21; see Acts 24:5.
7   Luke 20:20–26.
8   Matt. 27:2, 11–4; Mark 15:3; John 18:29–30.
9   Luke 23:3.
10   Acts 23:26.
11   Matt. 27:18.
12   Mark 15:7.
13   Luke 23:19.
14   Maddox, *Purpose of Luke-Acts*, 8.
15   See Acts 1:1.
16   See Acts 5:42, 7:48–50, 24:6.
17   1 Cor. 15:3, 12–17.
18   Luke 24:25–27; see Luke 24:44.
19   Luke 24:20.
20   Acts 1:1.
21   See Gal. 3:1.
22   Acts 28:30.
23   See Acts 28:14–15.
24   E.g., Acts 2:17–21.
25   E.g, Acts 15:23–29.

CHAPTER 31

OTHER EXPLANATIONS FOR *LUKE–ACTS*

U.S. Federal Judge Wayne Anderson of the Northern District of Illinois once remarked from the bench while I was sitting in his courtroom that "cases are not lost on their strong points but on their weak points."

The thesis of this book, that *Luke-Acts* was written to a Roman official charged with gathering facts for Paul's trial as a legal brief to acquit and convert, may seem convincing to the reader who has not considered other possibilities. Yet it is only one of numerous theses as to its purpose which have been advanced in the last century. Therefore, to fairly argue the viability of the evangelistic legal brief hypothesis, and to test that thesis as rigorously as possible, let us now explore alternative theories which are at variance with it. I have relied in part on the bibliography for the alternative explanations for the writing of *Luke-Acts* offered by Robert Maddox,[1] although with some paraphrase and not in the same order he lists them. We will examine their relative strengths, weaknesses, and compatibility with the premises of *Paul on Trial*.

1. Luke wanted to write a history of Christianity and he wrote about people and events he knew most closely. In writing this history, Luke also intended to show that "divine intervention" was "one of the credentials of the Christian movement."[2] Both formulations are true but insufficient. Like eyes in a dimly lit room, so the collective perceptions of scholars over the twentieth century have come, with time and focus, to discern with some certainty what was once only vaguely apprehended. Yes, Luke has written a history, if "history" is loosely defined as "a generally chronological account of who, what, when and where." Similarly, the credentialing of Christianity through miracles is unquestionably a major emphasis which is found not only in *Luke-Acts* but throughout all the Gospels. H. J. Cadbury's observation that Luke was writing because he was so inclined is compatible not only with an evangelistic legal defense thesis, but with just about any other explanations for the writing of *Luke-Acts*. The pertinent question is, "*Why was Luke so inclined to write?*" Time and opportunity are necessary requirements, but something more must have moved Luke to provide the particular "edited history" that is *Luke-Acts*.

Cadbury's observation about the "credentialing" of Christianity is a bit more pertinent. Luke's credentialing actually has two purposes. In his Gospel he, as do the other Gospel writers, argues that Jesus is Messiah because of his miracles and resurrection. Thus, his first purpose is to persuade people to believe. In *Acts*, however, the miracle accounts also serve as a challenge to the verifiability of the narrative, which is Luke's second purpose. This verifiability aspect increases throughout *Acts* as the miracles asserted come closer and closer to the time (A.D. 62) and place (Rome) where *Acts* it is to be read or as the miracles relate to Roman officials or locations because they can more easily be investigated.

2. *Luke-Acts* was written to show Paul's theology and actions were part of mainstream Christianity of the first century and not an aberrance.

> Robert L. Brawley's Luke seeks to reunite Pauline Christianity with Judaism to draw authentic Jews toward Christianity and authentic Christians toward Judaism! This rapprochement requires the rehabilitation of Paul, which is the main burden of Acts. In the face of Jewish and Jewish-Christian criticism, Paul must be shown a faithful Jew, in direct continuity with the unimpeachably Jewish Peter . . . [Luke uses] many standard legitimation techniques of hellenistic literature . . . to defend Paul.[3]

Brawley and others who hold to this explanation are fundamentally correct. Luke wants to show that the Christians are true to Judaism and that Paul is a true Jew. Their conclusion fits precisely with a legal agenda to show that the Way is not an illegal religion. However, the Brawley thesis is flawed to the extent it suggests a theological readership of Christians or Jews and fails to recognize *why* Luke sought to show Paul as a faithful Jew.

3. *Luke-Acts* was written to explain the universality of the gospel with an emphasis on Gentiles, women, and the enemies of Israel being included in the kingdom of God *and to legally defend the church*.[4] Jhan Moskowitz's synthesis makes great sense and comes closest to agreement with the evangelistic legal brief conclusion in many ways. Obviously, the legal defense hypothesis is fully consistent with the conclusions of this book. Also, the universality of the gospel is a patent and principal theme of *Luke-Acts*. Moskowitz's weakness, however, is stressing concurrent themes. If universality of the faith is *per se* a principal theme, rather than a part of the legal apology, then it is a theological argument not relevant to a readership of Roman officials, but only to the church. Consequently, certain chapters of *Acts* are written to instruct the church. Suddenly, Luke remembers he is writing to Roman officials so he shifts to the political/legal innocence of his protagonists until he next remembers he needs to swing back to an audience of believers. The conflict is reconciled by realizing that the universality theme subserves rather than coequals the legal agenda. It addresses a fact which would have been obvious, ominous, and puzzling to Roman officials: Gentiles were becoming believers in the God of Abraham and the Jewish Messiah and joining the Jews who had the same faith, yet without those Gentiles being circumcised or adopting many other external marks of Jewishness. The universality theme takes the facts concerning Gentiles and puts them in a legal framework: This faith is legal; it is legitimate Judaism.

4. *Luke-Acts* was written, partly, for "pastoral" reasons[5] or to confirm the gospel "to those of wavering faith"[6] and "**With the motif of fulfillment**, the author of *Luke-Acts* proclaims and explains the accomplishment of God's purposes in the life and ministry of Jesus and the earliest Christians."[7]

Because the actual audience appears to have been nonbelieving Roman officials, these explanations are inconsistent with a legal brief conclusion. However, the insights which recognize that Luke is confirming the verifiability of miracles are fully consistent with a legal brief explanation which would assert the truth of the facts it recites.

5. *Luke-Acts* was written to explain the relationship of "Israel" and "the Gentiles".[8,9] Maddox apparently accepts the gist of G. Lohfink's analysis but considers that "his solution is methodologically incomplete"[10] because it fails to explain the importance of the imprisonment and trial section, Acts 21–28. As has been argued throughout this book, the legal defense of Paul and of Christianity absolutely necessitated a full explanation of the relationship of Gentiles to Judaism. The understanding of *Luke-Acts* as an evangelistic legal brief thus accommodates and encompasses Lohfink's thesis by viewing Acts 21–28 as the culmination of the previous sections of *Luke-Acts*.

6. The "aim of [of *Luke-Acts*] is to allow the readers to perceive the reliability of the message they have heard. It is a work aimed at reassuring the Christian community about the significance of the tradition and faith in which it stands."[11] Maddox's own conclusion is strongly consistent with the evangelist legal brief thesis on one important legal level: *verifiability*.[12] The same aspects of *Luke-Acts* which establish the reliability of the events recounted in it, presumably to assure Christians, may be a direct assertion to Theophilus of the factual accuracy of those events which give the basis for the legal defense on behalf of Paul and Messianic Judaism.

Of course, I disagree with Maddox's assumed audience, because of:

A. The numerous pro-Roman government episodes throughout *Luke-Acts*.

B. The description rather than explanation of theologically fraught events such as:

   1. The Ascension.

2. The kingdom teachings of Jesus after the Resurrection.

C. The detailed legal arguments of Acts 21—28.

D. The carefully explained financial dealings.

E. The failure to ever attribute the attacks against Paul to satanic or demonic influences.

F. The military/political/fiscal ramifications of Gentile believers not becoming Jews.

G. The continual emphasis on the legal innocence of Jesus, of Paul and of other believers in circumstances of civil unrest.

All these seem more tailored to Roman officials than Christians. Further, a Roman investigator would have *far greater capacity* to verify than any Christian.

7. The chief purpose of Luke-Acts is evangelism.[13, 14] This thesis is fully consistent with the concept of a legal brief written to convert the judges and readers. The theory is, of course, incomplete because it fails to explain much of Acts 21–28 where the evangelistic message is muted and the forensic thrust is accentuated. The theory is also incomplete because it does not readily explain the Israel/Gentiles theme nor the universality theme. All that the proponents of this view need realize in order to see how valid their insights are is that lawyers can be evangelists and evangelists can write legal briefs.

8. Luke wrote to defend Paul at his trial;[15] and

9. Luke wrote to defend Christians in the eyes of the Roman government.[16] These two explanations (8 and 9) are the flip side of the evangelism thesis (explanation 7). In addition to recognizing that an advocate is halfway to being an evangelist by virtue of his training, the proponents of these theories need only realize that a defense for the individual (Paul) constitutes a simultaneous apology for the larger group (the church) and vice versa.

10. Luke wrote to proclaim Christians as witnesses to the world,[17] witnesses in the legal, evangelistic, and martyr sense. Rosenblatt does not assert that her thesis is a comprehensive explanation of the purposes or intended readership of *Acts,* but her conclusions are on dead center. There is no reason all four theories (7, 8, 9, and 10) cannot be connected and united to give us the fullest sense of Luke's purpose.

11. Luke wrote to convince Theophilus to identify publicly as a Christian. According to Winter, Theophilus was a high-ranking Roman official who was considering making a public identification as a believer in Jesus.[18] Luke wrote him, in part, to assure him that such a step would not violate Roman law. The inclusion of Gallio's decision, Acts 18:15, and the statement that Paul taught "unhindered" for two years in Rome, Acts 28:31, are cited in support of his theory. Winter's deductions are consistent with the "Jesus has made Judaism universal" legal argument but particularly fail to account for the ending of Acts in A.D. 62. If Theophilus needed official Roman assurance that it was acceptable to identify as a Christian, he would have waited until he saw the result of Paul's trial. Further, would Luke ever have expended such efforts in writing *Luke-Acts* to convince a skeptic of the legality of faith in Jesus *if the determination of such legality* was dependent not on his research or his argument but on the ruling of Nero?

On the other hand, if Nero had already ruled on Paul's guilt or innocence, then the ruling of the emperor would have been by far the single most important event to the faith declaration of the timorous Theophilus. The ruling and, indeed, all of *Acts* would need to be explained in the context of that ruling.

12. _Luke wrote to solve a crisis of faith in the church_ stemming from the delay of the anticipated Second Coming.[19] This explanation rests on quite different premises than the evangelistic legal brief theory. First, if *Acts* was written in A.D. 62 as I have argued, then the delay is not nearly the concern it arguably could have been if *Acts* were written twenty to thirty years later. Second, key passages supporting such an interpretation, such as Acts 1:6, "Lord, will You at this time restore the kingdom to Israel?" can as well be taken as an assurance to Roman authorities that the followers of Jesus were not being sent out to foment rebellion but to share the faith: "you will be my witness" (Acts 1:7). On the other hand, passages which support the legal brief understanding, such as Acts 25:25–26, "It was clear to me, however, that he had committed no capital crime," are hard to relate to a delayed Second Coming hypothesis. Third, the audience of *Luke-Acts* under this theory must be Christian, but the internal evidence analyzed throughout this book points strongly to a primary readership of non-Christian Roman officials.

SUMMARY OF ALTERNATE THEORIES

The many theories concerning the writing of *Luke-Acts* and its assumed audience overlap. Those which emphasize the legal defense theory are essentially accurate but do not completely appreciate how other themes support the legal objectives. The proponents of the universality, Israel/Gentile, historical, and verifiability of events theses also all have correct insights, but to the extent that those themes are seen as equal or superior to rather than reinforcing the legal purposes, they are overemphasized.

The evangelistic purposes of *Luke-Acts* are independent of and, if successful in reaching Theophilus, Nero, or other Roman officials, complementary to the legal objectives. Those purposes are most typified in Paul's second trial before Felix when Agrippa exclaims: "You almost persuade me to become a Christian."[20] Accordingly, it can be fairly concluded that the emphatic assertion of Jesus as Messiah permeates even the legal brief format and defense of faith purposes. Put another way, the proclamation to Theophilus of what Luke believed to be truth about Jesus was an inextricable part of winning his case, but he still was writing a legal brief to defend Paul and the Jewish Christians against specific charges.

Theses based on an assumption that Christians are the intended audience of *Luke-Acts* are inconsistent with the conclusions of this book. We can best learn from *Acts* not by seeing it as a catechism or epistle, but by seeing it as a forthright assertion to Rome of the truth and Jewishness of faith in Jesus the Messiah. Now all the evidence has been introduced. Let's summarize what it tells us.

---

1   Robert Maddox, *Purpose of Luke-Acts.*

2   H. J. Cadbury, *The Making of Luke-Acts*, (London, 1927), cited in Maddox, *Purpose of Luke-Acts*, 1.

3   Steve Mason, "Chief Priests, Sadducees, Pharisees and Sanhedrin in Acts," in *Acts in Palestinian Setting*, 122–3.

4   Jhan Moskowitz, various unpublished Bible study lectures (Chicago: 1995, 1996). I am deeply indebted to Moskowitz for arousing and informing my interest in the purposes for which *Acts* was written.

5   S. G. Wilson, "The Gentiles and the Gentile Mission in Luke-Acts," Society for New Testament Studies Monograph Series (1973), 85f.; see Rosenblatt, *Paul the Accused*, 94.

6   W. C. van Unnik, "The Book of Acts, the Conformation of the Gospel" *in Sparsa Collecta,* Part I (1973), 360–3.

7   David Peterson, "The Motif of Fulfillment and the Purpose of Luke-Acts" in *Acts in Literary Setting*, 83.

8   G. Lohfink, "Die Sammlung Israels: eine Untersuchung zur lukanischen Ekklesiologie" in *Studien zum Alten und Neuen Testament*, vol. 39 (1975), cited in Maddox, *Purpose of Luke-Acts*, 11.

9   See also C. K. Barrett, *Acts, The International Critical Commentary* (Edinburgh, U.K.: T.T. Clark, 1998), introduction p. 40, "The mission to the Gentiles is his chief concern, and [Luke] wishes to show that it received the backing of all elements within the church."

10 Maddox, *Purpose of Luke-Acts*, 11.

11 Ibid., 186; see Fitzmyer, *Acts of Apostles*, 59.

12 Affirmed also by Fitzmyer, *Acts of Apostles*, 59.

13 F. F. Bruce, *The Book of Acts* (London: 1954), 17–24, cited in Maddox, *Purpose of Luke-Acts*, 30, and J. C. O'Neill, *The Theology of Acts in Its Historical Setting*, (London: 1970), 172–185, cited in Maddox, *Purpose of Luke-Acts*, 20.

14 See Barrett, *Acts*, introduction p. 49.

15 A. J. Mattill, "Naherwartung, Fernerwartung and The Purpose of Luke-Acts, Weymouth Reconsidered," *Catholic Biblical Quarterly*, Vol. 34 (1972), 276–293, cited in Maddox, *Purpose of Luke-Acts*, 20.

16 B. S. Easton, *The Purpose of Acts* (London: 1936), also reprinted in *Early Christianity, the Purpose of Acts and Other Papers*, F. C. Grant, ed., (Greenwich, Ct.: 1954) and E. Haenchen, "Judentum und Christentum in der Apostelgeschiehte" in *Zeitschrift für die neutestamentliche Wissenschaft*, vol. 54 (1963), 155–187, both cited in Maddox, *Purpose of Luke-Acts*, 20. Easton at p. 9 actually goes so far as to assert, "Chapters 13 to 28 may be regarded as a case-book in Roman law."

17 Rosenblatt, *Paul the Accused,* various references.

18 Bruce Winter, divinity faculty, Cambridge. Private conversations. Following is part of an e-mail I sent Dr. Winter regarding this issue.

    Bruce, I am writing to explain why I think your theory about Theophilus does not fit all the evidence. . . . We agree that Theophilus was a high ranking Roman official. You believe that he was considering open identification with the church but feared that in so doing he might incur "guilt by association" or other repercussions. (I think you left open the question of whether Theophilus had actually come to believe.) You point to Luke's words in Acts 28 and particularly verse 31 which indicate he was "unhindered" as evidence that his preaching was not illegal and that Gallio's decision in Corinth, Acts 18, had legitimized Jewish Christianity. . . . Assuming I have caught the essence, here is my reply:

1. Failure to prosecute [while Paul is in Rome] does not establish legality.

2. Gallio's ruling [made under the emperor Claudius] was certainly highly important, . . . nevertheless I cannot even imagine that it would be binding on Nero—an influence certainly, but not binding. Consider not only the history of Christianity under later emperors, they certainly did not feel constrained by Gallio's decision, but Luke does not even quote Paul as raising that precedent before Felix, Festus or Agrippa!

3. I think you also opined that the space given to the Gallio and Agrippa (Acts 26:31–32) rulings was too little to support a forensic hypothesis. Your point is thought provoking. Perhaps the answer is that the decisions really were succinct or perhaps Luke knew that Theophilus would have access to the official transcripts if he felt the need for elaboration and thought that the best use of his space was for development of the factual background.

4. The ending of *Acts*, Paul awaiting trial, is highly inconvenient to your theory. If Theophilus is wavering and truly was looking to Roman authority to signal whether it was ok to identify as a Christian then he certainly would have waited for the outcome of Paul's trial! Luke would not have undertaken the *Luke-Acts* magnum opus if Theophilus could be so easily swayed.

5. If *Acts* was written for Paul's trial it makes perfect sense to end in A.D. 62 but if it is written to convince a fearful Theophilus the ending date is quite a coincidence. After all, if Nero had rendered a judgment in Paul's case by the time *Acts* was written, it would have been *mandatory*, under your theory, for Luke to have discussed the ruling.

6. Why doesn't Luke give Theophilus some *theological* instruction, in *Acts*, on the importance of acknowledging Jesus publicly? You might respond "Isn't Luke 12:4–9 sufficient?" I would reply "Yes!" Why write the rest of *Acts* to persuade when Jesus has already commanded? Jesus didn't make any "wimp" disciples; I don't think Luke would have wanted to either.

7. The length of *Acts* is far more appropriate for the defense of the church's leading missionary in a case that could affect all missionaries and the entire church than just a letter to convince one cautious seeker. If Theophilus were needful of such encouragement why write instead of just talking to him? The only answer that seems plausible to me is Luke 1:4. However that verse only makes sense if putting something in writing adds to the certainty. For example, if I have told you that no one in Evanston likes green peppers on their pizza and then I write you a letter reasserting that statement I do not help you become more certain. However, if I give you the names and phone numbers of all the pizza restaurant owners in Evanston, you are made more certain because you have a phone and can call them to verify my assertion. Also, you know that I know you have a phone, so I can confidently say in my letter that you may know the certainty of what I have explained. In other words, unless Theophilus could verify the assertions made by Luke (by personal investigation, correspondence, or showing the letter to someone else who could confirm the truth), Luke's words in 1:4 are hollow. Theophilus would say to himself, "Luke knows I couldn't possibly know whether his accounts of Paul in Philippi, Ephesus, Corinth or Jerusalem are true!" *unless* Theophilus also had the resources to verify Luke's words. A related point on length: a lot of money was probably necessary to produce *Acts*: support for Luke, research, scribe, materials, copying, etc. The funds could more likely be raised from the folks described in Acts 28:15 and other believers in Rome if the goal was to free Paul and/or get the gospel to the emperor and his consilium rather than to influence one timorous official.

8. E.g. Theophilus, the putative investigator, might care a lot about the identity of Demetrius (Acts 19:24) or of Alexander (Acts 19:33–34), but why would Theophilus, the potential public identifier, care unless he had a lot of money to burn, was highly skeptical and couldn't wait for the result of Paul's trial?

9. You mentioned that Paul's trial would take, at most, a day. You may be right, but several considerations suggest that a far more extensive trial occurred. If so, it would be consistent with more extensive trial preparation such as the writing of *Acts*:

> A. The political implications of a decision by the emperor that Paul was not guilty because Christianity was a legal Jewish sect would be enormous. The Romans surely would realize that this movement could affect their military, their revenue, their slave system, their class system and their relationship with their non-Christian Jewish subjects. If not a long trial then certainly a long investigation would be appropriate to sort out the issues.

> B. Nero loved a show, especially one where he could be center stage.

> C. Somehow the Messianics gained enough prominence in the minds of Nero and the Roman public to make them plausible scapegoats for the fire of A.D. 64. A publicized and extensive trial of Paul is the best explanation I can think of to create such prominence.

> D. The existence of apocryphal letters between Paul and Seneca strongly suggests that Paul's trial was a matter of widespread public interest and knowledge.

> E. Passages such as Col. 4:3–4 and 2 Tim. 4:14–17 also suggest that the trial would or had involved Paul's personal testimony in addition to the legal issues.

10. *Acts* was preserved by the early church. Is not it more likely that copies would be made and circulated of a document prepared for Paul's trial than for a private "epistle to Theophilus"? . . .

19   Maddox, *Purpose of Luke-Acts,* 21, 100–145 cites a considerable number of sources for this position.
20   Acts 26:28.

CHAPTER 32

SUMMATION

Most excellent reader, you are the jury. You have been on a wide-ranging journey, met some fascinating people, and heard powerful testimony. Let us consider what you have seen and heard. I will try to be brief.

We have attempted to prove that when Luke wrote the book which has come to be called *Acts*, he was writing a legal defense for his mentor, Paul, against the charges pending against him in Rome around A.D. 61–62. Although his immediate audience was a Roman pretrial investigator, Theophilus, who evidently held the office of *a cognitionibus* (investigator) under Nero, Luke wrote hoping his work would be widely read within the Roman government, including Nero and his advisers Burrus and Seneca. Because the resolution of these charges implicated the future of the entire church, Luke's defense of Paul also necessarily required a defense of Jewish Christianity itself. Although Luke wanted and hoped to help gain Paul's acquittal, he also intended to present the gospel to his readership through the medium of his brief.

Before we move to controversial points, let us review the undisputed facts and uncontrovertible conclusions, which are obvious from the text or are widely held by scholars regardless of their religious or scholarly viewpoint:

1. *Luke-Acts* is one book.

2. *Luke* moves from the birth of Jesus through his life, passion, and resurrection. *Acts* then selectively chronicles the spread of the faith in Jesus, leading to exclusive focus on the missionary activities of Paul, and concludes by narrowing further to the particular legal proceedings against Paul before various Roman officials.

3. *Acts* ends in Rome with Paul awaiting trial before Nero.

4. *Luke-Acts* was written to a Gentile Roman reader (or readership).

5. Many of the details unique to the Gospel of Luke pertain to issues which would be of concern to Roman officials, such as the attitude of Jesus and

his followers to taxation, Roman government, and the use of force.

6. In *Acts* several decisions and comments of Roman officials affirm the legality of the Way and/or the innocence of Paul and his companions in particular circumstances.

7. *Luke-Acts* was written in Greek, the language of Roman government at least equal to Latin in official usage.

8. Luke wrote as if his initial reader was knowledgeable of the Greek language, Roman politics, Italian geography, and some Roman legal procedure.

9. Theophilus is the named reader in *Luke* and *Acts*. In *Luke*, he is addressed as "Most Excellent", a title used for Roman officials.

10. Few, or probably very few, Roman officials were believers in Jesus when *Acts* was written.

11. A major, if not the primary life purpose of the man Luke was to share the gospel.

12. The gospel is presented repeatedly in *Luke* through the life and teaching of Jesus and in *Acts* through the words of Peter, Stephen, Paul, and the Hebrew prophets.

From these undisputed facts, we can see that the evangelistic legal brief hypothesis is not only plausible but fully consistent with the evidence. If you are applying a measure for decision making which simply says, "The conclusion is more likely true than not," I suggest you need read no further: You may conclude that *Acts* was written as an evangelistic legal brief.

If you want greater certainty, if you want to foreclose in your deliberations other reasonable theories, then let us think about some of the issues that have been questioned by some or not considered by others who have studied *Acts*:

1. <u>Jewishness</u>. Luke wanted the reader to see the faith in Jesus as authentically Jewish rather than a new religion. You have seen this through his frequent use of scriptures and his constant contextualization of the Jewishness of the Messianists. You have also seen this in the way Luke has put so many controversies in an intra-Jewish context. Finally, you have heard the *religio licita* defense (faith in the Messiah is legal Judaism) echo throughout the encounters and trials of *Acts*.

2. <u>Gentiles</u>. The grand theme of *Acts*, that the gospel is universal, is shown by Jesus' declaration, "You shall be my witnesses . . . unto the ends of the earth" (Acts 1:8), by Luke's featuring of an Ethiopian eunuch, a Roman centurion, and many other Gentile converts, and by the encounters with so many of the religions and philosophers of the age. Knowing that the assertion, "the God of Israel has brought salvation to all mankind through his promised Messiah,"[1] is also a defense to the charge that faith in Jesus was illegal, we see numerous details in *Acts*

thought by scholars to be extraneous to any legal purpose are in fact an integral part of a legal argument.

3. <u>Charges</u>. The chart on the charges against Paul indicates that numerous legal charges were made against Paul and other Christians by various accusers from across the empire. Moreover, these charges correlate precisely to the prohibitions of Roman law as we understand them.

4. <u>Refutation</u>. An analysis of the text has shown a systematic refutation/defense of these charges.

5. <u>Countercharges</u>. The chart on the countercharges against Paul's opponents suggests Luke was vigorously defending Paul by impugning the character and explaining persuasively the motivation of Paul's accusers.

6. <u>Roman Legal Procedures</u>. The accounts of Paul's trials before Felix and Festus reveal procedural irregularities and violations which would have been apparent to an official knowledgeable in Roman law. Because Luke mentions them without elaboration, it is reasonable to conclude that Luke believed his reader to be legally sophisticated.

7. <u>Judicial Readership</u>. Chapter 3 on The Investigator has shown that there are numerous questions about "Christian" belief or behavior which a judicial readership (investigator, magistrate, or lawyer) would care about and the answers to which would be already known by or of no interest to a Christian readership. An examination of the text of *Acts* has shown that Luke answers these questions.

8. <u>Details</u>. A review of numerous details shows that the nonbelieving Gentile Roman attuned to legal thinking, rather than the Christian Gentile Roman, was Luke's intended reader. Such details are as glaring as the omission of almost all teaching by the resurrected Messiah (Acts 1:4–8); as apparent to a Roman as the comparison of Acts 1:9 to the ascension of Romulus or/and the comparison of Acts 14:11–12 to the story of Philemon and Baucis; and as emphatic, to a Roman legal official, as Luke's recounting that a ship transporting Paul was named after the Gods of truth and perjury (Acts 27:11).

9. <u>Rewriting</u>. The evidence that *Acts* was redrafted (see comments on Acts 8), together with the Roman practice of rewriting legal documents, suggests both that *Acts* was a brief and that it was not an "epistle to Theophilus."

10–11. <u>Witnesses and Trials</u>. The identification of key individuals is consistent with their introduction as potential witnesses. The unifying threads that *Acts* is a "Book of Trials" and Rosenblatt's conclusion that *Acts* is a book of witnesses, both in the evangelistic and forensic sense, fully support the evangelistic legal brief hypothesis of this book.[2] The use of the result in many of the trials as precedents showing the innocence of Paul and the Christians is straight from "Legal Writing 101." The identification of the Jewish Alexander from Ephesus in Acts 19 as a man put forward by Paul's opponents to speak before the angry crowd of artisans and the reference to "Alexander the metalworker who did me much harm" in 2 Timothy is either a deliberate identification of a hostile witness or an extraordinary coincidence.

12. **Speeches**. The content of *each* of the twenty-nine speeches is shown to be consistent with specific legal and/or evangelistic goals. The form of speech quotation as good brief writing technique is explained and shown to serve the defense objectives. Stephen's speech, a centerpiece of Acts, is shown to be a forensic construction edited in form and content to further four legal arguments on behalf of Paul.

13. **Documents**. The thirty-three documents referenced in or implicit to *Acts*, *particularly those eight documents, other than scripture, likely to exist* when *Acts* was written, uniformly contain information legally relevant to Paul's defense. Exhibits A and B, the letter from the Jerusalem Council concerning Gentiles and the report of Commander Lysias exonerating Paul, both quoted verbatim in *Acts*, are particularly powerful evidence that *Acts* was written as a legal brief. Reference to documents extraneous to the agenda proposed for *Acts* does not exist.

14. **Verifiability**. The miracle encounters, trials and events which Luke has selected for *Acts*, including the names and identification of individuals, precise locations, and public nature of events reveal a pattern of verifiability under Roman record keeping systems and/or Roman investigatory capabilities.

15. **Military**. The favorable portrayal of Roman soldiers and centurions throughout *Luke-Acts* answers both the perceived threat to Roman military security of Gentile conversion to Messianic Judaism and also serves to make the evangelistic message more acceptable to a readership of Roman officials.

16. **Women**. The apparent prominence of women, and their parenthetical but deliberate inclusion in the text as evangelists and prophets, is explained through women who are not a threat to Roman social order: Lydia, a dealer in purple cloth, Priscilla, with her husband Aquila, four daughters of Phillip. The prominence of these women is also depicted not as a departure from Judaism but as a fulfillment of prophecy from Tanakh.

17. **Authority**. Luke's stress on the authority of the apostles coming from God and being independent of the Jerusalem Sanhedrin suggests he is arguing the legitimacy of the Nazarene sect for forensic purposes.

18. **Barnabas and Mark**. The roles assigned these evangelists in the text are precisely tailored to a legal defense agenda for Paul. The role of Barnabas ends abruptly when his actions no longer affect that agenda. The role of Mark continues as it plausibly remains relevant to Paul's defense.

19. **God-fearers**. The prominence given God-fearers throughout *Acts* is shown to comfortably fit Luke's legal agenda.

20. <u>Money</u>. Luke's explanation of the early church's use of money, goods, and land to provide for common needs[3] and help the poor[4] is consistent with the thesis that he has to defend against charges that the believers have formed *collegia*, associations illegal for non-Jews.

21. <u>Slavery</u>. The account of Paul and Silas giving deliverance from a demon to the Philippian slave girl shows that Paul was not inciting civil unrest and Christianity did not teach slave rebellion.

22. <u>Rome and Rioters</u>. The preoccupation/obsession, if not paranoia, of Rome regarding civil order and rioting is seen to well explain Luke's careful explanation of the riots which in some way were associated with Paul's ministry.

23. <u>Transitions</u>. Even the choice of transitions in Luke's writing are consistant with a legal agenda because they continually emphasize the growth of the church.

24. <u>Theophilus</u>. The known or inferred details concerning Theophilus and the hypothesis he held the office of *a cognitionibus* or was otherwise a judicial investigator consistently fit with the narrative structure and nuances of the text.

25. <u>Nero, Seneca, and Burrus</u>. What is known concerning the personalities, responsibilities, and politics of these men fits with the conclusion that Luke wrote with the hope, if not intention, that they would also read his defense of Paul. The inclusion of proconsul Gallio, Seneca's brother, as a prominent exonerator of the Way is a *very strong* piece of evidence for this assertion.

26. <u>Gospel of Luke</u>. Scores of unique details which distinguish *Luke* from *Mark* and *Matthew* are consistently compatible with the hypothesis that it was written to give factual background and legal foundation for Paul's trial before Nero.

27. <u>Paul's Letters</u>. The numerous details in Paul's New Testament correspondence are evidence corroborating that Luke was very close to Paul physically while he was in prison. The letters tell us Paul's primary goal was to share the gospel, but he also hoped to be released from prison. *Acts* has shown us that Luke was Paul's disciple and thus highly likely to share Paul's goals. The *omission* of any reference in *Acts* to Paul's letters strongly undermines other theories about the composition of *Acts* but is consistent with the legal brief hypothesis.

28. <u>Opportunity</u>. An examination of the circumstances of Paul and Luke in Rome around A.D. 61–62 shows they had the time, sources, resources, and motivation to collaborate in producing *Luke-Acts*.

29. <u>Hebrew Scripture</u>. The numerous passages from Tanakh quoted in *Acts* all can be seen to support a legal defense, particularly those that foretold the inclusion of Gentiles into the faith of Israel.

30. <u>Archaeology</u>. Luke's thoroughness and accuracy in geographic details as attested by archaeology suggests a writer concerned that his references would be scrutinized.

31. <u>Genre</u>. The inability of a century of scholarship to identify a genre for *Acts* has, by process of elimination, shown that a new explanation is needed. A new category, the evangelistic legal brief is that elusive genre.

32. <u>Other explanations</u>. The alternative explanations for the purpose of *Luke-Acts* all have serious problems. However, most of those explanations are supportive of or at least consistent with the evangelistic legal brief hypothesis. Some of the facts and inferences from alternative explanations point in more than one direction but, almost always, one of those directions is forensic or evangelistic. Many of the facts and inferences point *only* to a legal brief written to evangelize.

CHARGE TO THE JURY

Esteemed juror, you have heard the evidence. As you weigh it you may rely on your general experience and knowledge of history, religion, and human behavior. However, you are requested to set aside, so far as is reasonably possible, your preconceptions about this particular controversy and focus upon the evidence before you, principally the text of *Luke-Acts* proper. Your charge is to decide the truth of the allegation: "*Luke-Acts* was written as a legal defense of Paul as he awaited trial before Nero and was intended to bring the gospel to Theophilus even as he gathered facts concerning the charges against Paul." The implications of the truth of the allegation may challenge your worldview significantly enough to require subsequent serious investigation. However, whether those implications disturb, anger, or reassure you, your duty is to decide the truth of what is before you rather than reject what the evidence proves because of where it may lead.

Dear reader, allow me to be frank: unbiased jurors in the realm of religious inquiry are rare. Can you be one? As you have sifted the evidence, hopefully you have discerned that I, like you, seek truth. If you have preconceived that the Resurrection is or is not historical fact or if your understanding of Christianity or Judaism agrees or conflicts with the implications, those preconceptions or understandings may color your judgment. Lean against your biases, scrutinize the evidence, and allow it to speak to you. *Acts* tells its own story. Before you finalize your decision, please read the commentary chapter headings aloud to yourself. Every heading contains words written by the witness Luke. His words. Member of the jury, consider these matters carefully. Then render your verdict.

---

1 A paraphrase of the message of Acts.
2 Rosenblatt, *Paul the Accused*, various references.
3 Acts 4:32—5:11; 6:1–6.
4 Acts 11:29; 20:33–5; 24:17.

BIBLIOGRAPHY

Alexander, I. C. A. "Acts and Ancient Intellectual Biography." *The Book of Acts in Its Ancient Literary Setting*. Grand Rapids: Eerdmans; Carlisle, U.K.: Paternoster Press, 1994. **46**

Barnes, T. D. "An Apostle on Trial." *Journal of Theological Studies* 22 (1969). **132**

Barrett, C. K. *Acts, The International Critical Commentary*. Edinburgh, U.K.: T & T Clark, 1998. **31, 215, 216**

Barrett, C. K. *Luke the Historian in Recent Study*. London: 1961. **31**

Bauckham, Richard. "James and the Jerusalem Church." *The Book of Acts in Its Palestinian Setting*. Grand Rapids: Eerdmans; Carlisle, U.K.: Paternoster Press, 1994. **55, 117, 119**

Boak, Arthur. *A History of Rome to 565 A.D.,* 3rd ed. (New York: The Macmillan Company, 1943). **101**

Bruce, F. F. *The Book of Acts*. London: 1954. **216**

Bruce, F. F. *New Testament History*. Garden City, N.Y.: Doubleday, 1971. **1, 41, 102, 119, 133, 134, 166**

Cadbury, H. J. *The Making of Luke-Acts*. London: 1927. **213**

Clarke, Andrew. "Rome and Italy." *The Book of Acts in Its Graeco-Roman Setting*. Grand Rapids: Eerdmans; Carlisle, U.K.: Paternoster Press, 1994. **169**

Easton, B. S. *The Purpose of Acts*. London: 1936. **216**

Encyclopedia Judaica. Jerusalem: Keter Publishing, 1971. **73, 88**

The Expositor's Greek New Testament. Grand Rapids: Eerdmans, 1979. **183**

Fiensy, David. "The Composition of the Jerusalem Church." *The Book of Acts in Its Palestinian Setting*. Grand Rapids: Eerdmans; Carlisle, U.K.: Paternoster Press, 1994. **126**

Fitzmyer, Joseph. *The Acts of the Apostles*. The Anchor Bible series. Garden City, N.Y.: Doubleday, 1998. **3, 22, 49, 61, 64, 215**

Geisler, Norman, and Howe, Thomas. *When Critics Ask.* Colorado Springs: Victor, 1992. **124**

Gempf, Conrad, "Public Speaking and Published Accounts." *The Book of Acts in Its Ancient Literary Setting.* Grand Rapids: Eerdmans; Carlisle, U.K.: Paternoster Press, 1994. **150**

Gill, David. "Acts and Roman Policy in Judea." *The Book of Acts in Its Palestinian Setting.* Grand Rapids: Eerdmans; Carlisle, U.K.: Paternoster Press, 1994. **162**

Gill, David. "Macedonia." *The Book of Acts in Its Graeco-Roman Setting.* Grand Rapids: Eerdmans; Carlisle, U.K.: Paternoster Press, 1994. **xviii**

Gill, David. "Acts and Roman Religion." *The Book of Acts in Its Graeco-Roman Setting.* Grand Rapids: Eerdmans; Carlisle, U.K.: Paternoster Press, 1994. **112, 134**

Grant, F. C., ed. *Early Christianity, the Purpose of Acts and Other Papers.* Greenwich, Conn.: 1954. **216**

Gruber, Dan. *The Church and the Jews.* Hanover, N. H.: Elijah Publishers, 1997. **152**

Gruber, Dan. "The High Priests Who Condemned Jesus." (www.elijahnet.org) **2**

Gruber, Dan. *Rabbi Akiba's Messiah.* Hanover, N.H.: Elijah Publishers, 1998. **xiv**

Gruber, Dan. *Torah and the New Covenant.* Hanover, N.H.: Elijah Publishers, 1998. **119**

Haenchen, E. "Judentum und Christentum in der Apostelgeschiehte." *Zeitschrift für die neutestamentliche Wissenschaft,* Vol. 54 (1963). **216**

Hornblower, S., and Spawforth, A. "Roman Law." *Companion to Classical Civilization.* Oxford and New York: Oxford University Press, 1998. **12**

Johnson, Jerome. *At the Right Time: Dating the Events of the New Testament.* Havre de Grace, Md.: Bath Kol Books, 1998. **xviii**

Judge, E. A. "Judaism and the Rise of Christianity: A Roman Perspective." *Australian Journal of Jewish Studies* 7:2 (1993). **97**

Kearsley, R. A. "The Asiarchs." *The Book of Acts in Its Graeco-Roman Setting.* Grand Rapids: Eerdmans; Carlisle, U.K.: Paternoster Press, 1994. **141**

Ladoucer, D. "Hellennnistic Preconceptions of Shipwreck and Pollution as Context for Acts 27-28." *HTR* 73 (1980). **181**

Leon, Harry J. *The Jews of Ancient Rome.* Philadelphia: Jewish Publication Society of America, 1960. **2, 119**

Levinskaya, Irina. "Diaspora Jews." *The Book of Acts in Its Diaspora Setting.* Grand Rapids: Eerdmans; Carlisle, U.K.: Paternoster Press, 1996. **13**

Levinskaya, Irina. "God-Fearers: The Literary Evidence." *The Book of Acts in Its Diaspora Setting.* Grand Rapids: Eerdmans; Carlisle, U.K.: Paternoster Press, 1996. **129**

Lohfink, G. "Die Sammlung Israels: eine Untersuchung zur lukanischen Ekklesiologie." *Studien zum Alten und Neuen Testament,* Vol. 39 (1975). **215**

Maddox, Robert. *The Purpose of Luke-Acts.* Edinburgh, U.K.: T & T Clark, 1982. **44, 45, 197, 209, 213, 215, 216**

Marshall, I. Howard. "Acts and the Former Treatise." *The Book of Acts in Its Ancient Literary Setting.* Grand Rapids: Eerdmans; Carlisle, U.K.: Paternoster Press, 1994. **15**

Mason, Steve. "Chief Priests, Sadducees, Pharisees and Sanhedrin." *The Book of Acts in Its Palestinian Setting.* Grand Rapids: Eerdmans; Carlisle, U.K.: Paternoster Press, 1994. **162, 214**

Mattill, A. J. "Naherwartung, Fernerwartung and The Purpose of Luke-Acts, Weymouth Reconsidered." *Catholic Biblical Quarterly,* Vol. 34 (1972). **216**

Moskowitz, Jhan. Various unpublished Bible study lectures. Chicago: 1995-6. **214**

Nobbs, Alanna. "Cyprus." *The Book of Acts in Its Graeco-Roman Setting.* Grand Rapids: Eerdmans; Carlisle, U.K.: Paternoster Press, 1994. **107**

O'Neill, J. C., *The Theology of Acts in Its Historical Setting.* London: S.P.C.K., 1970. **216**

Palmer, Daryl W. "Acts and the Ancient Historical Monograph." *The Book of Acts in Its Ancient Literary Setting.* Grand Rapids: Eerdmans; Carlisle, U.K.: Paternoster Press, 1994. **46**

Peterson, David. "The Motif of Fulfillment and the Purpose of Luke-Acts." *The Book of Acts in Its Ancient Literary Setting.* Grand Rapids: Eerdmans; Carlisle, U.K.: Paternoster Press, 1994. **215**

Porter, Stanley E. "The 'We' Passages." *The Book of Acts in Its Graeco-Roman Setting.* Grand Rapids: Eerdmans; Carlisle, U.K.: Paternoster Press, 1994. **124**

Ramsay, W. M. *St. Paul the Traveller and the Roman Citizen.* London: 1920. **4**

Rapske, Brian. "Acts, Travel and Shipwreck." *The Book of Acts in Its Graeco-Roman Setting.* Grand Rapids: Eerdmans; Carlisle, U.K.: Paternoster Press, 1994. **15, 179, 181**

Rapske, Brian. "Paul in Roman Custody." *The Book of Acts in Its First Century Setting.* Grand Rapids: Eerdmans; Carlisle, U.K.: Paternoster Press, 1994. **Vii, 29, 57, 68, 69, 72, 77, 88, 125, 127, 154, 156, 161, 170, 181, 187, 195**

Rickman, G. E. *The Seaborne Commerce of Ancient Rome: Studies in Archaeology and History*, D'Arms, J. J., and Kopff, E. C., eds. Memoirs of the Amer. Acad. in Rome, 36 (1980). **179**

Robinson, O. F. *The Criminal Law of Ancient Rome*. Baltimore: John Hopkins University Press, 1995. **12, 13, 14, 15, 16, 33, 89, 100, 169, 179, 192, 206**

Rosenblatt, Marie-Eloise. *Paul the Accused, His Portrait in the Acts of the Apostles*. Collegeville, Minn.: a Michael Glazier book, Liturgical Press, 1995. **Xv, 62, 76, 100, 102, 215, 216, 223**

Rosner, Brian S. "Acts and Biblical History." *The Book of Acts in Its Ancient Literary Setting*. Grand Rapids: Eerdmans; Carlisle, U.K.: Paternoster Press, 1994. **46**

Rudich, Vasily. *Political Dissidence Under Nero*. London and New York: Routledge Publishers, 1993. **11, 101**

Satterthwaite, William. "The Background of Classical Rhetoric." *The Book of Acts in Its Ancient Literary Setting*. Grand Rapids: Eerdmans; Carlisle, U.K.: Paternoster Press, 1994. **3**

Segal, Alan F. *Paul the Convert*. New Haven: Yale University Press, 1990. **Xiii, 89. 139**

Strobel, Lee. *The Case for Christ*. Grand Rapids: Zondervan, 1998. **124**

Syme, Ronald. *Roman Papers*. Vol. I. Oxford: Clarendon Press; New York: Oxford University Press, 1979. **11**

Trebilco, Paul. "Asia." *The Book of Acts in Its Graeco-Roman Setting*. Grand Rapids: Eerdmans; Carlisle, U.K.: Paternoster Press, 1994. **Xiii, 139, 140-41, 142**

Tyson, Joseph. *Images of Judaism in Luke-Acts*. Columbia, S.C.: University of South Carolina Press, 1992. **13, 109**

Unger's Bible Dictionary. Chicago: Moody Press, 1983. **41**

van Unnik, W. C. *The Book of Acts, the Confirmation of the Gospel*. *Sparsa Collecta*, Part I (1973). **215**

Wilson, S. G. "The Gentiles and the Gentile Mission in Luke-Acts." Society for New Testament Studies Monograph Series (1973). **215**

Winter, Bruce, divinity faculty, Cambridge University, Cambridge, England. Private conversations. **216**

Winter, Bruce. "Acts and Food Shortages." *The Book of Acts in Its Graeco-Roman Setting*. Grand Rapids: Eerdmans; Carlisle, U.K.: Paternoster Press, 1994. **98**

Winter, Bruce. "Acts and Roman Religion." *The Book of Acts in Its Graeco-Roman Setting*. Grand Rapids: Eerdmans; Carlisle, U.K.: Paternoster Press, 1994. **134**

Winter, Bruce. "Official Proceedings and Forensic Speeches." *The Book of Acts in Its Ancient Literary Setting.* Grand Rapids: Eerdmans; Carlisle, U.K.: Paternoster Press, 1994. **14, 15, 16, 25, 45, 159**

Winter, Bruce. "Gallio's ruling on the legal status of early Christianity (Acts 18:14-15)." *Tyndale Bulletin* 50.2 (1999). **133**

Winter, Bruce. "The Importance of the Captatio Benevolentiae in the Speeches of Tertullus and Paul in Acts 24:1-21." *Journal of Theological Studies.* 42 (1991). **161**

Author Web Contact

John Mauck can be contacted at paulontrial.com, where additional copies of *Paul on Trial* can be ordered.

INDEX